"Anyone who puts her children and the ecology of the planet ahead of herself is a singular person in my book. But this is Janet LoSole's book, full of daring adventures, selfless volunteerism, and endless curiosity—a must for community-based travelers. *Adventure by Chicken Bus* is a delightful romp into Central America and an important story for our time."

—KARIN ESTERHAMMER
author of *So Happiness to Meet You: Foolishly, Blissfully Stranded in Vietnam*

"Helping children learn without school is always an adventure. Doing it while backpacking and adjusting to and respecting foreign cultures makes it an epic adventure. This family's story will keep you spellbound. It will make you laugh, cry, and hold your breath in fear, and help you appreciate both the value and joy of learning from life."

—WENDY PRIESNITZ
editor of *Life Learning Magazine*

"Janet LoSole's entertaining and instructive book about her adventures traveling for nineteen months through Central America with her husband and their daughters, ages eight and five, occasionally sends a chill down the spine of any parent, with harrowing tales like clinging to the edge of a shaky bridge over a river to avoid being hit by passing trucks while crossing the border from Costa Rica into Panama. But this story will also light a fire in the heart of parents who wish for their children to experience other places and cultures."

—MICHAEL LANZA
creator of thebigoutside.com and National Outdoor Book Award-winning author of *Before They're Gone: A Family's Year-Long Quest to Explore America's Most Endangered National Parks*

"Buckle up for an unforgettable ride; an emotional journey that takes the reader on an exciting family adventure like no other!"

—ALAN MALLORY
author of *The Family that Conquered Everest*

"*Adventure by Chicken Bus* is a fascinating look at one family's journey of international travel, cultural immersion, personal discovery, and learning together through it all."

—KERRY McDONALD
author of *Unschooled: Raising Curious, Well-Educated Children Outside the Conventional Classroom*

"Brave and inspiring, *Adventure by Chicken Bus* immediately draws you in with its honesty and color.... This book has so many important messages about parenting, caring for the planet, and daring to strive for something more from life."

—MIA TAYLOR
award-winning senior staff writer for *TravelPulse*

ADVENTURE BY CHICKEN BUS

ADVENTURE BY CHICKEN BUS

AN UNSCHOOLING ODYSSEY
THROUGH CENTRAL AMERICA

JANET LoSOLE

RESOURCE *Publications* • Eugene, Oregon

ADVENTURE BY CHICKEN BUS
An Unschooling Odyssey through Central America

Copyright © 2019 Janet LoSole. All rights reserved. Except for brief quotations in critical publications or reviews, no part of this book may be reproduced in any manner without prior written permission from the publisher. Write: Permissions, Wipf and Stock Publishers, 199 W. 8th Ave., Suite 3, Eugene, OR 97401.

Quote by Dr Marcolongo taken from www.iamat.org. Used with permission.

Excerpt from Association Save The Turtles of Parismina (ASTOP) www.parisminaturtles.org. Used with permission.

Resource Publications
An Imprint of Wipf and Stock Publishers
199 W. 8th Ave., Suite 3
Eugene, OR 97401

www.wipfandstock.com

PAPERBACK ISBN: 978-1-5326-8486-9
HARDCOVER ISBN: 978-1-5326-8487-6
EBOOK ISBN: 978-1-5326-8488-3
Manufactured in the U.S.A.   12/05/19

To Lloyd.

Most of all, to Jocelyn and Natalie.

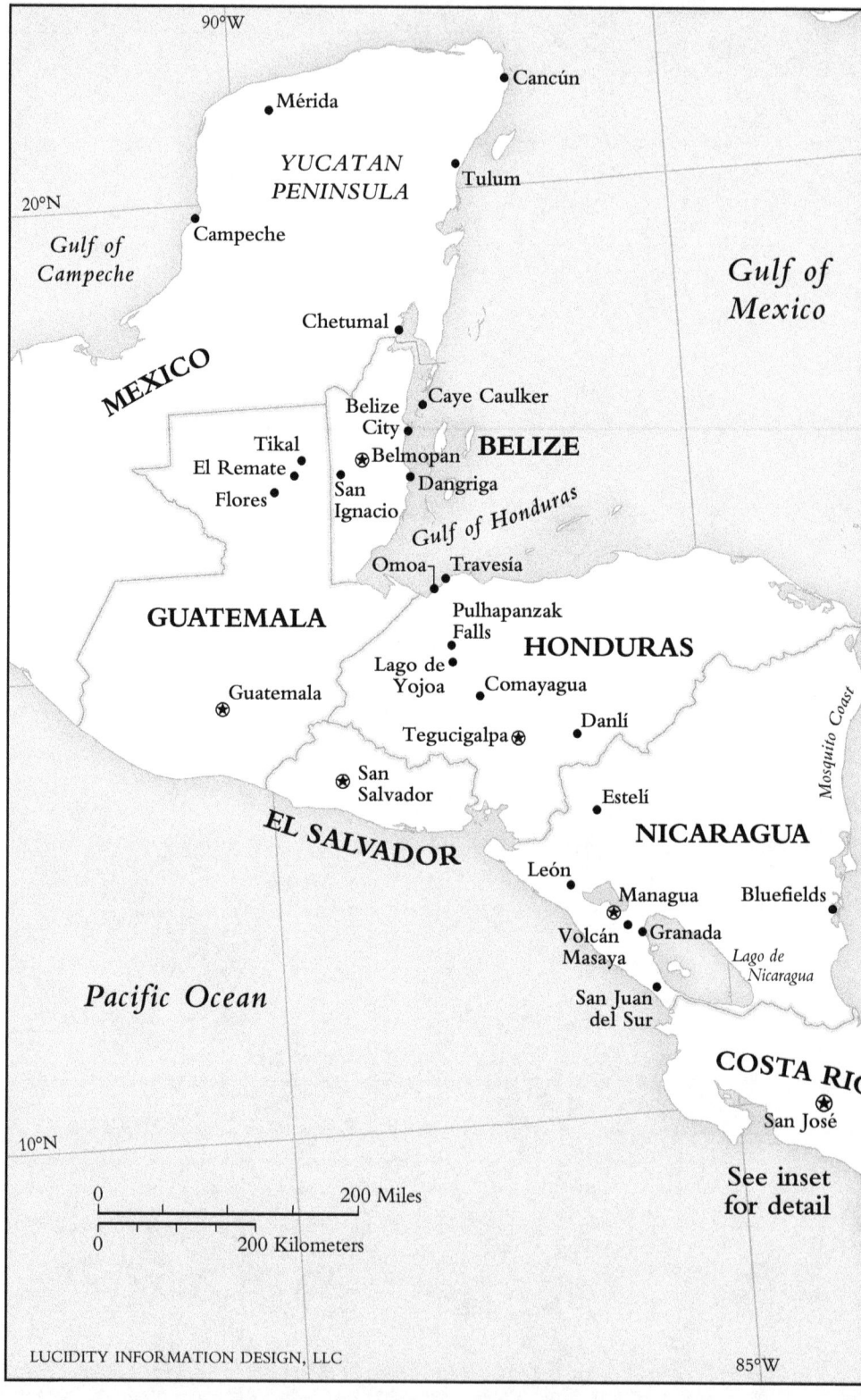

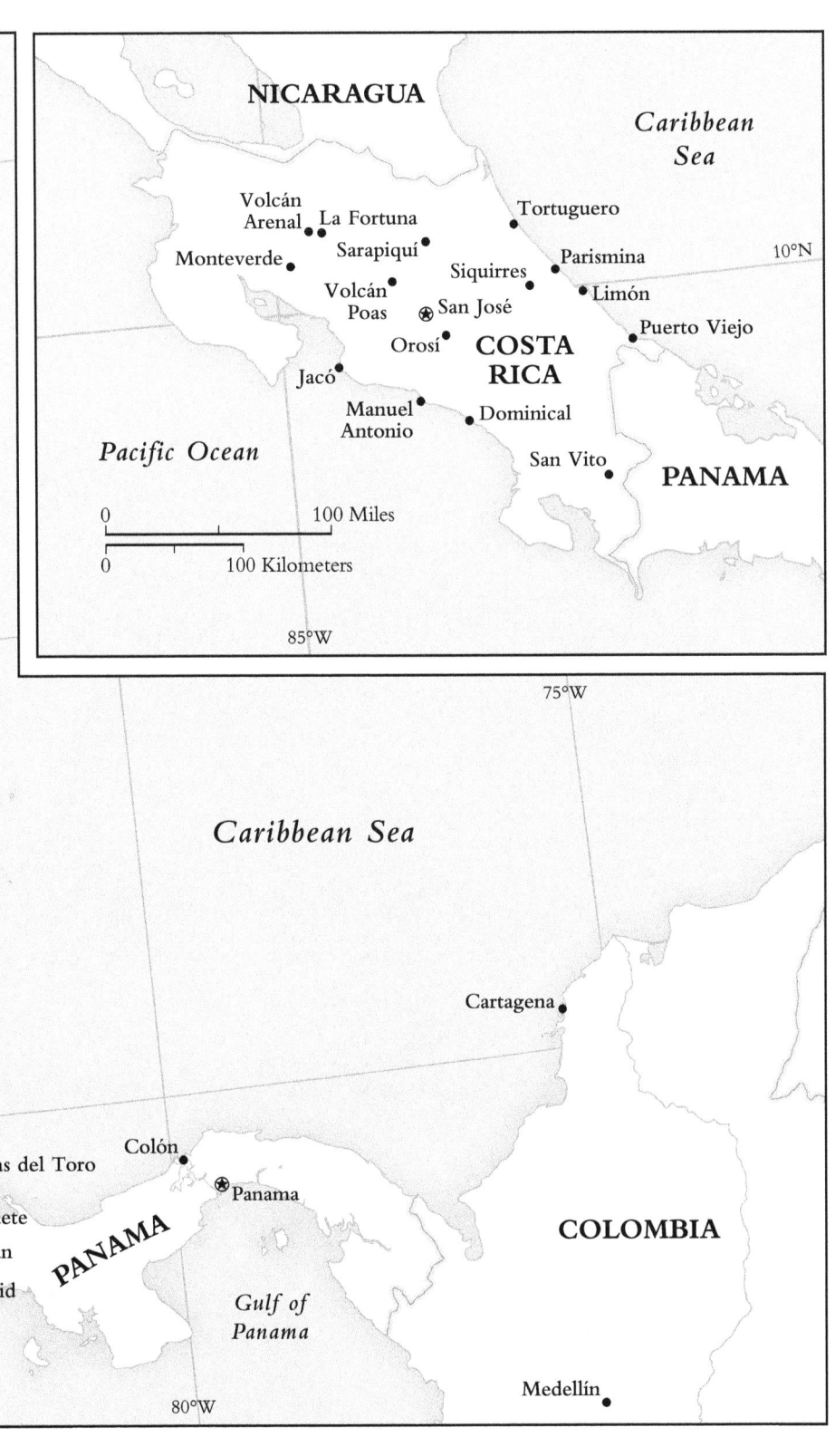

Contents

Author's note	xiii
Chapter 1 | Farewell	1
Chapter 2 | Baby Steps	11
Chapter 3 | Parismina	21
Chapter 4 | Tortuguero	38
Chapter 5 | Puerto Viejo	43
Chapter 6 | Entering Panama	54
Chapter 7 | Panama City	60
Chapter 8 | Jacó, Costa Rica	68
Chapter 9 | Settling Down	72
Chapter 10 | Summer Vacation—Back to Panama	100
Chapter 11 | Winding Down	125
Chapter 12 | Nicaragua	137
Chapter 13 | Honduras	156
Chapter 14 | Belize	174
Chapter 15 | Guatemala	177
Chapter 16 | Back to Belize	185
Chapter 17 | Mexico	191
Chapter 18 | Home	202
Epilogue	205
Bibliography	211

Author's note

Inevitably, things change. Since the writing of this book, some roads have been paved, and prices have gone up. Some names and identifying details have been changed to protect the privacy of individuals.

Chapter 1

Farewell

ON THE EVE OF the trip, I tossed and turned on my farting air mattress and worried. Visions of attacking crocodiles and venomous snakes weaseled into my brain. The empty house echoed around our sleeping bags laid out alongside small piles of clothes. Two years of planning had come down to this. Every possession sold. Jobs put on hold. Long goodbyes over. *Are we ready for this?* I stared at the ceiling, then I rolled over and faced Lloyd, to see if he was awake. Fat chance. He was breathing deeply, oblivious to my concerns.

When Mom and Dad had come to visit the girls one last time, Dad treated us all to ice cream. He played foot hockey with the girls in the parking lot of the ice cream shop, kicking stones across an imaginary goal line.

Mom shoved her hands in her pockets. "Dad's having nightmares. He's worried about the girls."

"You *know* Lloyd and I have loads of travel experience." I said it overloud, as if to convince myself we knew what we were getting into. I reminded her that we'd spent our honeymoon teaching in South Korea followed by a sojourn in Australia.

Of course, we've never backpacked with the kids. I kept that thought to myself.

At the farewell party in our garage, I'd ushered friends over in small groups to show them the map of Costa Rica tacked to the wall and explained our itinerary.

"We'll be arriving at the tail end of turtle nesting season, so we'll head directly to this area here," I'd said, pointing to the Caribbean coast, "to volunteer with a conservation project. After that, we'll return to the Central Valley to find jobs."

Some peered at the map, nodding; others pointed nervously to the region lying to the north.

"Nicaragua? With the girls? No. No way," I said.

But I wasn't stewing about going to Nicaragua the night before we left. I was thinking about keeping our two daughters, eight-year-old Jocelyn and five-year-old Natalie, safe and healthy while we taught English as a Second Language in Costa Rica.

WHY GO IN THE FIRST PLACE?

Before our oldest, Jocelyn, was born, followed by Natalie two years later, I told Lloyd I wanted to be a stay-at-home mom and, since we were both teachers, educate them at home. The goal? To focus 100 percent on the well-being of my family and to provide the girls with as many educational opportunities as possible without the confines of a government-imposed curriculum. Eventually, the notion to take a massive field trip somewhere exotic germinated one night when we realized that the original blueprint was going off the rails. With only one of us working, homeschooling demanded frugality. We'd embraced a Salvation Army standard of living, buying secondhand furniture from their thrift shop, but we could not survive without the credit card to get us out of financial jams. With a steadily rising debt load, Lloyd and I were forced to pick up night school contracts. This meant hiring a sitter. It also meant both of us were absent from putting the girls to bed at night. As a family, we were spending little time together.

The cost of having two cars on the road, it turned out, produced most of the deficit, $450 per month to be exact. When Lloyd lowered the calculator to announce this fiscal detail, we were stunned. Homeschooling appealed for many reasons, not the least of which was family bonding, and now our budget separated us from the girls more than we wished. Lloyd missed the girls terribly. He left before they woke up and, because of night school, did not see them until the weekend. He also complained that his values were being compromised every day we drove our cars. As an environmentalist, he worried about the message this practice was sending the girls.

He dropped the calculator on the table. "This is not how I want to live."

I thought for a minute. "Let's write down what means the most to us and go from there." As a couple, we had established a practice of writing down our long-term goals and working toward them. We worked well as a team, egging each other on and reviewing the lists periodically.

"You mean what will bring us the most happiness? What would we be doing if we had our wishes granted?"

"Yes, exactly."

We finished scribbling and then swapped papers. We looked at each other. The lists were nearly identical. At the top of each was one word: *travel*.

He sat back in his chair. "Well, this comes as no surprise."

"Nope." If there was one thing we never argued about, it was traveling.

On a snowy Christmas morning, just after I turned seventeen, my father placed a small rectangular box in my hands and gestured for me to open it. It was a French/English dictionary.

He's done it.

He'd brokered a deal with his boss to hire me as an *au pair* for the summer in France. The dictionary was confirmation. Seven months later, at the family's compound in the Ardèche region of south-central France, I met another teenager at the annual summer BBQ. The adults drank wine and debated politics; Sophie and I wandered off, found an empty picnic table, and, under a canopy of stars, discussed life in stilted franglais. She left with her mother the next day. "Viens me voir à Toulon." Come see me in Toulon.

That summer, I developed the resiliency to cope with homesickness and to handle a brief solo journey that I was permitted to take to visit a classmate in Liège, Belgium. A week later I boarded a train heading south to Toulon. Sophie met me at the *gare*. We hung out in Aix-en-Provence, Nice, and St. Tropez, strolling the sprawling pebble beaches and walking among the floating palm trees of the French Riviera.

That first summer in France instilled a lifelong yearning to get out among our world's people and speak their languages. Years later, studying French linguistics at York University in Toronto, I worked part-time as a parking attendant. I completed reams of homework huddled over a plywood counter in a barely heated booth. One evening, I looked up from my books and noticed my cubicle directly faced the flight path of aircraft leaving Toronto International Airport. It dawned on me how ridiculous it was to study languages from a text when I could get on those planes and learn them in the very countries they were spoken. Though I was three years into a four-year degree, I felt I had no choice. I dusted off my backpack and left. Jocelyn and Natalie had been raised listening to my stories of adventure, knew all about hostels, and rifled through our map collection and travel mementos when I cleaned out the closet.

As a child, Lloyd spent his days after school messing around in the barn, throwing rocks in the river, seeking out caves, looking for bear tracks. He camped and hunted with his father and grandfather. In 1992, at twenty-three, he was invited to tour Italy with his grandfather and the Perth Regiment Veterans Association. Forty-four veterans and their families boarded a coach and corkscrewed around Italy. "You haven't felt a lump in your throat until you've seen grown men cry," he told me. "We toured eleven cemeteries where allied soldiers were buried."

In Pompeii, Lloyd saw Mount Vesuvius, and geology grew into an obsession, demonstrated to perfection by the eight rolls of Italian topography (not a single human in any of the shots) he presented to me on our first date.

Lloyd and I met at Nipissing University's Faculty of Education, during a pick-up game of basketball. When our relationship turned serious, we presented each other with proposals. Mine was radical: get our degrees, complete one year of teaching at home, then another overseas. He was more traditional and suggested that perhaps getting married could be incorporated into the timeline.

"Oh, right." It was as romantic as that.

After graduation, we both found work—me as a French teacher, Lloyd as a substitute. We planned the wedding while we looked for international teaching posts. Back then, in ancient times before the internet, applying for overseas teaching positions was a matter of finding the right job at the right time. To wit, my college roommate called me one night and told me to look in the want ads section of *The Globe and Mail*, Canada's national newspaper. There, buried in a sea of ads, we read:

"International Teaching Jobs—send SASE to Rothesay, New Brunswick."

"Lloyd, if ever there was a hotbed of international teaching information, it must be Rothesay, New Brunswick." I thrust the paper under his nose.

"What? Where is that?"

Over the phone, Professor Thomas Mullins explained with great enthusiasm and a slight Liverpudlian accent, "Please send six self-addressed envelopes to me and I'll send you my newsletter."

When we received our first package, we knew we had hit the mother lode. The professor had cobbled together hundreds of want ads from schools around the world looking for ESL instructors. So, while we cut our teeth as rookie teachers in the Ontario elementary system, we were faxing our résumés to the four corners of the earth.

From among the dozens of job offers—including one from a school in Finland who called me as I was leaving for the church on our wedding day—we selected a language school in Masan Bay in South Korea, where we spent several months teaching English as a Second Language.

Domestic life set in after our return. Even after the girls were born the travel bug remained. It was time to set out again, this time with the kids, twelve years after Thomas Mullins had first helped us along on our first international teaching foray.

We originally chose Costa Rica after scouring the WWOOF website (World Wide Opportunities on Organic Farms), which lists locations of farms around the world that request assistance in exchange for room and board. I was excited to get back into WWOOFing. After we left Korea, Lloyd and I had weeded our way through the east coast of Australia. The WWOOF directory is organized by country and then district. To match a WWOOF site to your lifestyle—let's say, a family of vegetarians who homeschool—you scan the legend printed at the bottom of the farm's description. Typically, they look like this:

SfCiNa2ArcKyPhTtfWgtbLesDsGcH4Y5M1Z4

Do you notice, about one-third of the way from the left, the notation "Ky"? That signifies *Kids, yes*. Working back and forth between the legend and the listing, we noted that many of the farms registered in Costa Rica accepted children. To stretch our dollars, we hoped to WWOOF in between teaching stints.

I sat at the computer and imagined us out in the tropical sun, planting lemon trees and cooling off in the Pacific after a long day.

Wait. Remember raking macadamia nuts in Australia's oppressive heat? Won't I be following the girls around to make sure they were not walking into a nest of snakes? WWOOFing, perhaps, would have to wait until they were a little older. But the *idea* of Costa Rica stuck. We dug a little deeper to see what it could offer us—a bored, burned-out family in a lot of debt.

Lloyd was barely in the door that night when I called out to him from the computer. "Hey, did you know that Costa Rica has no military?"

He dumped his bag and leaned over my shoulder to view the website, not even stopping long enough to take off his coat.

I read aloud. "Costa Rica abolished its military forces in 1949 and since then has devoted substantial resources to investment in health and education."[1] These facts appealed to our Quaker sensibilities toward peace and nonviolence.

He began reading along with me. "Its population of 4.4 million people enjoys a literacy rate of 96 percent and a life expectancy of 79.3 years." He stood up. "That's about the same as Canada!"

---

1. Costa Rica Embassy, "Costa Rica at a Glance," para. 4, http://www.costarica-embassy.org/index.php?q=node/19.

Ticos, the affectionate term for Costa Ricans, benefit from cradle to grave health care, just like Canadians. As a mother of two young children, these initial findings were paramount to my comfort level. Still, we agreed (if there was one thing we never argued about . . .) that a dry run to Costa Rica during the holidays would determine whether we could manage the peculiarities of traveling with two children and would allow us to network for employment.

We toured a Quaker school in a mountain town called Monteverde, an enclave famous among fellow parishioners, known as "Friends" in Quaker tradition. Fleeing from conscription into the Korean War, American conscientious objectors founded the community due to its cooler climate and fertile soil. Their stewardship extended to preserving a swath of land, the Monteverde Cloud Forest Reserve, now considered a major eco-destination.

The director was pleased to see us. We'd been communicating by email, engaged in a complex application process. We exuded professionalism and cheer on the tour to complement our written submissions. Then we attended Meeting for Worship in a dark-paneled, open-air room. We settled into the silence on hard benches while hot gusts whistled through the trees. After twenty minutes, I took the girls to First Day School, the Quaker equivalent of Sunday School. Together, we decorated napkins for the luncheon after Meeting.

Hiking back to town, we passed teachers' housing, provided to staff for free.

"The salary's not much," I said to Lloyd.

Later, on the terrace of our pension, he took out a pen and scribbled on a piece of paper. "On the other hand, the cost of living is low," he said, showing me the numbers.

A few days later, we hired a driver to take us down the mountain to Puntarenas. From there we crossed the Gulf of Nicoya to relax and celebrate Christmas in the small village of Montezuma. We swung in hammocks. Read lots of books. We walked the beach daily. The receding tide sucked the water shoes off the girls' feet. A twenty-minute hike brought us to an oasis we called Shangri-La, a freshwater pool fed by mountain runoff. We reposed there for hours. The girls puttered with their dad while I gazed at the ocean, not twenty meters away.

We were sold on Costa Rica.

Back home I dove headlong into researching everything about the living conditions there. I tapped into a listserv, populated mostly by retired expats. They were generous with their advice. Based on their anecdotes and Lloyd's calculations, we wondered if we might be better off financially in

Costa Rica than in Canada. To that end, Lloyd and I discussed, at length, the possibility of making the move permanent.

To make an informed decision, we would put the country under the microscope. At the same time, we dedicated this odyssey to the girls as a homeschooling field trip to learn about biology, social studies, geography, history, environmental science, language arts, and international relations. All we had to do was deposit the girls at the location and let their day-to-day surroundings perform the incidental instruction. Without so much as a lesson plan, they would learn another language, for example.

The larger educational picture, however, encompassed values. Lloyd felt we were only paying lip service to environmentalism while driving two cars around. We intended to rely on public transit whenever we could. It also mattered a great deal to us to have the girls exposed to a way of life that might be deemed difficult. Witnessing economic differences and social inequality had a profound impact on me during my youthful excursions. I wanted the girls to understand how others lived and to respect the privilege into which they were born.

Traveling requires confidence. We hoped to instill conviction in their abilities to travel while they were young. Lloyd and I also wanted to prove to other families that *you can travel with children*, and to encourage them to reject the expectation that one must work without ceasing until retirement. And we would satisfy our travel addiction, the four of us spending long hours together, exploring, day in and day out—a vision of freedom, lodged in our minds, for all our sakes.

SETBACKS

We returned to Canada from our practice trip to Costa Rica emboldened to make our dream come true. As we saw it, two major hurdles stood in our way: debt and job security. We were $18,000 in credit-card debt. Deficit reduction was simple: work more hours and spend less; so we persevered with night school, and Lloyd added a summer school contract to his timetable.

Spending less proved more challenging. Weeks before departure, my clunker breathed its last breath. Because it was impossible to run all over town to get things done without a car, we reluctantly agreed to have it fixed for $500. Nevertheless, Lloyd, the consummate accountant, paid down the credit card debt every month. Then we learned the school board would grant Lloyd a leave of absence, guaranteeing him a teaching position when we returned. We were stunned, therefore, when the Quaker school in

Monteverde informed us that we were not even being slated for interviews. We felt we had received every reassurance to the contrary.

In a nutshell, we were a family with nowhere to go. In a few months, neither Lloyd nor I would have a job in *any country*. I crumpled under the stress of it all. Lloyd remained confident and insisted we resume looking for opportunities in Costa Rica.

After Meeting for Worship that Sunday, we broke the bad news to Friends. "Just go anyway," they said. Truthfully, I felt a little frustrated by this attitude. With no income for two years? As a mother of two girls, this seemed irresponsible and immature. Taking off at twenty-one to backpack around Europe for a year is one thing, but two years living on a prayer? But Friends knew us as adventure-seekers, given our travel history, and encouraged us not to give up.

In the end, it was Lloyd who established a calm attitude about the whole thing. "We're going after all," he announced. "Something will turn up."

One morning, after a night of sleeplessness, I took the girls to the local parent-child drop-in. It was near-blizzard conditions and the place was empty. The facilitators were eating their lunch in the kitchen, so when the girls ran off to play, I was left by myself. In despair, I lay down on the floor of the community center and looked up at the ceiling, pleading with the universe for something concrete to unfold. To my surprise, the lines on the ceiling, the ones that bisected at odd angles and stretched from one side to the other, formed the perfect outline of an airplane.

Another strange image kept cropping up in my mind while we were churning through websites and emailing potential employers. "I'm seeing us standing on the shores of a vast ocean with friends," I said to Lloyd. I knew that these people were American and that we were standing on the beach in their country. The vision was recurrent and vivid. I had no inkling what it meant.

Not many people knew the circus act our minds were performing, sifting through dozens of scenarios and recalculating our finances. We behaved as though we were leaving for two years, as announced to friends and family. Over winter break, we enrolled the girls at gymnastics camp. By the time Lloyd had dropped them off, I had a pot of coffee waiting and a notebook open. We spent every minute surfing the internet and making calls to schools seeking English teachers. After assorted correspondence with language schools in San José we were bluntly told, "If anything, you're overqualified."

Music to my ears.

Reassured by our prospects, we breathed a sigh of relief that our trip was still possible after all. After exhaustive research and plenty of emails, we felt confident that a few schools would at least interview us once we were in Costa Rica. But because we had been waylaid by false hope before, we forced ourselves to consider the possibility that none of it would pan out. And that's how we made our way, with no definitive plan to support the family and a vague itinerary mapped out for the first three months.

Once I wrapped my mind around Lloyd's vision, I was fully committed. After all, he was the breadwinner. If he didn't feel insecure, why should I? Ultimately it was the comments from Friends who planted the seed of "just go anyway" that permitted me to push past my insistence on financial stability. However, since the security of steady employment was nebulous at best, we devised a fiscal plan that allowed us to travel for up to one year without any income. All that remained was financing one additional year.

Frugality was the key. Budget backpacking has distinct advantages over upscale forms of travel. Students do it well, living on a shoestring budget for months, getting around as the locals do, eating their food, shopping at their stores, relying on them for information and assistance. In return, budget travelers put currency directly into the hands of the villagers and develop friendships with individuals of all stripes. This amounts to community-based tourism. Not content just to sightsee, we expected to integrate, live as the locals did, have real-life experiences that would enhance our understanding of the culture. How did all those other countries make it onto our itinerary? It happened organically. I laugh now when I think about how I reassured friends about the girls' safety.

"How close is it to Honduras?" they'd asked at our garage party.

I tried to put them at ease. "We'd never take the girls anywhere close to a place like that."

Like any mother, I was uneasy. My primary concern centered on the health and safety of the girls. The more I spoke to friends about my discomfort, the more I received words of reassurance. One told me, "Families go on missions in the middle of Africa and come back safe and sound."

Thereafter, I prepared for this trip with a fanaticism that consumed every waking moment. Niggling details demanded attention—acquiring health insurance and medical supplies, completing minor repairs to the house, and screening tenants to rent the house while we were away. The insurance company refused to cover the house for damages with us so far away. It took one year to find a firm that would insure us for five times the price. Their stipulations demanded we hire both a property management firm to collect rent *and* a maintenance company to manage repairs.

Check.

When the summer arrived with its typical oppressive humidity, the girls and I loaded up our backpacks with stuffies and took walks around town to acclimate to the added strain on our bodies. I especially worked on getting Natalie used to physical discomfort. She was strong and agile for her age, but after bursts of energy she dissolved into tears from thirst or heat.

Check.

The possessions we had accumulated in eleven years together were departing our lives with nary a second glance. I held a perpetual garage sale from April until August. We sold all: fridge, stove, washer, dryer, clothes, toys (except for the few that traveled with us), books, beds, tools, shelves, televisions, firewood, and lamps. In the final weeks, we ate everything left in the cupboards and gave away extra spices, coffee, tea, and household cleaners. We rented the house to a single mom who worked for an appliance repair company. She was scheduled to move in at the end of the summer with her two boys.

Check.

The only new acquisitions were backpacks for the girls and air mattresses for everyone. Lloyd and I bought two thin "equatorial" sleeping bags. For the girls, I sewed sleeping sacks and for all four of us, air-mattress covers. The air mattress covers were shaped like giant pillowcases, and the sleeping sacks were shaped much the same. I saved money by making the sacks out of old sheets that were too shabby to sell. For nearly two years, we used these items hundreds of times.

Check.

To pad my thinner résumé, I enrolled in a TESOL course (Teaching English to Speakers of Other Languages). As proof of pure universal synchronicity, I discovered that the course was being taught by none other than Professor Thomas Mullins himself.

Check and double check.

At the end of August, we closed out the garage sales, packed unsold leftovers in bags, and returned them whence they came—the Salvation Army—and scrubbed the house to a sheen. We went to bed on air mattresses stuffed inside handmade covers. I turned back to stare at the ceiling. At length, I drifted off, comforting myself with the words of Dr. Marcolongo, founder of the International Association of Medical Assistance for Travelers (IAMAT). He states:

> The need for peace and understanding between the peoples of the world has never been as great as now. Peace can only come with understanding, and travel is an important means of acquiring it.[2]

---

2. Marcolongo, "Message from the Founder," para. 3.

Chapter 2

Baby Steps

Goodbyes over, tears shed, beer guzzled, we handed over the keys to our tenants and left Canada behind on a hot August morning in nervous anticipation and on empty stomachs. American Airlines' no-meals policy for short flights turned Natalie and me sour. At the Miami airport we had two hours before our connecting flight. I noticed that other travelers evaded the overpriced fast food offerings by wisely packing a lunch. I'd overlooked this seemingly inconsequential task because we had sold all worldly possessions and *had nothing to pack a lunch in*. When we landed my mood was black with hunger. I surveyed the waiting area at Juan Santamaría International Airport and spotted Vicente, who had been sent to deliver us to Villa Alajuela. We had stayed at Vicente and Gabriela's bed and breakfast last year on the practice run.

"Bienvenidos!" he said, taking the girls' packs.

Natalie collapsed against me in the van. We rolled in just as a light rain began.

Gabriela greeted us. "Are you hungry? I've ordered pizza."

We devoured it and then we all went to bed, but I lay awake, unable to sleep. Facing up to the next two years was sinking in. Our adventure had begun.

"Mommy?" Natalie called out to me in the blackened room. "Where are you?"

I crawled into her bed and then stared wide-eyed at the ceiling, my heart pounding. *What the hell do we think we're doing*? In the morning, the regular bustle of seeing to everyone's needs distracted me from my misgivings. Plus, the girls' enthusiasm was infectious. They poked around, fondling the lobster-like claws of the heliconia plants and chasing geckos. I dashed off a couple of emails to family back home, letting them know we'd landed safely.

Villa Alajuela B&B rests on a hill overlooking a bend along the main road to the popular Parque Nacional Volcán Poás. As hard as it was for Lloyd, we decided to save exploring Volcán Poás for another time, choosing to trek into the center of Alajuela by public bus.

Like many Latin American towns, Alajuela follows a square block pattern, with a large cathedral anchoring the Parque Central. Shops and market stalls lined the streets just inches from the roadway. We wandered through the streets, turning sideways from time to time with our backs against the exterior walls of the shops, like criminals hiding from the fuzz, to let the crowds pass. Others circulated fluidly, sometimes stepping down onto the road to avoid an obstacle without breaking stride. For us, the simple act of hand holding was a challenge.

Perhaps because they were homeschooled, both girls did not lament leaving any friends behind. Jocelyn, who had just turned eight, spent most of her time engaged in imaginary play and enticed Natalie to construct kingdoms with their toys. She also often went off in her mind to a fantasy world instead of looking where she was going. In Alajuela, the lack of typical public safeguards made her daydreaming a relatively big concern.

"Please pay attention to where you are going," I said, dodging potholes. We looked like strutting chickens, lunging over gaps in the sidewalk or ducking to avoid low-hanging signs. Noise blared from every direction: horns, engines, music, shouting. We clapped our hands to our ears and gave up any attempt to speak to each other.

A man stood at the entrance of a small eatery known as a *soda* in Costa Rica, hollering out the day's special, a dish of rice and beans with salad and plantain—translated literally to mean "married man": "Casado con bebida mil quinientos!" Casado with drink fifteen hundred! For lunch, we gorged on their gigantic portions before waddling in the direction of the terminal to pry loose some information about buses to San José.

Public transportation in Costa Rica is inexpensive. On our practice trip, we'd relied on taxis and private drivers to get around. Now we shucked the luxuries we could no longer indulge in if the money was expected to last. So, we all had to put into practice the lugging and stowing of four backpacks in the heat. Our training sessions back home helped some. Even Natalie was expected to carry her own belongings. She was solid and wiry, favoring vigorous activity and strenuous exercise. Until she got tired. Or hungry. Or hot. Then we scrambled to avoid a full-scale meltdown. The tropical setting guaranteed that she would face extreme heat, fatigue, or thirst. I'd learned to pack drinks and organize our days around her need for downtime in the afternoon.

The next morning, we said goodbye to Vicente and Gabriela and embarked on our first trek, venturing a pathetic twenty kilometers to San José, giving a whole new meaning to the term "baby steps." I felt rather proud as we whizzed down the Pan American highway to bunk for a week at a hostel called Costa Rica Backpackers. In my twenties I could travel overnight, sleeping upright on a train leaving southern Italy destined for Denmark, and shake it off at the other end with a shower and hot coffee. Now, as an "older" backpacker responsible for the health and safety of two children, acclimatization was the priority.

At Costa Rica Backpackers, we were given the key to our room and wished good luck to find it. Our paltry room was crammed with just a single set of bunk beds and a small wooden locker no more than one foot in height. We made it work by wedging the girls' air mattresses under the bottom bunk. We stowed packs at the foot of our beds. Each pack held the individual's clothes, books, toiletries, air mattresses, air mattress covers, sleep sacks, and shoes. Lloyd brought with him the four-man tent, some tools, and an air pump, and I carted the travel guides, health books, medicines, vitamins, first aid kit, and laptop. The girls traveled with a few toys including a handful of Lego pieces, some Barbies, and Jocelyn's beloved Pepper, a stuffed St. Bernard. This comprised the entirety of our possessions.

In the morning, we propped the air mattresses upright against the wall to make room to shuffle into each other and change. The benefit of this claustrophobia was a greatly reduced rate; in fact, they didn't charge us for the girls at all, a practice we were always grateful for over the next year and a half.

We shared a bathroom and shower with a dozen travelers in our wing. Both facilities offered a lesson in cultural practices that require explanation. First, one does not flush one's toilet paper in Central America. The narrow pipes do not provide an adequate conduit through which much . . . uh . . . debris can flow freely. On any given day, therefore, the wastebasket was overflowing with used toilet paper. For nineteen months, we discarded, rather than flushed. A backpacker friend emailed me when we returned to Canada and reminded me, "Flush the toilet paper."

Second, "hot" showers are achieved courtesy of a contraption colloquially known as a "suicide shower." These devices, resembling an automotive fuel filter, are suspended at the end of a pipe that juts out of the wall just above eye level. Wire runs along the pipe, attached by tape or string until—and here's where it gets confusing—it intersects with a bunch of other wires and mashed up balls of electrical tape. This system somehow powers the heating element encased inside the "fuel filter" to heat the water as it flows (or dribbles) out of the showerhead. On the one hand, it makes more sense than heating hot water all day unnecessarily in a tank. On the other hand, suicide showers are safe only if you don't adjust it mid-spray. The girls, being short, were safe. Lloyd, at six feet, ran the risk of electrocution when he reached up to wash his hair.

Early the next morning Jocelyn woke us early by maneuvering her air mattress and changing into her swimsuit. "Let's go to the pool, Natalie."

I chased after them with sunscreen and towels while Lloyd found coffee. When he returned, he unfolded a copy of the "Eventos" section of the local newspaper and slid it over to me. After a few passes, I could translate enough to say: "I think it says the children's museum stays open until four o'clock and there is a performance at the Teatro de la Danza on Saturday." I tapped an entry in the guidebook. "Let's make sure we hit the tourist office, too."

That afternoon, we became proficient at the layout of downtown San José after wandering aimlessly looking for the Museo Nacional inside which the tourist office was concealed. Racks of glossy brochures featured overpriced tours to places we'd never dream of going, such as whitewater rapids (the girls were too young) or Papagayo Resort (we were too poor). We crossed our fingers that an outdated bus schedule that listed departures for the Caribbean was accurate. In a week, we were expected by the Parismina Sea Turtle Commission.

To escape the heat, we visited the Museo de los Niños, one of the best children's museums we have ever visited, it turns out. When the Central Penitentiary shut down in 1979, it was left abandoned and haunted until 1994 when it reopened under the vision of Mrs. Gloria Bejarano de Calderón as an educational center for the children of Costa Rica.

The irony could not escape Lloyd's notice. "When you think children's education, you automatically think prison."

The girls raced around old jail cells exploring rooms representing different themes, such as the Milky Way, the human body, and aviation. In the human body jail cell, the expert planners had designed a chair that, when sat upon, let loose a series of burps and farts, a real inspiration for future biologists.

Jocelyn beckoned for Natalie to join her at a house furnished with shelves full of books and knick-knacks and a small table set for the evening meal. "Let's pretend we're eating supper," she said.

An employee walked over to a control box and pressed a button. The floor shook violently beneath them, sending dishes and books cascading to the ground. The exhibit was designed to educate children about the destructive power of an earthquake based on the levels of the Richter scale, but the girls thought it hilarious and beseeched the young man to hit the button over and over again.

The following morning, we walked down to the Teatro de la Danza where we saw an all-dance version of *Genie and the Magic Lamp*. My friend Helen had introduced us to musicals like *The Sound of Music*, *Oklahoma*, *The Music Man*, and *The Wizard of Oz*. If the girls had their way, they would have mainlined the movies on a continuous loop directly into their veins—they loved musicals that much. Raised as athletes, Lloyd and I had vague notions that such a world existed. Even so, we recognized that the performers of the Teatro were exquisite in their ability; the lead dancer's gyrations produced a bucket of sweat, his makeup dripping blue down the front of his white blouse. Lloyd remarked, "I can't believe this only cost us six dollars."

Even with these highlights, San José was a warren of frenetic shoppers on their way to the *mercado*, and about a million buses, to our small-town eyes, spewing black sooty exhaust into our faces. In the cramped supermarket, we bumped around, straining to read the Spanish labels. Jocelyn exclaimed, "There's too many people!" On top of that, we choked and gagged on the exhaust that wafted in from the main bus terminus, out front. When we left with our groceries, we darted in and out of the busy streets, half dragging the girls, worried that the cars wouldn't see us.

"How long before we sprain an ankle on these sidewalks? Lloyd asked.

Back at the hostel, the air buzzed with travelers spilling into town to begin their journey, like us, or resting up after completing one. San José was like that, a geographic jumping off point inside Central America. I felt Panama was shafted in the process. Panama City, with the nearby canal by far the major attraction, lies too far away, and most incorrectly assume there is little to do there.

I was captivated by the stories from travelers who breezed in from Nicaragua or who had flown in from Colombia. The hint that the entire region was well-suited to backpacking was taking root. We'd thumbed through the guidebooks until they were dog-eared, never once contemplating the adjacent countries because, of course, they were too dangerous. We allowed for brief forays into border towns in Panama to renew our visas but nothing more adventurous than that.

Young sojourners, curious at the sight of a backpacking family, questioned us no end. Many assumed we were rich, and others scratched their heads at the notion of homeschooling. Anyone from Canada or the States reacted with a knowing, "Ah, you're homeschooling." Europeans, (where homeschooling is less common and, in some countries, illegal), asked us to explain. One young man from the UK commented, "I can't imagine coping with the stress of traveling on top of the responsibility of educating your children."

Lloyd replied drily, "We figure we can do both at the same time."

People are surprised to learn that homeschooling can be accomplished without the use of an official, text-based curriculum. In fact, many families adopt a system called "unschooling" where children learn through natural life experiences. We intended to use this approach on the road. We felt it would be senseless to interrupt their natural learning by making them read about China, for example, or complete work that had no relevance to their current lives. The entire trip was designed as an opportunity to participate in hands-on learning, and their first lesson was science.

On the Caribbean side of Costa Rica, the advent of the rainy season coincides with the end of turtle nesting season. We hoped to wheedle into the narrow slot between the two seasons for a few weeks before returning to the Central Valley, where Costa Rica is densely populated, to look for teaching jobs. However, we were determined that everyone remain healthy. We knew the Caribbean side presented challenges due to the humidity and lack of roads, and because Costa Rica has suffered outbreaks of dengue (some extremely serious) since 2000, we were mindful of protecting ourselves from mosquito bites.

After a week, we left San José. The members of a turtle conservation project were waiting for us to help them in their efforts to rescue the endangered sea turtles of Parismina.

LIMÓN

Our research uncovered intriguing information about the hamlet of Parismina, a Caribbean island village visited annually by nesting sea turtles. Remote and cumbersome to find, we planned to break up the journey by stopping at Limón, further south of Parismina along the coast.

San José's Gran Terminal del Caribe, where coaches shuttled folks to the coast, sat below street level in a concrete basin of heat and humidity. Our bus rumbled out of the city only when every last seat was filled. Even though there was no air conditioning, passengers slammed windows shut against the violent rain that obliterated the sight of the Cordillera Central mountain range. Once we emerged from Parque Nacional Braulio Carrillio two hours later, the rain let up, and the driver pulled in to a rest stop.

Over the din of the engines, I shouted to Lloyd, "You grab some drinks. I'll take everyone to the bathroom. Ready? *Break.*"

I nearly failed at convincing the girls to get back on that heat-chamber of a bus for the final leg that careened out of the mountains and into the boggy Caribbean lowlands. I felt a little guilty about it, for the temperature on the bus truly seemed a health hazard. Jocelyn's tummy burbled from motion sickness until she became distracted by a little boy of about four who fell in love with Pepper.

For ninety minutes I fanned myself with a copy of *La Nación*, Costa Rica's Spanish language daily, until we disembarked in Limón. "Sweat is dripping down the back of my legs," I remarked to Lloyd.

"Zip off the bottom of your cargo pants," he suggested.

"Oh," was all I could think to say.

We formed a scrum and decided that Lloyd would stay at the terminal with the girls while I tried to find Hotel Rey, recommended in our guidebook. Bad idea. Street signs don't exist in Costa Rica. Directions center on the number of meters you are from a major landmark. Hotel Rey, I was told, was "fifty meters west of the southwest corner of the mercado." Of course, these instructions assumed that I knew where the mercado was in the first place and that I understood that fifty meters represented a portion of a city block and not actual meters (in Costa Rica, fifty meters is half a block, 100 meters is a block; it does not equate to 100 linear meters).

After a few of these wild-goose-chase directions, I gave up on finding Hotel Rey. Back at the terminal, Jocelyn, Natalie, and Lloyd drank from their bottles of water, enjoying the floor show—hawkers who sang out "Pati! Pati! Pateeeeeeeeeeee!"

Market stalls ran the west wall of the bus station. Corporate marketers in developed nations spend millions on slick ad campaigns, but merchants in Limón's market employed attention-getting gimmicks and annoyance to attract customers. This method almost worked; we seriously considered buying some pastries, hereafter known as "pateeeeee."

At that moment, saving us from an unnecessary gastronomic expenditure, a gentleman approached us. "Excuse me, do you need any help?"

"Do you know where the Hotel Rey is?" Lloyd asked.

"No, I don't."

I flipped through my guidebook. "How about Hotel Internacional?"

"Yes. I'll take you there."

When he pulled up to the front door of the hotel, Lloyd offered him a little money, which he accepted, and then we shook hands and said goodbye. The kindness ended there. The reception at Hotel Internacional was beyond indifferent. The front desk clerk slouched with chin in hand and pointed, without speaking, to the rate board, which listed prices much higher than those quoted in our guidebook. Still hopeful after a greatly reduced rate at Costa Rica Backpackers, I asked for a discount for the girls.

"No."

To illustrate how uncharacteristic this behavior is, in nineteen months of travel (nine of those full-on, chicken-busing, hostel-sleeping, hard-core backpacking), we were refused a reduced rate a total of three times, and two of those originated from American hoteliers.

Back out on the street, I rejoined the family who were sitting on bags, piled askew. I told them what had transpired.

Lloyd shielded his eyes from the sun. "Well, that's too much. Go across the street to that hotel."

I took Jocelyn's hand. "This time, I'm taking one of the girls with me, to get a cute-kid discount." At the Hotel Continental, my heart sank when I saw the head-in-hand, and thought I was seeing double; the woman at reception looked exactly like the previous one. Had she run around the back and entered without us noticing? When I asked about their rates I explained, in my bad Spanish, how we had previously been given reduced rates for the girls in San José and can't you see how cute my kid is?

She shook her head. "We don't do that here."

After the gift of an air-conditioned ride from the kindness of a stranger, we were back at square one. "We need to find Hotel Rey I guess."

Later that night, going through my guidebook, I mentioned to Lloyd, "Says here that the same family owns Hotel Internacional and Hotel Continental." The head-in-hand resemblance was thus explained.

We paced the streets, following the city's grid like Pacman, advancing and backtracking until we found Hotel Rey and stood looking up at the reception on the second floor. We must have looked a sight, because a dusty, old shifter with a patchy grey beard and wiry hair offered to carry our bags up the two flights of stairs for a small fee.

Hotel Rey proved quite a contrast from Costa Rica Backpackers. The girls said nothing as they stared at the colorless walls and ratty furniture, but after the day's hopeless pursuit, the whisper of a chance to lie down was a welcome relief. The dilapidated beds squeaked in defiance as we dumped our packs and looked around. I sent the girls to snoop around the lobby. I knew I could count on Jocelyn to take this new and exotic locale and invent a narrative that would capture Natalie's attention for a few minutes while we got organized.

The small lobby hung over the street directly above Limón's hectic comings and goings. Lloyd spied a grocery store from the balcony. "I'll be back in a minute. I'm off to buy cold beer and snacks."

The owners of the hotel—a Chinese family consisting of many people—lived in the back, their apartment entirely exposed to the public by curtainless, glass walls. The girls didn't know which way to turn, out the front balcony to ogle the street or inside the lobby to watch the traffic up and down the stairs while tolerating guests who patted them kindly on the head.

Lloyd and I relaxed on the balcony in the lobby with cold Imperials. Across the street, people at an open-air gym exerted themselves on treadmills and stationary bicycles. Lloyd chugged his beer. "You couldn't pay me to work out in this heat."

Eventually, we gathered up empty beer cans and water bottles and went out for a walking tour of the city. We ambled down to the central market and then crossed town to the shore. The girls teetered along a low wall that bordered the beach, arms out to the sides mimicking an airplane. Lloyd walked beside them. When they lost their balance, they touched a hand down on his shoulder to steady their gait.

"Girls, this is the Caribbean Sea," Lloyd said.

They stopped. "What?"

Limón's waterfront does not inspire postcards. The beach was strewn with garbage and the dark grey sea was barely distinguishable from the charcoal sky. Costa Rica possesses miles of beautiful shores, but cruise ship passengers disembark in Limón, a busy port town, and board shuttle buses flinging them to far away sites like Sarchí or Sarapiquí.

As we made our way back to the hotel, we looked for better accommodations to reserve for the following month's annual festival, when Limón lets its Caribbean hair down for "Carnival," centered around Columbus Day on October 12th. We narrowed it down to Hotel Miami, located right next door to Hotel Rey.

The spacious lobby was laid with cool white tile, stretching all the way to the back kitchen. "This place is gonna cost an arm and a leg," I snorted. The immaculate hallways gave way to a row of rooms with bright walls painted in pastel shades. The girls gasped at the television sets. When the front desk gave me the price, I pressed her to repeat it. "Is that per night or per person?"

"Per night."

Lloyd leaned in. "We're paying the same price at Hotel Rey."

The woman handed me a business card. "Call closer to Carnival to reserve a room."

Back at Hotel Rey, we tried to settle in for the night. "Ahhhhh, relaxing in Cell Block 4," Lloyd said, referring not so much to the four windowless walls as for the one bare light bulb that dangled above the bed. The walls did not even make it all the way to the ceiling. The last two feet were enclosed by lattice that allowed in all the light from the street and the noise along with it.

You're asking, no doubt, why we didn't bail on the Hotel Rey and move next door to the cleaner Hotel Miami? I blame the heat. We could not bring ourselves to descend two flights of stairs and then ascend to the check-in at Hotel Miami with all our gear.

We would not even allow the girls to take a shower in the grimy communal bathrooms. We also forbade them to use the dusty, threadbare hotel blankets. Instead, we laid out the sleep sacks alongside each other on the double bed. "Lie down on top of the sacks," I told them.

"What about jammies?" Jocelyn asked.

"No, keep your street clothes on," I said. Then, I gestured to the sleeping sacks I had sewn from light, cool fabric to use as de facto sleeping bags and asked Lloyd, "Am I not smart?" but he was busy examining the doorknob and trying to enter the locked room from the outside to test its security. In the middle of the noisy night, the absurdity hit me, and I burst into a fit of giggles. *Fleabag hotel.*

In the morning, Lloyd complained. "Was someone chopping food all night?"

The four of us sat up groggily on the beds. We could hear all manner of sounds emanating from neighboring rooms. Jocelyn raised her head and announced, "Somebody farted."

Thus ended our brief introduction to Limón, the Costa Rican transportation system, the oppressive heat, and the art of finding a decent hotel (always check one more). We trudged down the street to the terminal and sat at a little table eating pastries that we bought after being attracted to a corner kiosk by a hawker yelling, "Pati! Pati! Pateeeeee!"

Chapter 3

Parismina

As part of a hands-on biology lesson for Jocelyn and Natalie, we devoted three weeks to assisting an organization called ASTOP (Asociación Salvemos las Tortugas de Parismina) in saving endangered sea turtles. After feeling like a contributor to environmental problems, Lloyd felt obligated to support this effort. By email, we had arranged to stay in the village of Parismina and participate in turtle patrols.

The village of Parismina lies along a marine thoroughfare that rambles from Limón to the Nicaraguan border. Settlements along this route are accessible solely by boat. However, getting there by lancha, a canopied motorboat, to the tune of eighty dollars was out of the question.

At this point, we had targeted our expenses at $600 per month and planned to dip into this fund to pay for food and accommodation. Tours and transportation were extras, but thrift was Lloyd's middle name, and traveling like the locals cut our costs by more than 90 percent.

I imagined myself reclining in a lancha breezily taking in the sites along the canal. Then again, the difference between bus and water fares was too substantial to ignore. Daunting though it seemed to us, it was the way of life for locals, so we opted to finish eating our pateeeeee and hop back into the oven that doubled as a bus.

We backtracked to Siquirres and transferred to a bus bound for Caño Blanco. From there, a lancha would ferry us the short distance to Parismina. Siquirres is about the same size as Limón, and the image of an egg frying on the sidewalk comes to mind when I think of it. The pleasantly plump lady who ran the soda at the main terminal took one look at Natty's sour face and hugged her. Jocelyn joined in, wrapping her arms around the pair of them. The owner then brought out plates of food and cold drinks to placate us while we waited for the afternoon bus to Caño Blanco.

An old man with greasy hair tucked into a faded cap and a stubbly, grizzled beard wheeled by, balancing his grimy Styrofoam cooler on his adult-sized tricycle. "Huevos de tortuga. Huevoooooooooooooos."

I jerked my thumb at him. "Lloyd, he's selling turtle eggs."

Lloyd scowled. Sadly, most of the egg vendors we saw that day were old men and appeared to be poor. They probably had no other source of income. Technically illegal, selling endangered sea turtle eggs—one cog in the wheel of the underground economy—goes to the heart of the problem. How does one deprive people of their right to an income and survival even if it impacts the survival of another species? In Parismina, we hoped to find the answer to that question.

At noon, we were directed to wait in line with an ever-growing assembly of people. "There's no way they can fit us all on one bus," I asked, "is there?" Some passengers dragged enormous burlap sacks of potatoes while holding the hand of a small child or cradling a nursing baby. We bunched in with them, weighed down by our overstuffed backpacks, hair stuck to our heads, and still in our sweaty clothes from the day before.

Lloyd turned to a young student next to him and gestured toward the bus. "All of us, on that bus?"

The young man looked at him as if he was from another planet. "Of course."

At one o'clock, the crowd surged forward, jostling to board a "chicken bus," a colloquial term used to describe the run-down, discarded school buses from North America sold to Latin American countries, where they are repainted in riotously bright colors, outfitted with stereo speakers, and upcycled with more seats to accommodate man, woman, and child along with their potatoes, avocados, and chickens—and in this case, a family of Canadian backpackers.

Lloyd was relieved of having to fold himself into a seat when the driver insisted he take the big adult packs and stand with them on the back stairs. That left me with the girls and their gear to board the bus which was now standing room only. Claustrophobia threatened, but I swallowed my fear when I saw the girls laughing at each other, plastered into the armpits of their neighbors. A young mother gathered her little girl onto her lap to free up space for one of us to sit down and the three of us took turns sitting on the seat, standing up, or squatting on a backpack.

During the commute, ticos were smiling, laughing, or being helpful to each other. Even when my camera bag fell out of the overhead bin and bonked a lady squarely on the head, she merely smiled and handed it back to me. The driver picked his way slowly over hard-packed dirt roads. Pitching and rolling along lonely stretches, I glimpsed sleepy jungle backwaters through thick fronds. At times, the driver lurched to a stop for passengers who indicated they wished to get off by amiably calling "Parada," or "Stop" as in "This is my stop," not the imperative "Stop!"

After one of the paradas, a shout rang out from an older gentleman who hobbled off the bus on bowed legs to retrieve his sack of produce from another passenger who had mistakenly disembarked with it. He walked down the road and waved his arms good-naturedly to summon the fellow back. We waited patiently as he reboarded the bus and stood in front of us for a moment to bask in triumph before chuckling and dragging his load of wayward vegetables behind him.

These delays did nothing to annoy the weary crowd. Closer to the end of the journey, seats opened up, and I sent the girls back to their father; the locals hung on to their sleeves as they stumbled down the aisle. Jerking from side to side, I realized that Lloyd and I would be the recipients of the life lessons we had anticipated for the girls. Taking local transportation reveals a great deal about a culture as witnessed by the ticos' indifferent attitude to the hardship of the commute. "They are the very definition of tolerance," I said to Lloyd later.

After two bone-jarring hours, we bumped into Caño Blanco—the end of the line. The bus turned around here and went back to Siquirres. The lancha skipper greeted us at the docks, took our bags and the girls, and deposited all of them on a bench. We wormed in beside them. The fifteen-minute ride afforded spectacular scenes that rose above us on the lush river banks. Lloyd pointed out cormorants drying their wings on jutting stumps. A water buffalo grazed quietly on reeds, undisturbed by the buzz of the motor. He lifted his head and looked right at Natalie, who was studying him. When the animal turned away, she shot me a look, her eyes wide and her mouth shaped into an "o" of wonder.

Parismina is technically an island, bordered on one side by the Caribbean and the other by the Río Parismina. The breeze we had relished puttering along in the lancha gave way to stifling heat when we docked. Our clothes stuck to us like rice paper. The air held the scent of cooking fires. We shouldered our packs and followed the crowd along the dirt path that led into the village.

Stray, skinny, mangy dogs sauntered by. Modest, cinder block houses leaned against each other. Corrugated metal roofing, jagged and rusty, topped most buildings. Older homes—built with wooden slats, warped from years of baking in the sun—exposed great gaps. Windows held no screens, nor were there many doors. Save for a lone pick-up truck that drove around collecting garbage, no vehicles graced the island.

Folks ambled along the crisscross of dirt tracks that followed no discernible direction. Some trails, etched in the scorched earth, bisected front yards, if that was the most convenient route from point A to point B.

We went largely ignored until a young girl of about twelve came by to escort us to the village.

"Good afternoon," she said in Spanish. "I will take you to Don Rodrigo's campground. Do you need something to drink?" She pointed to a *pulpería*, a sort of mom-and-pop grocery or convenience store, where an old woman sat on a stool near the window selling chips and pop. I felt as though the sun were baking my brains right inside my skull, but I couldn't bring myself to drink anything sugary, so I said, "Let's just go directly to Don Rodrigo's."

Putting off hydration was a mistake. I spent the next day in bed with faint nausea and extreme fatigue. It would not be the last time I suffered from underestimating my need for hydration.

Bunking at Rodrigo's, on the other hand, was no mistake. We rented a small, A-frame *cabina*, complete with built-in shelves and four beds, one of which was wedged in a loft perpendicular to the others. Beautifully maintained grounds spread out like a green carpet from the door of our cabina to a block of clean, communal, cement block showers. Next to that was a rustic, open-air kitchen, comprised of a rusty, ant-infested fridge, four picnic tables, a sink, and a two-burner hot plate.

The nightly rate was ten dollars. Though the beds were thin and the cabin a little dusty, Lloyd pointed out, "No mosquitoes are getting in here," as he examined one of several air vents Rodrigo had covered with fine netting.

The girls picked out their beds and then ran outside to explore, immediately tripping over the campground dog, Chispa, Rodrigo's intelligent mutt that followed them everywhere and slept protectively outside our cabina at night, barking at every crab that came within twenty-five feet.

That afternoon, we went to the center of the village to stock up on water, covering the distance in about three minutes. The skinny dogs, looking doleful and neglected, elicited pity from the girls. They were consumed with the desire to pet them.

"Don't touch any animals, please," Lloyd warned.

"Why not?" Natalie asked.

We couldn't explain to a five-year-old that rabies transmits through saliva, usually via bites, so instead I said, "We don't know if they are friendly to children."

"What about Chispa?" Jocelyn asked.

"He's okay because we know him. The others are off limits."

At the island's only grocery store we looked at the selection in dismay. Rice and beans, pasta and oatmeal, but few vegetables, adorned the shelves. Fruit was left rotting in crates and refrigeration appeared dedicated to ice cream and water. We drank and drank and drank. None of us was urinating. I battled mild queasiness and kept a close eye on the girls for signs of lethargy.

Back at the campground we cleaned ourselves up, a grand feat of scrubbing away two days of grime from fleabag hotels and sweaty buses.

Our main objective in Parismina was to support ASTOP, increase our understanding of the culture, and learn Spanish. For example, I hoped to learn how to make coconut oil from one of Rodrigo's neighbors. For a small fee I joined the family—an ancient, blind man, his daughter, son-in-law, and his two great-grandchildren—in whipping up a batch of homemade coconut oil. The grandmother worked across the river at the pricey Río Parismina Lodge. Each morning the grandfather, who cared for his blind father-in-law, waded into the sea that lapped into his backyard, to catch fish.

Like many others in the village, they lived simply. What little electrical current they could afford was used to power their lone light bulb. The government provided clean drinking water and free health care from a doctor who visited the community twice a week. This family had chickens for eggs and reaped fresh papayas and mangoes that fell at their feet. They used coconut pulp to make oil and sold it to make a few *colones*. Coconut pulp was also used to feed their chickens, and they grew avocados and harvested yuca. They prepared hot meals on a raised cook stove fueled by burning coconut husks.

Massive palms cast speckled shade on the lawn. Out of the corner of my eye, I saw crabs skulking from behind hicaco bushes. We grated the coconut pulp, added a small amount of water, and squeezed the milk by hand into a battered pot. The concoction bubbled over a small cook fire while the family chatted with me genially in Spanish. The little, blind patriarch smiled in my direction with blank, glassy eyes.

After a few minutes, the liquid changed from milky white to a translucent, oily amber and exuded the distinctive odor of coconut. My host decanted the cooled oil into a recycled water bottle. I voiced my muchas gracias, paid the fee, and said adiós.

I walked back to the campground, silently congratulating myself and Lloyd on coming to Parismina. Living in an isolated community without the luxuries of air conditioning, reliable refrigeration, and access to a well-stocked grocery store forced us to cope as the locals did. These were precisely the types of contrasts we were searching for.

The rhythm of the town fascinated us. Walking and cycling were the sole methods of human locomotion. Each day at 4:00 p.m. on the dot, the townspeople assembled a motley team at the soccer field for an hour of the world's most popular sport. Behind the soccer pitch, another group banded together for a pick-up game of volleyball. Combined with all the walking and bike-riding, Parismina stood to be the fittest town in the western hemisphere. Even so, the conservation of energy set the pace. Everyone moved slowly and deliberately. I attributed it to two things: the extreme heat and the lifestyle of a people unencumbered by the demands of the nine-to-five world.

One morning Rodrigo brought over fifteen sweet limes, a breadfruit, and a bunch of water apples harvested from trees on his land. He could see that we were trying to learn their ways, so he lent Lloyd a small machete and encouraged him to chop down fruit whenever we wanted. He especially encouraged us to consume the clear liquid of the coconut (known as *pipa* in Costa Rica) which provided much-needed electrolytes to our poorly acclimated Canadian physiologies. Every couple of days, Lloyd chopped down the cocos, drained and chilled the clear, syrupy liquid, and made me drink it, which probably saved me from getting sick, if truth be told. Rodrigo also taught us how to harvest the starchy tuber known as yuca, and after a few tries Lloyd got the knack of using the machete without severing any fingers.

Natalie craved the water apples so much she often implored her dad, "Lift me up?" and, using Lloyd as a human ladder, she climbed up to pick them herself. From the ground, all I could see was Lloyd with his arms raised over his head and two small feet in his hands.

Thanks to the loan of the machete to harvest fruit, Lloyd made gallons of fresh juice. Then Val, an American expat and the village nurse, showed me how to use a tortilla maker and I became an expert at grilling cheese tortillas for lunch.

Rodrigo noticed my dismal efforts at hand-washing our clothes, as the locals did. "You can use the washer," he said, indicating a twin tub throwback to the sixties where clothes were loaded into the left-hand drum and then manually transferred to the right-hand receptacle to spin out the water. "Drain the water into the yard," he instructed.

One morning after washing up, Lloyd dropped into a chair in the kitchen with a cup of coffee and a toasty cheese sandwich and watched swallows circling a bush, swirling like Tasmanian devils in a rapid spiral. He was unwinding, relieved of the stress of hours and hours of teaching, day and night. "Well, it seems we are doing a little living off the land." He gestured toward the orchard with his mug.

I leaned against the half-wall that enclosed the kitchen. "We *are* living like the locals, aren't we? It certainly suits our budget." The nominal fee Rodrigo was charging us for our cabina, and the abundance of free fruit allowed us to live on just $150 a week.

Some find Costa Rica expensive. After roaming all the way to the Yucatán, we disagree. The four of us could live as cheaply as two because hostels rarely charged for the girls and our vegetarian diet reduced food costs substantially. We also prepared almost every meal ourselves, eating in restaurants only occasionally.

Of course, it was easy to scrimp in Parismina. One restaurant served the entire island. There were no clothing shops or internet cafés or pharmacies; there was simply no market for them. The closest shopping district was back in Siquirres, several hours away. Everything that couldn't be grown or caught was shipped from the mainland on the lancha, even building materials and televisions.

The dinky pulperías provided a scant supply of necessities such as milk and plantain. Fruit was abundant at Rodrigo's, but the heat left vegetables limp and unappealing. For a family of non-meat-eaters, the lack of veggies was a problem. Lloyd arose at 5:00 a.m. one morning to stock up on supplies, vegetables, and rent money in Siquirres. When he returned after the twelve-hour ordeal, he plunked his pack on the kitchen table and said with a hint of sarcasm, "Wait until you hear what happened to me." This is his narrative:

> I depart Parismina on the 5:00 a.m. lancha to catch the bus at Caño Blanco. We stop first at the home of a cheese-making family. To my surprise, Val embarks there. We strike up a conversation and Val suggests we eat breakfast together in Siquirres as neither the bank nor the markets will be open yet. Over a hearty plate of beans and rice called *gallo pinto*, she suggests splitting a taxi to return to the docks at Caño Blanco after our shopping spree since she will be carting several cans of paint for the school back to the island with her. I agree. Then, I set off merrily for the bank to withdraw money for rent and food, after which I intend to shop at the market for produce, then the grocery store for staples and items such as a can opener and a good knife.
>
> With Val's directions fresh in my mind, I go off in search of an automated teller. I am informed there are two in town. As I round a corner, I see a long lineup at the ATM. At least forty people have queued before me. I immediately reverse course only to discover thirty people queuing at the second ATM.

Knowing the market closes at 10:00 I worry that I will not make it there in time to pick up the produce I have been commissioned to buy. In the back of my mind, I remember that Val will be waiting for me at 1:00 to make the trek back to the docks. As I have a small amount of cash, I decide to make the market a priority, so I blow off the second ATM. Along the way I stumble upon the main grocery store called the *Palí* [rhymes with pa-teee], and I nip in to purchase the staples first.

I notice the grocery store has its own ATM. As a stupid foreigner, I have no clue how the system works. The machine only spits out a receipt which I am instructed to take to the cashier who calls the manager to authorize a payout of twenty-five thousand colones. Armed with the knowledge of this process, I dare to do it again, but the normally gregarious ticos are now giving off bad vibes due to my depriving them of any cash with which to do business, for I have cleaned out their till entirely.

I still don't have enough money and time is running out on the market and my return rendezvous with Val. I abandon the plan to complete purchases at the Palí and head directly to the market. I pass both ATMs and notice nervously that the lineups remain long. I'm at the market by 9:15 and buy ten pounds of spuds, five pounds of carrots, five pounds of onions, and three cabbages and load them into my backpack by ten o'clock.

Now I am off to do some banking, but first, I stop in the shade to redistribute the weight and desquishify the veggies. I bump into Val, who asks if I mind delaying departure until 2:00.

At ATM #1 I am disheartened to see forty people still waiting in line. I hurry by it and veer east to the Palí to get staples: peanut butter, pasta, pasta sauce, rice, and jam along with the knife and can opener.

After that, I check ATM #2 and mercifully, its lineup has dwindled to just fifteen people waiting in the full egg-frying-on-the-sidewalk sun. I wait in line here, trying in vain to protect myself from sunburn with only a baseball hat and my collar flipped up to protect the back of my neck. But my collar is not enough. I rotate the brim of my cap to shield my Anglo skin against the blaze and try my best to cope with one bottle of water.

I wait patiently as the queue recedes and when I am just three people away, the ATM shuts down. I have just lost forty-five minutes. I elect to go inside the bank where I see the line is snaking around the lobby and out the door. Perhaps fifty to sixty people are there, but I reason that at least the bank will not run out of money.

For *two hours* I shuffle forward with the bulky vegetables as heavy as a dead body on the floor at my feet. The line shrinks and I drag the corpse ahead, then step forward. Again and again, drag the dead body, step forward.

I begin counting down the people waiting in line at 25 . . . 24 . . . 23 but become aware of a cultural idiosyncrasy that impedes my progress. When pregnant women or senior citizens enter, they immediately jump the line, with no complaints from anyone. And so it goes 24 . . . 23 . . . 22 . . . old man jumps the line . . . 23 . . . 22 . . . 21 . . . 20 . . . pregnant lady . . . old man . . . 22 . . . 21. I check my watch. The one o'clock bus to Caño Blanco has left, and I have one hour to get money and meet Val.

At the teller, I present my Visa card and ask for a $300 cash advance only to be told that I am in the wrong line. The clerk sends me to customer service where I take a number and get in line behind fifty people. Panic sets in, and I entertain thoughts such as, *Should I go home and come back the next day? Will my wife kill me?* In a moment of dread, I make a split-second decision. I drag the dead body out onto the street to go to ATM #1. It is now 1:15.

With twenty people in line there I think I might have half a chance, but after forty-five minutes in line I am at the wire deciding whether to blow the whole thing off, when Val walks by.

"I'll wait for you," she reassures me.

By now I am truly perishing in the heat. I have no more water and no more hope. I am getting closer and closer to the bank machine. I hear a lot of cash coming out. This line up has been here all day. Money will run out. I will have to come back tomorrow. Either I will die of sunstroke or my wife will kill me.

Then, it is my turn. I crowd into the small telephone-like booth with the dead body and after having hours to get my bank card ready, I gap it totally and dig frantically for it. I am horrified. It is not there. I feel the glares of those behind me as they watch the gringo feeling himself up for his ATM card, hidden in his money belt, down his pants. I see people peering over shoulders and sense that they are telepathically telling me to hurry the hell up. With seconds feeling like hours, I find my credit card tucked away in a different slot after the Palí.

With a sense of relief no words can describe, the machine spews out cash which I stash in my money belt. I pick up the dead body, so heavy by now after dragging it for hours that I must set it up on the counter to get it on my back. I make my way to the paint shop where Val is patiently waiting. We clock in at Parismina at 5:00, twelve hours later.

At least we learned a few things from this debacle: plan your hard cash needs well in advance (on the Caribbean side, ATMs were either not reliable or nonexistent) and always ask if you are in the right line up.

"Girls, I think I may have scored a horseback-riding and cheese-making tour," Lloyd said as he unloaded vegetables.

They looked at him, bug-eyed with excitement.

"Mom, can we go?" Jocelyn asked.

"Are you willing to get up at five o'clock to catch the lancha to Caño Blanco?"

The girls clasped hands in wild anticipation. "Yes!" they said in unison. In fact, neither one had any concept of how early that was.

Deeming it a worthwhile and cultural event—a direct mandate of the trip—we signed up for the tours. The girls could scarcely wait the two days. When we stepped off the bus in Caño Blanco, an entire family was waiting for us. The matriarch was a thin, hard working woman named Catalina who ran the cheese-making operation with three farm hands. Her son worked in a barn behind the main house making handcrafted furniture. The daughters, all single mothers, scurried after toddlers in the main house. They treated us to a typical, hearty breakfast of gallo pinto and fried cheese, then escorted us to the farm for step one in the cheese-making process: milking.

We threaded our way past the carpenter's shop and forded a moat by inching across a log. Catalina set a stool down in front of a set of swollen udders and said to Jocelyn, "Grasp firmly, now pull."

"Like this?" she asked after a few dribbles came out.

"Let me show you." Like the old pro she was, she squirted an inch of milk into the bucket with only a couple of tugs.

Natalie got down on the stool in front of a waiting cow and milked it so successfully that within twenty minutes she had nearly an inch in the pail. I begged off, claiming I had photos to take.

The girls linked up with some children home on a mid-morning break from school, tramping around in the manure and playing with puppies and piglets.

Then we moved on to step two in the cheese-making process: curdling. Lloyd and Catalina poured the milk into buckets and left it to curdle. Since the curdling would take time, we edged back across the log to saddle the family's horses and ride to a nearby botanical garden called Jardín Tropical. Lloyd immediately realized he had a problem. "I'm too tall for these horses!" With his long, lanky legs, his stirrups behaved like a gynecological instrument gone awry.

Catalina waved off his concern. "We're not going far."

We were forced to ride tandem with the girls for their safety. Each of us had one hand on the reins and the other wrapped around a child. Off we cantered down the Siquirres road bathed in the full, hot sun. Lloyd's horse refused to walk, preferring to trot, or pull up short for no reason. After twenty minutes, he complained, "Where is this place?"

We had seen a few tour buses go by (where the heck were they going?) but had come across no other signs of life along the road, except for a few monkeys who swung low to laugh at us. The girls, secure in their saddles and a parent's clutches, were oblivious to our struggles to control the horses with one hand while trying to avoid passing out from the heat. Lloyd, usually patient and kind to a fault, was insufferable. "I can't go on. I have to get off and rest."

Catalina wasn't having it. "We will get there soon," she said.

Forty-five minutes later we rounded a corner and entered the luxuriant grounds of Jardín Tropical. Lloyd tried to listen carefully to our guide identifying the diverse plants, but his body was in knots.

"Are there any poison dart frogs here?" Natalie asked.

"Indeed, there are, right this way," replied the guide, bowing low, as if the girls were royalty, one arm across his waist, the other palm up and sweeping broadly, indicating a path. He led them to a small stand of broad-leafed trees and gently lifted a giant frond to expose two poison dart frogs clinging to the underside by their sticky pads.

The frond cast an emerald glow across the faces of the girls. They studied the frogs intently, but when one moved slightly it startled Jocelyn. "Oh!" she cried.

When a tour bus pulled in, the guide dropped the frond and went to greet the new arrivals.

Turning to Lloyd, Natalie said, "The frogs were hard to see."

"That's because they are camouflaged," Lloyd pointed out.

"Smart frogs," she said.

Lloyd left the girls and limped over to me. "I'm seriously thinking of asking that tour bus driver to take us back to the farm."

I looked at him incredulously. "Honestly. You are worse than the kids."

He kicked a rock in frustration. "I *know*."

In the end, he relented and mounted his horse, muttering angrily to himself. It was all I could do not to laugh out loud at the sight of him, knees to his armpits, bouncing along the rocky road. From time to time, to give his knees a break, he removed his feet from the stirrups and let them dangle, almost touching the ground.

I was developing a grim mood myself, but at least *I* tried to put on a brave face. "Just about five more minutes now, Jocelyn. What's that you say? You're hot? Yes, it is rather warm, isn't it?" And so on.

With that part of the tour over, it was time to return to the cheese-making process. Step three: pressing. With newly bowed legs, we hobbled to the barn to dump the curdled milk, now clumped into blobs, into wooden squares to form the cheese into blocks.

After milking, curdling, and clumping, Catalina announced, "Y eso es el proceso de queso." And that is the cheese process. We thanked her profusely for her time, paid her, and limped to the house to wait for the afternoon bus that had departed Siquirres some two hours before and was due to show up at any moment to shuttle us back to Caño Blanco.

On the veranda, the daughters gave us fresh juices and cut open unripe, sour fruit from the yard and sprinkled it with salt. We saw this delicious combination of sour and salty across the region. With such an abundance of fruit, the locals had learned how to eat it at every stage of ripening.

It had been a long day for us, and that rickety bus burping down the road toward us was a welcome sight! Still, we had made some great friends, and there was a touching moment when one of the little toddlers, affectionately called "Papi" by his grandma, wept when he realized the girls were leaving.

TURTLE PATROLS

At dusk, the townsfolk of Parismina gathered at the crossroads of two footpaths that converged at a beer stand–cum–night club. While children ran and played in the twilight, adults sipped cold beer on the branch of a tree. On Saturday nights, the crowd moved inside to cut a rug to the lilting sounds of Bob Marley. The rest of the week, people went to bed and got up in harmony with the sun. The only constituents who stayed out all night were the volunteers of the Asociación Salvemos las Tortugas de Parismina.

According to ASTOP, the three species of sea turtle coming ashore in Parismina—hawksbill, leatherback, and green—are on the brink of extinction. The website declares: "Costa Rica . . . announced a law in 1999 that strictly banned sea turtle poaching and the sale of turtle products. A decade later, thanks to ASTOP, poaching dropped from 98% to 38%."[3]

Back in Canada, when I'd emailed the link to Lloyd at work, he burst in the door that night, jubilant. "I can't stop thinking about this place." He

---

3. ASTOP, "Our Story," para. 2, http://www.parisminaturtles.org/association-save-turtles-parismina/about-us/.

scrolled through the website on his laptop with the girls on either side of him.

"Are we going to see the turtles, Daddy?" Natalie had asked.

"Definitely."

ASTOP had struck a committee to oversee volunteer recruitment and the operation of a turtle hatchery to stem the slaughter of female turtles for soup and the pilfering of turtle eggs. To the north lies Tortuguero National Park, which shelters nesting turtles under its National Park protection status. But Parismina falls just outside of the park boundaries and receives only occasional assistance from the Coast Guard in the form of armed patrols; the volunteer committee did most of the work.

A crucial component to the success of the hatchery and protection program was luring foreigners and their cash to the island. With these eco-tourists pumping money into the local economy, it became more profitable to keep the turtles alive and returning than to sell the coveted eggs on the black market. Volunteers registered with the program for a nominal fee to fund the local guides who patrolled the beach every night.

Sea turtles lay their eggs only at night. Since most plundering took place under cover of darkness, patrols commenced at 8:00, 10:00, and midnight and lasted four hours, following the chocolate sand beach for six kilometers. Participants watched for the telltale signs of nesting turtles: two thick dark lines in the sand.

Donning pants and long sleeves to repel mosquitoes, we rendezvoused at the guard shack for our first patrol on a muggy, overcast night. Lightning ripped silently through the clouds, heralding the start of the rainy season.

The walk along the beach was pleasant, for a while. But ninety minutes later, we had not been rewarded with any turtle sightings, as can sometimes be the case. For the locals, the lengthy patrols barely registered a blip on their exercise radar, but five-year-old Natalie found it overwhelming. Lloyd and I took turns piggybacking her on the return hike. Drenched in sweat, dog-tired, and disappointed, we flopped into bed.

The next night, Lloyd accompanied the guides alone. At midnight, he woke me. "I saw *three*."

That did it for me; I signed up for another patrol that night.

I was greeted by a beautiful high school girl named Julieta and her senior patrol partner, Fernando. Fernando handed me a walkie talkie, two plastic bags, a flashlight, and to prevent contact with harmful bacteria, a pair of latex gloves. We were no more than twenty feet from the guard house when we came across a young turtle in the early stages, digging out a hole to bury her eggs. We approached cautiously from the side, then moved to stand behind her. From just one foot away, I observed the entire process from beginning to end, unnoticed by her.

She developed a rhythm to her digging, bending one back flipper under her rear as if making a British curtsy. Then she dug her pointy flipper into the sand, curled it into a spoon and flicked outward. Her head receded into her shell, and her lungs exhaled in a great whoosh. The opposite flipper repeated the motion. Bend ... curtsy ... flick ... exhale, bend ... curtsy ... flick ... exhale.

Fernando detected when the digging was complete and the laying about to start. He gestured for me to put on the latex gloves, reach into the hole, pull out the eggs and plunk them into the plastic bag. I strained the length of my outstretched arm to pull out egg after egg. Because we were behind the turtle, she was ignorant of my stealthy robbery. As she laid her eggs, unknowingly plopping them right into my hand, I scooped them out without her ever noticing.

Fernando noted, "This is a young green sea turtle. See how small she is?" He touched her gently. "She should not lay so close to the sea."

The eggs, shaped like oversized ping pong balls, felt soft and delicate, almost flimsy. This female managed to lay ninety-eight eggs. Probably less than 1 percent would make it into adulthood. We retreated quietly, giving her room to bury what she assumed were her eggs, then measured her and checked for tumors. This smallish green turtle measured one meter from stem to stern. We watched her turn 180 degrees and flip clumsily back to the sea, and because her track marks led right to the nesting site, we walked a few paces to bury the eggs in a more hidden spot. Then we got down on our hands and knees and swiped the sand back and forth with our arms, raking it as best we could to cover our tracks, to foil the poachers who continued to prowl the beach. We reserved about half of the eggs to bury in the protected sanctuary of the hatchery, which was surrounded by fencing and watched over by a member in the guard shack. Further north in Tortuguero National Park, poaching isn't as much of a threat as everyday menaces, including crabs, birds, and even ants.

Chatting with the guides as we walked farther down the beach, I learned that the hourly wage for patrolling the beach wasn't great, but it went far in a town like Parismina. "You'll not come across a more dedicated and knowledgeable bunch," Lloyd said one night, tapping sand out of his shoe. Guides patrolled because they had grown up in Parismina and witnessed firsthand the drastic drop in the number of turtles that were part of the very fabric of their community.

After that first grueling patrol, I returned to Rodrigo's, peeled off my clothes, and stuck my sweaty body under the cold spray of the shower. A long-limbed frog, jammed into the corner of the stall, observed me with wide, blinking eyes.

Lloyd lifted his head when I crept into the cabina, and I flashed a thumbs up. He smiled and went back to sleep.

A few nights later I asked Jocelyn, "Would you like to go on a patrol with me?"

"Just you and me?"

"Yes. I don't think Natalie is ready for another long walk yet."

"Okay."

We packed water and flashlights and left for the guard house. Lloyd stayed behind to put Natalie to bed. A vacationing couple and their fifteen-year-old daughter joined us. That night we were rewarded with sightings of three leatherbacks. The guides showed particular attention to the children, pointing out the intricacies of the egg laying process and allowing them to touch the rough skin on the turtles' necks, giving them extra time to watch the turtles struggle back to the ocean before we moved on.

That evening, Jocelyn kept Lloyd up late, bubbling over in hushed tones as she told her dad about the turtles she had seen laying their eggs and how they bumbled their way back to the sea, wiped out and breathing heavily. As we had hoped, the stories inspired Natalie to go back out with Lloyd the next night. When they returned, she proudly reported to me, "I got to put on the glove and take the eggs out."

After that, Lloyd was out almost every night. He was in his element, sharing his childhood love—admiring wildlife out of doors—with the girls. The committee considered the patrols a success. One of the patrol organizers told me, "I can't remember when anyone had ever visited the island before the committee formed the volunteer patrols." Now we came in packs, ready to spend a pocketful of money.

A small airport was located at the far end of the island, and small planes transferred wealthy clients from San José to the Río Parismina Lodge, a sport fishing retreat on the mainland just opposite the island. Tarpon anglers, primarily from North America, thought nothing of shelling out $5000 for a week's stay at the lodge. I came across the airport just as a twin prop Piper Navajo was trying to land, dodging wild horses on the buckled runway. The employees of the lodge whirred over in golf carts to retrieve luggage. Villagers descended on the new arrivals, necklaces and bracelets draped over their arms. One of the guests, a giant Caucasian with dark sunglasses, patted a small girl on the head and, without once looking at her said, "Beautiful children." Then the group was shuttled to a lancha, spending as much as five minutes and zero dollars, in Parismina proper.

The final three patrols took place in the early morning to witness the next step in the process: the hatchlings. Lloyd and Jocelyn teamed up at 5:45 a.m. and returned with several sublime videos of the little gaffers flipping their way to the sea. Natalie, inspired by the videos, agreed to rise early for a patrol on a hazy Tuesday morning. Then, no guide showed up. The season was coming to an end and money to pay the guides had run out. They were now patrolling as volunteers. Still nervous about dealing with a headstrong five-year-old and a 5:00 a.m. wake-up call, I successfully convinced her to join me on the Wednesday morning. We were stymied again—no guide.

Our departure from the island was imminent. In two days, a lancha would ferry us to Tortuguero. Our last patrol was in danger of not happening. I was crushed that Natalie might not be able to see dozens of miniature turtles flapping pell-mell for the Caribbean Sea.

Later that morning, the four of us strolled along the main path to town. I told the girls, "You go on ahead. We'll catch up." A moment later, Lloyd and I rounded the corner of the campground and saw Jocelyn running back toward us, madly waving her arms. Immediately worried that Natalie had hurt herself, we yelled, "What? What?" and took off at a run. Ahead, on the lawn of the restaurant, Natalie was corralling a tiny baby turtle with her feet to protect it from Chispa. The baby had hatched, veered off in the wrong direction, and wound up at the edge of town.

Natalie was on the verge of tears. "What should I do?"

Lloyd picked up the baby, no bigger than the palm of a child's hand, and gave it to Natalie. She walked down to the beach, set it down on the sand and watched it flip itself silly in a frantic effort to escape into the sea. Every few seconds he popped his head out of the water to breathe. And then he was gone.

She turned and faced us. "There he goes!"

"You got all that, right?" I said to Lloyd.

"Oh yeah," he said, turning off the camera.

We ran into Martín, one of the project's founders, and told him what had happened. He took off to where the girls had seen the hatchling and uncovered four more babies tangled in the weeds; the girls found another off the main path to the campground. Later we learned that dozens had invaded the dance floor of a nightclub the previous night, and several had been retrieved from hotel rooms. The artificial lights of the buildings had disoriented their sense of direction.

The experience was enough to get Natalie to try one last time to go out on a morning patrol. I confirmed with the committee that a guide would be available, and this time Lloyd and Jocelyn joined us along with several other volunteers from around the world. Natalie participated in the entire process, uncovering a nest using the tape measure to determine its coordinates. Although some of the volunteers were in Parismina for only twenty-four hours, they graciously stood aside to let the girls take on the bulk of the digging, gawking and ooohing as the turtles awoke from their twilight state and fluttered out of the hole.

In a final and defining moment for our family, Jocelyn proudly proclaimed, "We *actually* saved the endangered sea turtles of Costa Rica."

This experience also provided the answer to the gnawing question of how to justify depriving someone of a source of income to save a species. Parismina had the solution: alter the source of revenue. "Some guides had formerly participated in stealing turtle eggs," Martín explained. "Now they play a part in protecting them."

A smart idea, grassroots at its best.

Chapter 4

Tortuguero

We left Parismina on an unbearably humid afternoon. Rodrigo wheeled alongside us to the docks to say goodbye. Chispa trotted sadly beside him. We had arranged for a Tortuguero-bound lancha to pick us up on its way north from Limón. This was the only way to accomplish the journey, really. Traveling overland from Parismina would not have saved us much money; the trip would have spanned many hours and required transfers from lancha to bus and back to lancha. We'd also have to account for all the drinks and snacks we'd have to purchase.

Our boat puttered to the dock with a few intrepid passengers aboard. They made room for us on the benches as we boarded. Birds cawed. Spoonbills mucked around in the water. Surly water buffaloes munched on river grass, regarding us with menacing faces. The banks rose sharply to a sea of green. The monochrome was broken from time to time by a clearing that signaled a farm. This section of the Caribbean lowlands remains almost undeveloped. In the 1800s laborers from Jamaica and other Caribbean islands immigrated to lay rail lines and work the plantations. Today Afro-Carib culture infuses the villages along the coast, with reggae music filling the air and English intermingling with Spanish. Whatever the reason that served to deter development, the wildlife appeared to appreciate it.

We swept into the crowded docks of Tortuguero in mid-afternoon and stared openmouthed at the difference. Trippers milled in clumps, inquiring into kayak rentals or canal tours. A few steps away, the center of town was chock-a-block with restaurants and tour operators touting their businesses. Whereas Parismina was a village of hundreds, with each cinder block house a respectful distance from the others, the town of Tortuguero was New York City by comparison.

We followed a maze of footpaths, most covered with boards to protect feet from mud, searching for the recommended hotel. The small, L-shaped inn opened onto a courtyard where scores of travelers congregated at tables parked under shady trees. Our room featured a well-wired suicide shower. For many in the developing world, cold showers are the norm, so I'm reluctant to admit that I relished the hot spray.

As I was toweling off, I opened the door to let the steam escape and overheard Lloyd lecturing the girls. "There was a scientist named Archie Carr who came to Tortuguero to study the sea turtles and because of him, the government made it illegal to kill the turtles for meat or steal their eggs. He convinced them to protect the turtles or else they would become extinct. Now the locals make a living by welcoming people like us to learn about them." The girls sat on the bed, not sure how to respond. "That's no small feat, girls. This town's economy used to revolve around sea turtle harvesting." He pointed to a picture hanging over the bed, depicting villagers holding spears raised above their heads while scads of decimated turtles lay in bloody pools on the beach.

Natalie looked queasy. "They used to kill them like that?"

"Yes," Lloyd said, "but not anymore. It's against the law now."

After the area bordered by Barra del Colorado Wildlife Refuge and the Río Parismina was declared a National Park, Tortuguero was able to access vital funding from government coffers and attained a coveted designation on Costa Rica's world-famous National Parks list. No one would dare kill a turtle under the scrutiny of that much international attention.

The next day, we called in at the Sea Turtle Conservancy, a research station that welcomed scientists from around the world to study within the National Park. The onsite museum depicted the lifecycle of the sea turtle, but having learned about the maturation and development of the sea turtle up close and personal in Parismina, we felt it was rather redundant.

Lloyd took the girls outside to the edge of the canal. Kayakers rowed back and forth, almost crashing into one another attempting to spot wildlife through the trees along the embankments. An otter popped her head out of the water, glanced at us, then disappeared below. "Maybe the animals are studying the humans. Did you ever think of that?" Lloyd asked.

On the way back to the hotel, Lloyd stopped off to buy a laminated pamphlet listing the wildlife of Costa Rica. "Oh look, Lloyd," I said drily, when we spotted a chicken roosting in a tree, "you can check that one off your list."

Residents, who must have been accustomed to foreigners wandering through their community, ignored us. As we ambled about the village, we were drawn to a soccer pitch covered by rusting corrugated metal where local teens were engaged in a match.

"Daddy, can we watch them play?" asked Natalie.

"Sure, they look pretty good."

The youth took no notice of gawking spectators. Parismina's children would develop this indifference in time, I suppose. It's a shame because the village offered something Tortuguero couldn't—a feel for the culture through homestays and turtle patrols. In Parismina, children mixed with Jocelyn and Natalie easily. In Tortuguero, the local children didn't even acknowledge ours; they were rendered invisible by their sneakers, logoed t-shirts, and cargo pants.

Most came to Tortuguero to see turtles, but we'd had our share of it. The next best place outside of the Amazon to see wildlife lay along the secondary canals. The girls were growing excited at the prospect of seeing animals in their natural habitat, fulfilling one of our primary objectives, to immerse them in science and biology. Lloyd sat at the picnic table outside our hotel room and went over the list of animals on the laminated pamphlet with both girls chatting about creatures they hoped to see on our canal tour.

Six weeks earlier, in San José, we had met a polite, soft-spoken young man named Tomas. He approached us timidly while we were supervising the girls in the pool at the hostel. He was quietly professional, respectful of our time as a family. He patiently explained his services as a tour operator on the Tortuguero canals and assured us that he would take us out in a canoe rather than a motorboat, so the animals would not become frightened. At that, Lloyd took an instant liking to him. Tomas told us that he traveled to the city often to market his tours. Even in a big city like San José, we ran into Tomas almost every day while he visited hotels looking for potential clients and after no more than one hour in Tortuguero, we ran into him again.

"Guys," I said over dinner that night, "Tomas must be meant for us. We bump into him everywhere."

"It isn't all that surprising," Lloyd said. "Tortuguero is actually *smaller* than Parismina."

The center of town was glutted with restaurants, hotels, and tour kiosks and in the heart of all this, Tomas and his brother, Tulio, operated their business out of a soda. His face lit up when he saw us, and he offered to take us on a walking tour of the village. We strolled through the mercado, listening to his explanations about the strange-looking fruit for sale and jotting down recommendations for restaurants. The sheer number of people was astonishing to me, purging an assumption I held about those who take package tours. I'd always thought that people long for a week of peace and relaxation, without having to cook or clean or think about the office. Here in Tortuguero, most came on a tour from San José and were not interested in relaxing at all. They were interested in one thing: seeing a giant sea turtle. I admired their efforts. The ride from San José was taxing and expensive, and because businesses operated on a cash-only basis in the village, calculating costs beforehand was essential. No obvious corporate presence violated the island apart from the companies that manufactured the motorboats—no McDonald's, no Starbucks, no Shell. Lloyd was pleased to see the lengths people went to spend their short vacation observing animals in their natural environment.

Tomas led us around a bend to his "office" to discuss tour costs. In the corner of a soda decorated with red gingham tablecloths, he and his brother laid out their paperwork to go over business. Partly because of his careful attention to us (he went out of his way to get life jackets for the girls) and partly because we wanted to support a local guide, we hired him to take us out the next day.

Early next morning at the main dock we met Tomas, Tulio, an older couple from Spain, and a young Danish student. We set out in two canoes for a four-hour tour of Tortuguero National Park. Tomas explained that he and Tulio were born and raised in the community. Lloyd could think of no one better equipped to take us out on the canals; they had been operating tours in the area for eight years and were expert canoeists, steering us away from noisy, motorized craft and into secluded, narrow channels. Lloyd snorted in disdain when a guide aboard a large motorboat plucked a river turtle out of the water and held it up for his clients to photograph. The turtle wriggled its legs in a fruitless attempt to escape. A dozen people whipped out their cameras while others clapped. Above the din of their engine, I think I heard Tomas snort, too.

Lloyd consulted his laminated pamphlet every time Tomas pointed to wildlife, especially abundant in some channels that were so confined the branches arched down, brushing the tops of our heads. A couple of times we were forced to lie back flat in the canoe to squeeze through tapered passages. The girls giggled and peered up over the rim of the boat. The brothers stopped paddling from time to time, letting us float through narrow tunnels so we could simply enjoy the panorama.

"Miren." Look, Tomas said. It took us several minutes before our untrained eyes discerned a well-camouflaged Jesus Christ lizard (nicknamed because of its so-called ability to walk on water) hiding in the jungle. The brothers were brilliant. At the end of their outstretched arms, we spotted lizards, iguanas, frogs, lanky spiders spread-eagled in webs between trees, as well as parrots and butterflies, including the famous blue morpho. Out on the main tributary, the brothers pointed out branches swaying in the treetops, indicating the presence of one of the three species of monkey: spider, howler, and white-faced capuchin.

At the half-way point of the tour, Tomas announced, "We will stop for a rest."

The brothers deftly beached the canoes at a secretive clearing, shrouded in a pocket of green, and presented us with fresh hot coffee decanted in a thermos. We chatted with the others—the retired couple speaking a Spanish of lisps and twangs, the Dane, flawless English. Tulio rounded up a tiny, poisonous, blue-jean frog from the brush to show the girls.

Back out on the canals, Natalie insisted, "I want to paddle now."

Tomas chuckled when he gave her an oar. "She remind me of my son, he live far away."

"Where does he live?" I asked.

"In Puerto Jiménez."

No two locales could be further apart in Costa Rica; they were literally on opposite sides of the country. My heart went out to him then, a soft-spoken, kindly young man working hard for a living, missing his child.

Lloyd considered the sixty dollars we paid for the tour an enormous bargain, measured by the forty-seven sightings of wildlife he ticked off on his pamphlet. The forty-eighth was checked off a few days later when we saw a domesticated toucan drinking from a water fountain. "I'm not sure that one counts," he said, but ticked it off anyway.

Later that night after we had thanked Tomas and his brother a thousand times for an excellent tour, we saw hundreds of people lining up on the opposite side of the island at the beach. Tour guides called out names and led groups along the sand to observe nesting sea turtles. The Coast Guard demanded the animals be given a much wider berth than those in Parismina. Tourists watched from a distance among dozens of other people, compared to our patrols in Parismina where often Lloyd or I were the only ones in attendance.

Tortuguero offered what Parismina couldn't, though: a little infrastructure in the form of coffee shops, hotels, and internet cafés. We felt buoyed that it could attract the sheer numbers of visitors that it does, given the transportation challenges. It was the end of the turtle season and *still* it was jammed with people seeking out a moment in nature.

Chapter 5

Puerto Viejo

Tomas negotiated an excellent fee on our behalf for water transport all the way back to Limón, but even then, the fares sliced our budget too thinly. However, we justified the expense because we had done so little spending in Parismina, primarily because there was nothing to buy. Locals rarely plow overland from Tortuguero to Limón; it's an excruciating trip, meandering inland through jungle and stopping several times over several hours. We had more than a year ahead of us; we feared turning the girls off backpacking forever by putting them through it.

Settling under the canopied lancha, Lloyd pointed to his wildlife pamphlet. "All we have left are crocs." We'd seen the tinier version of the species—caimans—on our tour with Tomas and it didn't take long to spot their monstrous counterparts.

We cut a swath along the channel for two hours before it widened south of Parismina. Logs riddled the brackish water. Basking crocs straddled them with wide-open mouths. They lay motionless, sharp werewolf-teeth jutting out of scaly mouths, eyes closed to slits. In that position, the awful creatures looked as if they were grinning. They jolted from their reverie when they heard us rounding the bend in the river and slapped into the water, disappearing, save for moments when their bulbous eyeballs broke the surface of the water. I secretly willed the boat to go faster, while the driver derived enjoyment by slowing down to point them out. Lloyd smiled and checked off the last entry on his pamphlet.

Four hours later, we buzzed into Limón. We took advantage of a kind Belgian couple who had ordered a minivan to meet them at the docks.

Seeing the girls with little backpacks melted their hearts and they offered to share their ride with us. The six of us pressed on to Puerto Viejo. It wasn't a very comfortable ride for the Belgians; they didn't dare move a muscle for fear of waking the girls, who had flopped asleep on their shoulders as soon as the van got going.

Puerto Viejo sits between two National Parks (Cahuita and Gandoca-Manzanillo) and is the last major settlement before the border of Panama, about thirty kilometers away. The town appeared stuck in an anachronism. Hordes of dreadlocked hippies circulated in bathing suits and flip-flops. Cars, scooters, bicycles, and pedestrians competed for the roadways with locals who still rode into town on horseback and tied their animals to a hitching post. When we rolled past the beach, our hearts sank. The rocky shore and dark, grey water were more reminiscent of Limón than the turquoise ocean we were hoping for. However, when we were dropped off at Rocking J's, a funky hostel eponymously named after the owner, our spirits rose. From the main road, the walkway leading to the interior of the hostel was laid with recycled tile that had been broken into little bits and re-plastered into vibrant patterns. Save for the kitchen, the bathrooms, and a few rooms, the entire hostel was open-air.

J maximized the use of space by erecting two long pavilions strung with rows and rows of hammocks and setting aside a rectangular section of sandy terrain for tent camping. We pitched our little four-man tent right beside the bathrooms in the north-west corner, encroaching slightly onto the main crab boulevard leading to the beach, (at night their silhouettes against the walls of the tent made them appear enormous). Backpackers from around the world, some displaying their national flag, camped side by side, in the true spirit of international relations.

Above the block of showers, lodgers ocean-gazed from hammocks strung across the balcony, and below that a thatched-roof shelter, also ringed with hammocks, evolved into a reading center. So, one could spend virtually 95 percent of one's day in a hammock if one exerted the effort.

The beach fronting the hostel was dusted with white sand and shaded by enormous palms. The ocean floor ranged from shallow, soft velvet sand, to crusty reef, to bottomless pools. Lloyd and the girls spent long hours exploring every nook and cranny of the reef and plunging into natural saltwater pools dozens of feet in depth. Pink swimsuit bottoms stuck out of the water, legs bicycle-pumped slowly, and snorkels wobbled vertically like drunken soldiers. They catalogued octopus, eels, starfish, and dozens of species of fish. I'd contracted a small foot infection and was advised to keep it out of the "bacterial soup." One day when I noticed the pus drying up, I joined them at the water's edge.

Lloyd urged me to come in. "It's simply amazing. I saw a lobster yesterday."

"Did you check it off your list?"

"You're funny," he said.

The clear, hot water was a balm to my sore muscles after all the late-night turtle patrols and backpack-lugging. I sat cross-legged at the water's edge, squinting against the sun's rays sparkling on the surface. I watched Natalie putter around me. Jocelyn swam with her dad in one of the deeper pools. So far both girls had exceeded my expectations. They could endure physically challenging activities like Parismina's multi-kilometer turtle patrols as well as long hours of inactivity aboard highjacked minivans.

Lloyd and I were still working out the kinks. Our main problem lay in the lumpy beds and heavy packs. The stress of the first few weeks was wearing off. Remaining hydrated was constantly on my mind. The girls became acclimated quickly, but we remained strict about their intake. Here in Puerto Viejo, we planned to take it easy.

I relaxed on the silky ocean bottom, bobbing lightly. Natalie asked, "Can we go to the big pool?"

"Where is it?"

"I'll show you." She took me by the hand and led me several meters out along the reef until the rocky crust gave way to a vast gulf of beautiful, clear water. We positioned our mouthpieces and goggles and took the plunge. She floated close to the reef. Underwater, she pointed out creatures to me: sea urchins hiding in the crevices, slithering eels, and fish of all shapes and sizes. I lifted my head and glanced over at Lloyd and Jocelyn, about twenty meters away. Lloyd was looking back. We grinned at each other. Yes, I think we would begin relaxing quite nicely here.

Every few days, Lloyd took the girls farther down the beach away from town, following a jungle path. It ended at an eye-popping white sand beach that stretched south toward Panama for hundreds of meters. The turquoise waves were not softened by the reef here, however, making it more exciting for the three of them, more nerve-wracking for me. I was concerned about riptides and powerful surf, but Lloyd was vigilant. He clasped their hands, and the three of them body-surfed onto the shore until they collapsed with laughter.

The opportunity to spend time with the girls was one of Lloyd's primary objectives for the trip. Because of his teaching commitments, he sometimes lamented how fast they were growing up. Jocelyn was becoming tall and lanky (like her dad). She had inherited my dark coloring passed down by my father's Italian heritage. Nearly black, thick hair, olive skin, and chocolate eyes made her indistinguishable from the locals. By contrast,

Natalie had fairer, lighter skin like her dad, with fine dark brown hair that fell into poker-perfect straightness after a shower. Like me, she was average in height and strong from the get-go, as I remember from her athletic attempts to escape my womb. She still napped in the afternoon, but if we addressed her hunger and fatigue, she could endure long hikes and spend hours in the tide pools. She was no princess, either. She paid no attention to getting her fingers dirty digging up baby turtles and was fascinated by the gigantic spiders we saw in the canals.

Jocelyn was more easygoing, able to handle hunger and fatigue when her sister was melting down because of it. She was never much of a complainer and rarely got bored. We used it to our advantage. When we plopped her next to Natalie on long bus rides, she immediately captivated her sister's attention by conjuring imaginary characters. Both adopted alternate personalities and created a make-believe world that could last for hours. I supported this dynamic as much as I could. Back home, when we were out of the house for a few hours, the girls begged me to delay dinner when we got home so that they could get their imaginary-play fix. I always agreed. In my opinion, children have been deprived of this kind of activity and spend too much time physically and mentally inactive. Jocelyn spent much of life in a daydream, though, and now for her safety, we encouraged her to pay attention more often.

One afternoon when Natalie went down for a nap, Jocelyn asked me, "Can I have an ice cream?"

I thought about it for a minute, thinking of refusing her. I wanted to soak my infected foot, but I hit on an idea.

I took Lloyd aside. "This is a good chance for her to learn some independence without relying on our eyes and ears all the time."

He agreed. "If you are willing to go to the pulpería across the street by yourself and ask for an ice cream in Spanish, then yes, go ahead," he told her.

Of course, she accepted our terms. We admonished her to look both ways before crossing the street. Then, after practicing a few words in Spanish with me, she marshalled her confidence and exited the gate of Rocking J's. Lloyd and I waited until she disappeared then hustled up to the balcony where we could see the entire scene from above. She waited for two scooters to whiz by followed by a trotting, wild horse. Then she crossed carefully, bought herself an ice cream and headed straight for the tent to show Lloyd and me her efforts. We murmured our approval, pretending not to be breathless from our rapid descent from the balcony. Any traveling family would do well to acknowledge distinct characteristics in this way before setting out on an adventure. We remained aware of each child's individual traits and adapted when necessary. Both girls exhibited temperaments that were both a challenge *and* a benefit.

For a change of pace one day, we rented bicycles to ride to Playa Punta Uva. A local shopkeeper leased us two bikes: a bike with a trailer, and a tandem. Jocelyn and I decided we could handle the tandem; Natalie, because she was still five, got a pass sitting in the trailer. Honestly, the equipment had seen better days, but it was the best we could do. The trailer appeared welded together using discarded metal tubes salvaged from broken-down carriages popular in the 1800s.

Before we left, I had worked out at the gym four times a week and still I could barely refrain from wheezing down the beach road. The asphalt varied from smooth pavement to rocks. Not stones, *rocks*. Lloyd swerved to avoid potholes, almost guaranteeing the trailer would hit them with full force. Natalie got jarred violently until Lloyd forewarned her by yelling "Pothole!" in time for her to lift her behind.

Jocelyn helped as much as she could, pedaling furiously from the back of the tandem. The rusty contraption was difficult to steer and after a bad bump I flew ass-over-teakettle into a ditch. Jocelyn was none the worse for wear, but I got caught underneath the jalopy looking up from the sharp, dry grass at the rest of the family who tried very hard not to laugh. The next day my tribulations were obvious; I was badly bruised, and along with various skin blemishes and a couple of boils, I was an ugly sight, to be sure.

At Punta Uva, we turned off the main road and followed the sandy street to the beach. To the right lay a few simple cabinas. Large palm trees erupted from bleached white sand to our left. We strolled over the grassy rise and were rendered speechless. This was it: the stuff of postcards. Images of only a handful of places on this adventure are burned into my mind's eye. Beautiful places on Earth that make my heart ache. Punta Uva is such a place. What's more, development here has resisted the onslaught of the corporate world. A couple of family-owned cabinas peppered the beach along with a local bar and a soda.

We hopped and staggered our way to the water's edge over boiling sand, plunged our feet into the ocean and looked up and down the coast with mouths agape.

Time stood still. Silence except for the breeze.

The rods and cones in my eyes struggled to differentiate the turquoise blue water from the cobalt sky. The tableau of powder white sand was framed by the green of the jungle looming from the shore. It seemed as though no other human beings existed on earth at that moment except for the four of us.

We zipped back across the burning sand and entered the local soda. We sat as close to the shore as we could and filled up on rice and beans and iced tea. When it came time to leave, I was almost in tears. Not so much because we were leaving this oasis as much as facing the bike ride back. "My legs feel like rubber bands," Lloyd said, but I won the best complainer award that day, claiming it from my husband, who was forced to relinquish it after the horseback riding fiasco.

The more we stayed at Rocking J's, the harder it was to leave. First, we had established a great community of friends with people of all ages from all over the world. Second, J's billing system was calculated on a factor of eight. Every eighth night was free, and once people figured out the math, plans changed and flights were rebooked. Our mornings at Rocking J's were active—breakfast early, then sunscreen, facemasks, and snorkels, then the beach. After that, Natalie had little trouble going down for a nap. Jocelyn and I reclined in the hammocks to read for a couple of hours in the afternoon.

Lloyd hung out at the dart board with two Americans named Steve and Derek. When I joined them one afternoon, Steve said, "I hear you're on a homeschooling field trip."

"That's right," I said. "We've only just begun."

Derek handed me a cold Imperial. "We've never met a family backpacking for such a long time."

Bob Marley played softly in the background. "Well we've never met other backpackers our age yet," I said.

"Actually, I'm retired," said Derek, stroking his grey beard. "Even though we live on opposite sides of the US, we spend a few weeks every year camping, usually in Arizona or Upstate New York."

Steve added, "This is our first year outside the US."

"We recommend Tortuguero," Lloyd said.

"He's been describing all the wildlife you saw on the canals," Steve said.

After enduring the viewing of eight rolls of Italian geology, I took pity on both men for having been subjected to the wildlife pamphlet.

Just then John, a rugged young man from Alaska, hobbled to us, bleeding and grimacing.

"Sit down," Lloyd commanded.

Steve, looking grossed out, asked, "What happened?"

"A bunch of us were swimming at that island offshore from the hostel," John said. "A teenage girl from Sweden fainted from the heat. I had to carry her back here. I've sliced open my big toe!"

"Go get the first aid kit, Janet," Lloyd said, examining the wound.

Lloyd and I united to clean the toe; John winced and sucked in his breath.

I muttered, "How can parents allow a girl that young to travel on her own?"

Lloyd wrapped the toe in gauze, tied it, and looked at me. "How old were you when you went to Belgium to visit your friend?"

Seventeen.

A few weeks later, in an email from the US, John reported, "I've still got the toe!"

When I told Lloyd about the email, he laughed. "Catastrophe averted."

The following week, Limón's annual Carnival celebration was scheduled. "Let's go as a day trip to celebrate Natty's birthday," Lloyd suggested.

"No Hotel Miami? I asked him.

"Well, we plan on coming back to Rocking J's anyway," he pointed out. "Why pack up all our gear for one night? Besides, Limón is only an hour away."

Before we left for Carnival, Jocelyn and I scoured Puerto Viejo looking for a bakery. After walking all over town, we came across a bread shop that agreed to make a cake for Natalie.

The young man who worked at the counter asked me, "Cómo se escribe su nombre?" How do you spell her name?

I took pains to write and rewrite and explain how to spell N-A-T-A-L-I-E in English. He chewed his thumbnail, studied my scrawl, clicked his pen and nodded.

"We will be back in the evening to pick it up," I said.

At midday, the main streets of Limón were filling with people. We circulated through the mud-covered midway, plopped the kids on the merry-go-round, then caught a movie at a 3D cinema. Afterwards, we splurged on a meal at a vegetarian restaurant. On our way home Jocelyn tried hard to refrain from spilling the beans about Natalie's surprise party with the gang back at the hostel. However, when we arrived at the bakery to pick up the cake, a sign on the door read: "Caique de Natalie—a la tienda de videos." Natalie's cake—at the video store. Because she could not yet read in either language, our secret was still intact.

Next door at the video shop, we pretended to peruse movie titles to disguise Lloyd's disappearance to the ATM. As in Siquirres, the machine was dry of cash, so he took off for the hostel to retrieve some money from our locker. Natalie looked beat after the long day and my heart fluttered a little at the potential meltdown and disaster awaiting us if Lloyd *didn't hurry the hell up*. He showed up breathless with a ten thousand colón note. The girl at the video shop refused it. "No tengo cambio." I don't have change.

Anticipating a catastrophic end to the day, I let the cat out of the bag, pulled Natalie into view and blurted, "It's for her birthday." At that, the girl melted and let us take the cake, asking us to leave some collateral and to promise to return the next day to pick it up and pay for the cake.

Back at the hostel, the crew shouted out, "Happy Birthday!" I sliced the cake thinly to feed my family and the company of vagabonds we kept. Nat was beaming while the crowd sang (their volume may have been influenced by a few bottles of beer). Suddenly, I realized that I had left some cake sitting out in the kitchen. I rushed back just in time to save it from millions of tiny ants who had breached the walls of the box and were virtually centimeters away from seizing it altogether.

I removed the cake from the box and put it in the fridge. When I returned to the party, I noticed each of my family members with their favorite people. Lloyd was with Steve and Derek. Natalie was going back and forth between Alicia, an African-American massage therapist, and Jennifer, who'd checked in from the US with her boyfriend, Eric. Whenever I was looking for Natalie, I looked for Jennifer's head poking above tent peaks, and she would indicate that Natalie was right there beside her. Jocelyn sat with Susan and Daria, two Australian sparkplugs who had conquered most of the world by backpack already. She'd been joining them in the early mornings on the balcony for yoga, led by Crystal, from Holland.

Even now, I believe I will remember our time at Rocking J's as a highlight of the trip. Per one of our objectives, the girls encountered people from around the world and persons of all linguistic backgrounds and skin tones. Fellow hammock-swingers included dozens of multilingual university students from Europe as well as environmentalists who blew into town for a few days of R&R from their jobs as turtle volunteers in Parque Nacional Cahuita. I do think we had some counter-impact on them, demonstrating how children can be interesting, funny, intelligent, and capable of "roughing" it with their adventurous parents. There were enough over-forties, like expats from the US who had left in the '70s and never returned, or traveling buddies Steve and Derek (or me and Lloyd for that matter), to show that adventuring is possible at any age. The only thing missing from our lives was interacting with the locals, and that was about to change, thanks to El Puente.

ONE NIGHT IN THE JUNGLE

For two years we researched activities we could do as a family in Costa Rica, from volunteer placements to beach holidays. On one discussion board, I discovered an organization known as El Puente (The Bridge), a not-for-profit organization founded by Nanci and Barry Stevens. El Puente supported the local Indigenous Bribri by operating a soup kitchen three days a week and raised funds to offer microloans to families. I emailed the Stevens to inquire about visiting El Puente, and Barry and Nanci invited us to attend one of their tri-weekly soup kitchens. We were eager to have the girls engage with local kids, and Nanci felt the same way about the young Bribri she knew, some of whom had never met foreign children. As soon as we arrived, the kids drummed up a game of catch in the front yard, and Lloyd and I helped to cut up vegetables. With my Spanish still mediocre, I unwittingly invited my whole family to spend one night with Abril, Ignacio, and their five children in the KeKoldi Indigenous Reserve.

The Reserve, known for migrating birds of prey, curves around the base of the Talamanca Mountains at the edge of town. The next morning, we agreed to meet the family at Nanci and Barry's, then trek forty-five minutes into the bush to a clearing overlooking the valley. The hike was not long as much as sheer uphill. We slipped on muddy trails, hanging onto vines for balance. Jocelyn and Natalie were captivated. Every odd-looking fruit captured their attention and the call of birds halted them as we climbed further into the jungle. At the family's homestead, Ignacio showed us around. He had fabricated two sleeping quarters, raised about three feet from the ground. Bamboo stalks cut into lengthwise strips were laid out on the floors, forming an undulating surface. The dorms, topped with thatched roofing to keep out the rain, were open-air, typical of structures in this warmer climate. Ignacio's family all slept together in the larger room. A small kitchen was attached to it, complete with a raised fire pit for cooking and a sloped rock that acted as a washboard for washing clothes. Nearby, Ignacio had fashioned a bathroom using planks laid out across a pit with a convenient hole carved out for "deposits."

Ignacio explained that the Costa Rican government had bestowed this expanse of land to the Indigenous of the area in the seventies and they, in turn, were permitted to reside there without disturbance. Ignacio was proud of his people and loved living in the jungle. "We have everything we need." Although we could hear eighteen-wheelers screeching their brakes as they passed El Puente below us, he said, "Here, it is muy tranquilo."

Their children, ranging in age from two to eleven, and ours sat together shyly on a log. Neither group spoke the same language but before long they were hopping off and on the log, laughing. They moved to the guest dorm, climbed on top of the bamboo rafter, lay flat on their stomachs, and hung their heads upside down over the edge so their hair fell over their faces. When they tired of that, the Bribri children pulled out coloring books and crayons and passed them out. They were simply the most well-behaved, soft-spoken children we had ever met. Not a raised voice among them, no fighting, only smiles and giggles. They were fascinated by Lloyd's digital camera when he pulled it out to show them our videos of the turtle patrols.

Ignacio showed us where Abril grew herbs and a few vegetables. Chickens and pigs scurried along dirt paths, foraging for grubs. The site was situated close to a stream for drinking, washing, and cooking, as close to town as possible so the kids could walk to school. Ignacio's and Abril's children were among the first of the Bribri to attend.

Ignacio pointed out several poison dart frogs, dangerous ants, and a snake that he claimed still posed a health risk seven years after being bitten by it. I had spent a sleepless night worried about this very possibility. Realizing that the Bribri and millions of other families in the world raise their children in much more dangerous surroundings, I swallowed my fear and insisted the girls wear their boots the entire time we were in the jungle, and I never let them out of my sight.

Abril cooked us a simple meal of beans and rice, and we ate by candlelight, cross-legged up on their sleeping platform. Afterwards, the children sat in a group and colored quietly.

The oldest boy, Jorge, came over to the adults and whispered to his father. Ignacio looked at Lloyd curiously.

In stilted English, Jorge asked, "Lloyd, how many years?"

In English, Lloyd responded, "Thirty-six."

Astonished, Ignacio made Lloyd stand beside him, then asked me to translate what Lloyd had said.

"Treinta y seis."

Ignacio and Jorge stared at each other, disbelieving. Ignacio explained that Lloyd looked much older because he was so tall. Ignacio, at thirty-five, stood a full foot shorter.

When it was time for bed, we followed the path to our sleeping quarters. We had brought our air mattresses, sleeping bags, bug suits, and insect repellent on Nanci's sage advice. Despite the warm temperature, we all wore long pants, long-sleeved t-shirts, and bug suits, leaving only our hands unprotected. (The girls showed me bites on their fingers in the morning.)

Of the four of us, Lloyd was the most excited about spending time outdoors in the fresh air. "One night in the jungle, how awesome would that be!"

Lying on the bamboo floor positioned us perfectly before an astounding scene of the lush green tangle of wilderness. We were reluctant to shut our eyes to the sight, but eventually we drifted off to sleep in the arms of Mother Nature. Throughout the night, our slumber was interrupted by animal sounds. Not by birds or howler monkeys but by the family's scavenging pigs and the damnable rooster *cock-a-doodle-dooing* all night long. So much for the sounds of wildlife.

In the morning, we paid the family a small fee which would contribute to Abril's gardening project then made our way down the mountain to Nanci and Barry's. To prevent me from tumbling, Ignacio had Jorge cut me a walking stick. This family makes this same trek every day to rendezvous at El Puente, with the children walking thirty minutes farther to the closest school.

Nanci and Barry accept anyone willing to volunteer. Contact them here to find out how you can help: https://www.elpuente-thebridge.org/.

Chapter 6

Entering Panama

On my darkest nights back in Canada when I entertained thoughts about danger, I never imagined sidestepping tanker trucks by clinging to a bridge overlooking a rushing river.

But I'm getting ahead of myself.

Persons of most nationalities must leave Costa Rica after three months for seventy-two hours to renew their tourist visas, so after using Rocking J's math of eight nights x four weeks, we had to vacate Rocking J's after thirty-two days of lounging and reading and swimming and socializing in Puerto Viejo. Everyone else worked in a "border run" to Panama, and returned three days later, but once we got looking at the maps of the two countries, we wondered about voyaging all the way to Panama City to see the famous canal before returning to Costa Rica. "We'll never be here again," I argued. "It might be the only opportunity to see the canal in our entire lives."

Lloyd acquiesced. "I guess I got to stay overnight in the jungle," he said. "Why not?"

The short jaunt to the border town of Sixaola was pleasant. The town, not so much. Locals hounded us as soon as we got off the bus, offering to escort us to immigration. We ignored their presence, cleared immigration without incident, exited Costa Rica, and faced the old banana bridge that spans the Río Sixaola, to enter Panama. As was our habit, we proceeded single file—one adult in front, then Jocelyn and Natalie. The remaining adult brought up the rear, to better supervise the girls.

This time, I was out front. I turned to Lloyd, dumbfounded. "Are they kidding?"

We had heard horror stories about the banana bridge. At Rocking J's, a young American college student asked us, "Are you crossing at Sixaola?"

"Yes, why?" I asked.

"Umm," she said, biting her lips, "it's tricky. Be careful with the girls."

I had no idea what she meant, and our imaginations did no justice to the reality of the situation.

"Girls, stay close!" Lloyd shouted.

A dilapidated chain link fence that bulged at spots where the weaving had come apart shielded us from falling into the river. The Costa Ricans had erected a pedestrian walkway beside the fence, but halfway across the no man's land, the walkway ended, and we walked along the bridge itself, sharing old railroad tracks with vehicles crossing the border. The tracks had been ripped up, exposing railway ties separated by gaps ranging from a couple of inches to almost a foot. The ties supported planks about eight inches in width. We walked across the planks balance-beam style some 125 meters to the other side, our heavy packs weighing us down, down, down.

We soldiered on, dipping and rising with the pulse of passing vehicles. The girls knew to stay quiet. One enterprising adolescent would not be deterred. He insisted on "helping" us through immigration procedures and stuck with us on the bridge. About two-thirds of the way across, three full-sized tractor trailers barreled toward us from the opposite direction.

"They'll wait until we're safely across, right?" I called back to Lloyd.

"Doesn't look like it. Follow the boy." Our young man beckoned us forward to a holding area—a perch, basically—a piece of plywood, jutting out over the river. A hole in the chain link fence had been cut to allow for this, and so we stood, the five of us, crammed together, clinging to the cut in the fence, bulging and buckled in spots and attached carelessly to the platform. The river rushed eastward below us. The long-haulers rumbled past and as they did, the boy reached over Lloyd's shoulder to pinch in his backpack to keep it from scraping the sides of the trucks.

BOCAS DEL TORO

Guabito was a typical border town mired in chaos, with rutted, muddy roads and men lurking around the customs office. Because Panama uses US currency as legal tender, we were directed to pay five dollars to get a tourist stamp then turn around and show it to the guy at the other desk. We didn't even take a step. The friendly officials were delighted to see children and waived their entry fee. We said goodbye to our young man amid passport stamping and filling out of forms. "Gracias. Muchas gracias," Lloyd said, pressing ten dollars into his hand.

He smiled and passed us on to a driver who offered to take us in his truck to the Changuinola docks, where we would catch a lancha to Bocas del Toro.

Negotiations with the driver were accomplished in loud voices to drown out the bedlam. We were a prime target for roving vendors, who shouted at us to buy whatever they were selling. In fact, in the fourteen crossings between seven countries, we warded off money changers, trinket sellers, drink peddlers, food and gum vendors, lottery ticket agents, luggage luggers, and taxi drivers, all of whom competed for our attention and dollars.

The girls were agog, eyeballing the chaos. "Go with Daddy. I'm going to buy drinks and snacks," I told them. Jocelyn, especially, had to be physically led to the truck by hand.

Lloyd loaded our packs into the cab of the driver's truck and buckled the girls into the back seat. It was slow slogging. Our driver threw his hands up in irritation when we came across lunar-sized potholes, which he maneuvered around by cranking the steering sharply to the left, then the right. Along the side of the road, strange looking cables hung overhead, parallel to us. Our driver came to a full stop where they crossed the road.

"What is that Daddy?" Jocelyn pointed to a clump of green bananas hooked to the cables by their stalks hanging down from a pulley. The bananas wheeled along, ski lift style, and passed in front of us.

Our driver explained, "The fruit from the fields travels to the processing plants over there." He indicated a metal-roofed rectangular building.

"Hey girls," I said, "Why did the bananas cross the road?"

"To get to the other side!"

❖❖❖

Our driver dropped us at the docks in Changuinola, a nondescript backwater where we had to wait a short while until a lancha materialized to motor us to the island. Bocas, as it's commonly known, rests on Isla Colón, one of many islands in the archipelago. Reputed to front pristine sand, hosting cheap and lovely accommodations, we learned that Bocas is a pretty little town whose activities were not centrally located. Participation meant a pricey boat trip to outer islands to see the untouched sand (a thirty-minute walk along a muddy beach), snorkel the reef (half dead from sediment), or enjoy a delicious lunch at a beachfront restaurant (overpriced).

We'd already taken part in all of this for free from the shore at Puerto Viejo or by butt-numbing bicycle ride to Punta Uva. Nonetheless, we elected to stay in town for a few days to unwind from our harrowing bridge crossing. Bocas was brimming with sojourners (many on border runs of their own), and the requisite number of hostels, pensions, upscale hotels, and outfitters to accommodate them. We had been on the road from Puerto Viejo since mid-morning, so we took a load off at a restaurant on the main drag. The rhythm of the town throbbed as we ate, then the rhythm of the town *pounded* as we ate. We looked at each other quizzically. "Do you hear something?" Lloyd asked.

The girls stood on the veranda and craned their necks down the street. "It's a parade!" cried Jocelyn.

Later, in bed, we furrowed our brows. We heard the same thrumming again. Our table at the restaurant looked out at the parade *rehearsals*.

"How can anyone sleep in this town?" Lloyd said.

I remarked that cultures unencumbered by the nine-to-five world would think nothing of losing sleep. He harrumphed and turned over.

The bands practiced all through the night. Their efforts were obvious on the day of the parade. Marching bands inched and shuffled their way through the small town of Bocas, dancing, twirling, and drumming. The lead percussionists, all strapping young men, jumped and hopped, and heaved their enormous drums into the air, sweating through their uniforms. What's more, the performers ranged in age from four to forty with the tiniest children marching in step for hours with people ten times their age.

Apart from this bonus cultural attraction, what we especially liked in Bocas were the shockingly low prices. I took advantage and bought bathing suits for the girls (now in tatters from all the snorkeling and body surfing) and flip-flops for less than a dollar. Lloyd came home with a six pack of beer that cost roughly three bucks. The high-speed internet was a huge benefit, enabling us to communicate with our tenants back home who had complained the garage was leaking.

Despite the great shopping, Bocas was a tourist town, and we'd had our share of that back in Puerto Viejo. It was time to set course for Panama City, a journey of ten hours that we planned to break up by stopping in David (pronounced "Daveed"). Buses destined for David met the lanchas in Almirante. I panicked when I saw the driver at the docks beckoning us to hurry up and board. We had barely eaten that morning because we had planned on eating at a *comedor*, Panama's version of a *soda*, while waiting for a bus, and since this leg lasted three hours, I asked the driver if he would wait until I ran into a nearby grocery store to buy food and water. He agreed. Lloyd got the girls settled, I loaded up with anything edible I could find.

We wound our way through the Chiriquí highlands on a mini-bus via a mountainous pass that cut in and out of the greenery. We were amazed to see people turn up at the side of the road to flag down the bus, seemingly out of nowhere. The presence of the Indigenous population became evident. Women adhered to traditional design, wearing loose-fitting, full-length, brightly colored dresses of orange, yellow, purple, or royal blue, embroidered on the bodice and the sleeves. The men dressed in a more assimilated style, in shirts, and trousers.

We rounded a bend in the hillside, and such a family flagged us down. They were five people in total, three children, the father, and a late-term pregnant mother. They sat directly in front of us. The father had his hands full with the baby. These people were so slight, all five of them could squish into two cramped seats, in contrast to Lloyd, who had folded himself into one entire seat at the back.

After much smiling and nodding of hello, I realized, looking down at my hurried purchases, that I had bought way too much food. We offered the family our bananas and chips. They accepted it without hesitation, responding with shy smiles. The disparity of wealth couldn't have been more apparent, and yet they received our offers with grace and asked for nothing more. Jocelyn and Natalie handed over small toys to the children who by now were overcoming their timidity and peered at the girls with sideways glances. The men of the two families communicated with one another using a common language: nodding, finger pointing, smiling and gesturing.

It was interesting, therefore, a little later, when a well-dressed young Panamanian foisted himself between Lloyd and me and repeatedly demanded money from us for the duration of our journey. I suddenly lost all ability to speak Spanish. Quite the study in human relations, I would say.

DAVID

David offers little to travelers other than respite from the long distances between destinations, but the cheap shopping is a huge attraction. As I piled the gang into a taxi, I spotted a vendor selling the popular *Condorito* comics that feature a loveable condor living in a small Chilean town. I bought five copies for next to nothing to use as a teaching tool for written Spanish.

The stopover proved that the world is indeed small. At the hostel, we ran into Eric and Jennifer, who had befriended Natalie back at Rocking J's, on the other side of the isthmus and in a different country.

Jennifer asked me, "Have you seen the grocery store yet?"

"No," I said.

"I'll watch the girls. You two need to go and see it."

We were simply agog. In the previous three months, we had shopped at dingy, dark, hole-in-the-wall, vegetable-rotting, dust-covered, bare-shelved stores. Even in Bocas, despite throngs of tourists, we were forced to undergo reconnaissance missions to find fruits and vegetables; after several passes, we had found some off the main drag on a side street.

Now we entered the pearly gates of shopping—a gigantic, air-conditioned, mecca of a supermarket, overflowing with produce. In fact, we went overboard and bought way too much, forcing us to stay in David a few days longer to eat everything. We used the delay to recharge our adult batteries. The girls frittered away the time watching *Animal Planet*, in Spanish. Four days later, thoroughly refreshed, we reserved our tickets to Panama City.

Chapter 7

Panama City

Stationed at a strategic international crossroad, Panama City is, hands down, one of the most geographically privileged metropolises in the world. The canal serves roughly fourteen thousand container ships delivering goods to the other side of the Earth annually, bypassing the Strait of Magellan, a sea passage separating mainland South America from the archipelago of Tierra del Fuego, thereby reducing transit by some 7,500 miles.

Getting there from David is straightforward if not painfully monotonous. Seven hours of highway separate the two cities, so we gathered up toys and snacks, and geared up for a lengthy bus ride. Fortunately, the buses have video screens showing violent and sexually charged movies for us all to pass the time. Lloyd and I shared supervision of the girls, covering their eyes or trying to distract them. In the meantime, the bus steward balanced on my armrest and feigned concern over the appropriateness of the movies to flirt with me.

Lloyd sat beside me, amused. "Is this guy coming on to you right in front of me?"

"It would appear so," I muttered out of the side of my mouth. "Care to do anything about it?"

"Nah, you're good."

Natalie dropped off to sleep fifty kilometers from the city and only then could I relax my efforts at preventing her from watching the movie. I was freed up to expend energy on avoiding the flirtatious steward.

The highway from David traverses the southernmost end of the canal over the Bridge of the Americas. For trivia buffs reading this, ships entering the canal from the Pacific do so from the south, transiting in a north-westerly direction, and clear the final locks south of Colón, the Atlantic sea port at the Caribbean.

Panama City's Albrook bus terminus functioned almost like an airport with the departures leaving from the ground floor and arrivals disgorging their weary commuters on the upper deck. Hawkers surged forward, bawling at us to stay at their hostel. Lloyd and I maintained an attitude of celebrity with this practice, treating them like paparazzi.

"I'll pretend I'm Harrison Ford," he said. "Who do you want to be?"

I couldn't respond. I had both girls by the hand, my head down. We pushed our way through the crowd. By now we were being screamed at like rock stars fleeing backstage. Hawkers stabbed flyers in our faces. We ducked the crowd and checked in to Backpacker International Hostel, recommended by Eric and Jennifer, who were traveling the region in reverse.

The owner of the Backpacker, an easygoing middle-aged woman (who called herself "the Mom") burst into grins when she saw the girls and insisted, "Los niños no pagan." Children don't pay. She led us on a tour, showing off the common lounge that opened onto a square balcony. The vista was as impressive as the one from the Bridge of the Americas, showcasing Panama City as a metropolitan center with skyscrapers and business in full swing, as evidenced by the bustle of rush hour traffic below. We took over a large dorm, which the Mom set aside exclusively for our family, then we went out to find provisions.

The next morning, we spotted a tourist information booth kitty corner to the hostel. The staff welcomed us with open arms as if we were long-lost relatives. For five days we rose early, had breakfast, and spilled into the kiosk with a tentative plan for the day. The staff usually saw us coming and stood out on the sidewalk waiting for us, then ushered us into the office with huge smiles. They compiled information on bus schedules, pressing notes into our hands with warnings about neighborhoods to avoid. Activities centered on Panama's rich past, but we set aside a full day for the canal. Lloyd and I weren't great at history; we counted on these excursions to fill the gaps in our teaching.

Though most well-known for the canal, the city's history boasts tales of piracy, pillaging, and infernos. The girls' curiosity was piqued when they heard that the original Panama City (now a World Heritage site called Panama Viejo) was a strategic holding area for gold, an irresistible attraction for pirates like Henry Morgan, who sacked the city repeatedly because of its precious inventory. Differing historical accounts claim that ships crept along rivers and lakes to ambush the city in the dead of night.

After Panama Viejo's destruction by fire (thanks to Morgan), a second settlement was built, now called Casco Viejo (also a World Heritage Site). A fortress encircled Casco Viejo, safeguarding inhabitants and inventory from pirates. Modern-day Panama City has evolved around the compound and stretches all the way to the original Panama Viejo site. We were headed there now, to take in the ancient ruins and museum.

Scaffolding buttressed some buildings in an ongoing restoration project to shore up the crumbling walls. The girls went berserk, running and climbing among the rubble, hiding from pirates and peeking out at the ocean through peepholes in the brick. Jocelyn had no trouble convincing Natalie that she could see ships heading for land.

Lloyd unpacked our lunch under a shady tree. "Bet you never thought we'd be adding history to this field trip." He plopped down with a satisfied sigh to watch the girls.

A member of the Policía de Turismo, a young, handsome man dressed in a crisp, short-sleeved uniform, came over to us. "Would you like a tour of the site?"

"Yes, thank you," I responded.

"When you are finished your lunch, please come and get me in the cafeteria over there." He pointed to a small building. "Please do not go to the museum without me; I will take you there," he added and walked away.

Lloyd was looking at the girls, ever vigilant. "Aren't you glad you insisted we bring generic backpacks instead of the expensive brand name types?"

Yes, I was. I'd wanted to act respectfully toward people who did not possess as much wealth. Learning about another culture, for us, meant assimilating—adopting the language, customs, and dress of the locals. The girls were climbing ancient blocks to the tops of roofless walls. I wondered if they would ever speak Spanish well enough to be mistaken for native speakers. Without any freckles and with heads of dark hair, their appearance, if they dressed like the little girls here, might lead people to believe they were Latina.

After lunch we found the police officer and he escorted us across the highway to the small Museo Panama Viejo. The young woman who led tours of the museum could not speak English, but since there was a scale model of the old city as it looked in the 1600s, the girls didn't listen to a word she said anyway. Lloyd and I strained to understand the guide's explanations as best we could while Jocelyn went off in her mind to Panama circa 1652.

The girls bounded out of bed each morning excited by the possibility of another day. Despite excellent directions from our friends at the tourist kiosk, Lloyd and I sprained our necks attempting to pinpoint a building in the labyrinthine streets and alleys that made up Panama City's inner core. A riot of noise and fumes engulfed us as we looked helplessly at the queue of graffitied chicken buses, called *diablos rojos*, or red devils, in Panama City.

"Maybe they turn up the music to camouflage the noise of the engine," Lloyd shouted over the din. It could be true. The buses were "retired" from North America after ferrying children to and from school for years before being handed down to Central American municipalities.

Drivers slowed down (notice that I haven't said stop) only to permit the loading and unloading of passengers. It was in this context that I, in my still-not-quite-fluent Spanish, struggled to shout a question to the driver who impatiently waved us aboard as if to say, "Get the hell on the bus, madam!" Thunderously loud music from speakers above the driver permeated every inch of our breathing space, so he hollered, "Los niños no pagan!" and beat a hasty retreat into the fast flow of traffic.

Apart from the stress of launching ourselves aboard a screaming, grating, hell-bound diablo rojo to wherever, we found a driver or two who would often indicate with a barely imperceptible nod that our stop was coming up, whereupon one of us would hurl ourselves from the coasting vehicle, turn and catch the girls, and drag them to the curb. The remaining adult was then free to jump as he/she saw fit.

We were wandering aimlessly looking for the bus to Mi Pueblito—My Little Village—when we met a Panamanian expat, now living in the US, who was in town visiting her daughter. "You'll never find it," she said, clutching the girls' hands and escorting us personally to our bus stop.

Mi Pueblito charmed the pants off the girls. It featured replicas of the three prominent cultures of Panama: Afro-Caribbean, Indigenous (Kuna and Emberá), and European through a collection of traditional buildings grouped around a horseshoe-shaped square. We let the girls loose to roam around with little supervision. At Panama Viejo (the ruins as well as the museum), and here at Mi Pueblito, we were the only customers. I sat on the hard pews of the faux Catholic Church watching Natalie puttering around looking at ornate stained-glass illustrations of Jesus following the Via Dolorosa. She sat beside me, resting her head on the back of the pew. I pulled her in close for a cuddle. She rested her arm on my leg and gazed at the ceiling. I relaxed against the cool surface of the bench, grinning.

"Is this what homeschooling is like?" Lloyd said, coming to join me.

"Well, no, we don't go to museums every day." I watched Jocelyn darting back and forth across the square, gravel flying underfoot, in and out of doorways to new worlds.

"I mean spending all this time together." He gestured to Natalie who was up, making her way around the Stations of the Cross. "It's fascinating to watch them learn."

I was not surprised to hear him say this. For years, he had spent long hours away from his daughters to allow me to spend every waking hour with them. Characteristically a natural, hands-on father, the separation killed him, but he valued the importance of providing a stable, nurturing educational environment for them. Our family time was precious because the four of us spent time together so infrequently. Sometimes, on the days Lloyd stayed in town to teach night school, I put the girls down for an afternoon nap even when they didn't need it so that he could put them to bed when he got home at 10:00.

"Care to tackle Catholicism?" I nodded in the direction of Natalie, now trying to read the placards lining the walls of the church.

He stammered his way through a few explanations, looking at me, a lapsed Catholic, from time to time for help. I came up beside them and offered a few corrections. Then we made our way to the gift shop where an older gentleman rewarded us with a Spanish guitar solo. He was undeterred that his audience was made up of four Canadians eating ice cream at a patio table.

"Can we come back tomorrow?" Jocelyn wanted to know.

"You like it here, but there are other things to see," I told her. A light rain had begun; we held the girls' hands as we made our way to the bus stop.

On the bus, Lloyd leafed through the guidebook. "We could sit out the rain in the Museo de Ciencias Naturales. Just a matter of finding it . . ." He trailed off, reading the map.

I danced to the front of the bus and asked the driver, "Dónde está el Museo de Ciencias Naturales?"

The driver then turned to the passengers, mentioning the museum. A discussion ensued. The entire bus of perhaps a dozen people debated, in animated, rapid-fire voices, the nearest stop to our destination. Once a consensus was reached, the driver stopped (yes, stopped) and told us, using grand gestures of the arm and hand, to walk down the street and turn left. Once disembarked, we turned around to see the bus still waiting for us to make our way, so we pointed off to the left to indicate our understanding. By now all heads were on the starboard side of the bus nodding affirmatively.

"Wave to them," I said to the girls, and we stood and watched all those passengers lean out the bus window to wave back.

❖❖❖

At least three museums are devoted to the history of the Panama Canal, including the Miraflores Visitors' Center at the Miraflores locks, some fifteen minutes from the city by bus. Our friends at the tourist kiosk informed us that a large vessel would be passing through at 12:30 so we timed our visit to coincide with this event. At the Miraflores locks, the closest to the Gulf of Panama, it's possible to witness the raising and lowering of the ships from several observation points. From the bleachers, we watched workers flood the lower lock with water to raise the ship and release her into the tributary leading to the Caribbean, a process lasting about fifteen minutes.

Inside, a short video in the amphitheater described the history of the canal and culminated with a fast-action sequence that depicted a complete transit from one sea to the other. Afterwards, the girls took over the museum and spent a long time at the exhibit that simulated driving a vessel through the canal. They talked to each other on the radios, set off every alarm there was, and "steered" through the locks. In Jocelyn's opinion, this was the best place, ever.

As we were about to leave, we heard an announcement that three ships were about to transit from North (Caribbean) to South (Pacific). We rushed back to the stands. What we saw was truly a spectacle. Two locks side by side facilitate ships' transiting from the Pacific to the Caribbean or vice versa. Closest to our observation point a cruise liner was transiting, gleaming white against the dark background of the locks. We waved at the crew and Natalie pleaded, "Can't we have a ride on that boat?"

God how I wanted to say yes. The best way to experience the canal is from the canal itself, in other words, on a boat. Tours originated at a nearby marina and ended in Colón, ten hours later. The price, however, was prohibitive.

"Mommy, there's another boat!" Jocelyn said. A puny American yacht had squeaked into the lock, dwarfed by the cruise liner. However, inching its way into the northern most lock, directly adjacent to these two ships was a massive container ship from China. This ship was a leviathan, dwarfing the other vessels by half. Two human eyeballs could barely take in the sight of her at one glance. I snapped off a plum shot of Natalie standing against the railing of the observation deck with the yacht in behind and the enormous *CHINA SHIPPING LINE* in the background.

At the end of every day, we cooked a simple meal and ate it on the balcony overlooking the city. Around this time, I was contemplating the second half of our adventure. I said to Lloyd, "I wonder if we could see the rest of Central America since we're already here." I had noticed backpackers clustering around the bulletin board, scanning notices advertising transit to Colombia. The Darién Gap, a thick, roadless expanse of jungle between Panama and Colombia, is besieged with dangerous animals, drug smugglers, and paramilitary soldiers. Traveling overland to South America is impossible; essentially the Pan-American highway ends at Yaviza, the southernmost community in Panama, and begins again in Turbo, Colombia. Those on their way to Colombia from the Mom's hostel in Panama City sought berths aboard sailboats or splurged and paid for a flight. In short, I was green with envy.

But here we are in Panama City, I thought, a locale that had never once come up in our discussions back in Canada. To return to Costa Rica's Central Valley, we knew we had a choice: leave Bocas and retrace our steps through hot-and-sweaty Limón, backtrack to egg-frying-on-a-sidewalk Siquirres, and weave through the Cordillera Central back to San José after renewing our visas in Guabito, and crossing *that* bridge, or proceed by zigging from Bocas del Toro to David, then zagging to Panama City, and passing back into Costa Rica from the Pacific side.

In Parismina we tried in vain to answer the question: Can we get from the Caribbean side of Panama to the Pacific? To illustrate how little the schools had in the island community, not one classroom had a map of Central America, and one had a road map of the United States, donated by expats.

It wasn't until we met the gang at Rocking J's that we learned accessing the Pacific through Panama was not only easy but common. The decision to detour to Panama City was a cinch after that. This was the most significant change in our thinking. We deviated from our original plan to stick exclusively to Costa Rica (except for the necessary and perfunctory visa runs) and opened our minds to the potential for seeing much more. We had our fellow and much younger backpackers to thank for that.

Perhaps they had us to thank about opening their minds as well. Increasingly we felt we were causing a mild and pleasant stir, showing up at hostels with two little girls. The young people were magnificent to them, asking all kinds of questions, treating them with great respect, and speaking to them in an intelligent and caring manner. In fact, those who treated them with less than the respect that they deserved were almost exclusively older, white men, grumbling about the noise they were making or furrowing their brows at some perceived misbehavior. No matter that our girls made far less noise than the late-night partiers or that they used pleases and thank you's more readily than folks five times their age. The younger generation of Europeans and North Americans were changing their attitude toward children (though we had a long way to go before we came close to the Latino attitude—they simply *adore* children).

Our days were full of gorging on history, but our evenings were rather dull. The hostel, located in the middle of a large urban area, offered no beach strolls, no hammocks, no local children for the girls to play with. After showering we hung out in our large bedroom reading books or completing crossword puzzles. Sometimes the boredom got the better of us.

Lloyd closed an *Archie* comic he'd read to the girls a dozen times. "Let's think of something to do."

Jocelyn pulled out a game of Password. We enacted a few scenes, some of us badly, and then wondered what next. It was still early.

"Let's play shadow puppets," Natalie suggested. "Daddy, where is your flashlight?" Then she directed us. "Everyone take turns making a shadow puppet and the others have to guess what it is."

Each person took their turn contorting their fingers into elaborate configurations.

"That's a crab."

"A deer."

"That looks like a camel."

When it came to my turn, I was fresh out of ideas. I warped my fingers randomly; Natalie shined the light underneath. "Ummmm . . . is this something?" I stammered.

Lloyd could contain himself no longer and burst out laughing at my ineptness so forcefully that he hiccupped. What must the other travelers in the hostel have thought that night when they heard shrieks of laughter coming from our room? Backpacking all over Europe in my youth had taught me to plan for these occasions. Tucked into a side pocket of my pack lay a deck of cards, a game of Password, pencil crayons, small note pads, dice, and puzzle books. But sometimes those get old. Desperate times call for desperate measures.

After a week, we left. The trek off the beaten path to Panama City opened a window into the history of the New World. We knocked ourselves out combing the sites and touring museums and took advantage of cheaper prices to stock up on a few necessities at the open-air markets and huge air-conditioned grocery stores. Opportunities in Costa Rica beckoned us back. Reluctantly, we bundled up our backpacks to prepare for the arduous journey west.

Chapter 8

Jacó, Costa Rica

For three months we lived rough, camping and learning about the locals' way of life. For that week in Panama City, though, the resources of the modern world became essential in dealing with a few matters. Leaking from a loose shingle in the garage had damaged some of our tenants' possessions. Instead of dealing with this simple problem, our property management firm showed complete indifference to the situation and had the gall to suggest we hire someone to fix the leaky roof ourselves.

"Isn't that their job?" Lloyd asked when he read the email.

They had also neglected to deposit two months' rent into our bank account. Since the property management firm had been hired to monitor and remediate any problems that cropped up during the two years we were on the road—on the directive of the insurance company—we took advantage of Panama City's telecommunications system to fire them by fax the morning we departed.

We had also received an email from a private school in Costa Rica that expressed an interest in interviewing Lloyd. In Puerto Viejo, I had translated a want ad in *La Nación*. "They're looking for an English teacher at a private school," I'd said.

"What else?" Lloyd had asked. "For what grade? Where is the school?"

"That's all it says. There's an email address to send your résumé to. That's it."

I'd photographed Lloyd posing in his only dress shirt in front of Rocking J's terra cotta wall so that he could attach the picture to his résumé when he answered the ad. (What the school didn't see in that photo were the swimming trunks on his lower half.)

Sitting at one of the Mom's computer terminals a few weeks later at the Backpacker, the response from the school popped up in my inbox. "They're requesting a meeting."

We pulled up to the hectic border post of Paso Canoas and bunched ourselves in with the burgeoning crowd. I slid four passports through a narrow slit in the thick Plexiglas window. The officer frowned and requested the entry receipts, which we had purchased at the Guabito office.

I stammered in Spanish. "I was told the children didn't need one. Here are two, one for me and one for my husband."

"No, you need four." He did not look up at me from his desk, and I could barely make him out behind the tinted window. "Twenty dollars," he said with indifference.

So, by breaking the rules accidentally we were charged twice as much for the girls. I had to wonder if he wasn't just pocketing the money himself, but a border is no place to quibble. I motioned to Lloyd that I needed twenty dollars as penance for our oversight. I slipped it through to the officer who stared at his computer screen for an eternity. The mob behind me swelled. *Whatever is he doing?* He stared at the console for so long I supposed he was playing a video game. Nervous sweat pooled in my armpits. One might ask, "Why don't they open more wickets?" But again, no good time to quibble.

At some point along the time continuum he stamped us out of Panama, then I turned to face the hordes and said, "I will now accept my award for the longest border transaction in history."

At least one woman laughed out loud.

We leapfrogged past the Osa peninsula, stopping overnight here and there to break up the journey. We were back in Costa Rica, land of rocky roads, monstrous potholes, and bone-jarring buses. Along Costa Rica's portion of the Pan-American Highway, we juddered over the Jekyll and Hyde roads. Here, a stretch of smooth tarmac, there, a length of gravel and dust.

Whereas we supplied the girls with every conceivable novelty to distract them from journey-boredom, Lloyd and I descended into brain paralysis staring out the windows for hours on end. At times, desperate measures led to silliness. This time, Lloyd opened his mouth and chanted, "Oooommm." He knew what he was doing; the washboard surface made his mantra sound like a jackhammer, "O . . . o . . . o . . . m . . . m . . . m . . ."

The girls had not yet reached the age where they considered their father lame, so they giggled. I turned my head to look out the window, refusing to dignify the act by laughing. But trying not to laugh just made it harder *not* to laugh, so I did, too, but begrudgingly.

We rolled into Jacó (pronounced "hocCO") on a hot afternoon, looking for the campground listed in our travel guide. A hard rain began when we found Camping El Hicaco located a block from the beach. Procuring rations meant negotiating a three-kilometer trek on the main drag that ran parallel to the ocean. We completed our set up under tarps, rushing to get done before the sun went down.

Lloyd contacted the school and arranged to meet with them. Then we encountered an unusual predicament. With nothing dressier than a white shirt, we were stuck looking for slacks in a beach town. We scoured the town and found a store that sold school uniforms. When we inquired about men's slacks the clerk showed us two pairs, only one of which was suitable if not too small. In the end, we reckoned that if he loosely tucked in his shirt and let it fall over the unbuttoned waistband and made sure never to bend over, he might have half a shot at looking presentable.

The trick must have worked because he was offered the teaching job at the interview. Thankfully, administration gave him a golf shirt adorned with the school crest that he could wear with shorts of his choosing (of which he owned a few that fit). Meanwhile, I resorted to taking the girls downtown to kill time during the constant cloudbursts. We sat for hours inside a mini-mall reading and drawing to pass the time away from the soggy campground. For two days we had endured cold showers in dark, cinder block bathrooms. Even in more modernized Panama, cold showers were the norm, but with all the rain, we could not face placing our cold bodies under cold water for the sake of hygiene. We were beginning to get a little ripe.

That night when we wiped our wet feet before bedding down, I said, "What I really want for my birthday is a hot shower. That's all."

Lloyd thought for moment, silently ticking off his fingers one by one. "Do you realize that we have had a total of five hot showers since August?"

"See what I mean?"

The next day I set out to find both a roof over our rainy heads and a shower with hot water. This time, I was determined to turn the shower on before agreeing to take the room. We had been duped by signs declaring: *¡Agua Caliente!* In truth, some of the showers had the hot water doohickey jutting out of the wall, but we'd monkey around with it to no avail, worrying about possible electrocution.

It took me the entire day to compile a list of options in our price range. Our biggest obstacle was finding one that was open for business. Owners were feverishly preparing their rooms for the busy season and were not yet ready for occupants, but one place looked promising. The reception area was under construction, and the pool was empty, except for four inches of guck at the bottom, but the rooms were spacious and clean, and the water in the shower was heated in a tank, not from a dangerously wired heater. My birthday was two days away. With a spring in my step I returned to the campground where I found the rest of the family huddled under the tarp, playing cards.

The girls were disappointed to hear that the pool wasn't yet functional, but the following day the rained stopped and the sun rose and swept slowly across the campground. "This is a good omen, girls," I said as we laid everything out to dry before we packed up. When we checked in to the hotel that afternoon, the pool was being vacuumed and filled.

"It is a good omen, Mom!" Jocelyn said.

Our corner room overlooked the Pacific through one window and the busy street through another. I cast my eyes to the shower. "Can I go first?" I said.

Of course, both girls agreed because they were thinking only of the pool, and Lloyd, who was thinking only of his marriage, said, "Oh sure. Go ahead."

On my birthday the following day, the girls and Lloyd cooked dinner in the communal kitchen while I relaxed with a book in the lounge. After supper, all three presented me with a fluffy towel depicting a large green sea turtle swimming in the ocean, and later, as if God himself was addressing me directly, a double rainbow glowed in the distance. I could not think of a better birthday.

Chapter 9

Settling Down

THE ITINERARY WE HAD roughed out over our dining room table back home came to an end in December. It was time to settle down and stretch our dollars and learn to live like the locals. We also needed a break from the intensity of backpacking. The girls were thrilled with it. For nearly four months their only hardship was long bus rides and a limited variety of food. Lloyd and I had their health and safety as well as financial matters both foreign and domestic to think about.

We knew that living in a community for a prolonged period was the key to perfecting the language and gaining a true understanding of the culture. In the backs of our minds, we also pondered relocating on a permanent basis. Since the school year in Costa Rica commenced in January, we were now faced with a few weeks in which to find long-term accommodations.

Residing in Jacó, however, was out of the question. Tourist season was nipping at our heels and Jacó is the busiest beach in the country. Think Fort Lauderdale on a surfboard. Living among English-speaking tourists would directly contravene our objectives. Worse, Jacó was plagued by the trifecta of tourist traps: partying, drugs, and prostitution.

A few days before Christmas, we were forced to travel to San José to see a dentist after Lloyd noticed a dark shadow on one of Natalie's teeth. We trundled off from the Jacó terminal, following the Carretera Costanera Sur, the South Coast Road, admiring the tropical-green countryside. About twenty minutes later, the bus turned off the highway, diverting into a village that was tico in every respect. A fruit and vegetable market overflowed with produce. The faded awning shaded crates of onions and potatoes stacked against the wall. The main pulpería came into view on my right while on my left I saw a nightclub called Discoteca Lucill. Next to that stood a recreation center with a covered basketball court, an open-air billiards room, and a public swimming pool.

People wheeled by on bicycles, dogs trotted aimlessly in the streets, chickens crossed the road. Why? To join the bananas maybe?

We covered the distance of the entire village in minutes, rolling counterclockwise, dropping off villagers here and there before linking up with the highway.

While I examined the town, the girls were chattering to each other, pointing out the strange sight of ropes strung from one side of the road to the other.

"Those are monkey bridges," Lloyd explained.

It made no sense to the girls. "Bridges aren't in the air," Natalie said.

"Well, how do monkeys travel?" Lloyd asked.

"They swing through the trees," Jocelyn said.

"Right, but what do they do when they get to a clearing?"

"They use their feet? On the ground?" Natalie asked. Then she said, "Oh! They'll get hit by cars!"

"Such a simple solution," he said to me, "but so effective."

After ninety nausea-inducing minutes, the driver pulled into a rest stop, but just before that, as the bus was slowing to turn off the highway, it crossed the Río Tárcoles and beneath us yawned the largest crocodiles we'd seen since Tortuguero.

"But I've already checked those off my list," Lloyd said to himself.

At the soda, a quartet of arcade machines drew the girls by their jingles. They pressed inoperative buttons with one hand and gulped down iced tea with the other. I joined Lloyd at a plastic table.

"I think we should send the girls to school." He'd been rambling on about the excellent facilities at the school where he had been hired, including an Olympic-size swimming pool, butterfly garden, air-conditioned classrooms, and a computer room. "You should come and take a tour with me when we get back."

"I don't know, I . . ."

"Look, it's only temporary, and it's a great way for the girls to learn Spanish," he pointed out. "Besides, it will give you uninterrupted time to write."

"Maybe you should become a lawyer," I replied. "You make a good case."

He insisted that the experience wasn't intended as an academic exercise as much as a cultural one. *Kids from around the world attend the school. Most of them are bilingual. Some classes are taught in Spanish only.* And on it went. Financially it was a tough decision; we wouldn't be getting much of a break on tuition, and was it in line with our goals?

A week later, Lloyd accompanied the girls and me on a tour of the school. I admit I was impressed. Naturally, the girls were in favor of it, after seeing the pool. After much hand wringing and gnashing of teeth, we decided to give it a try. Procuring accommodations now included the caveat: proximity to the school.

One day, on my return to the hotel from Jacó's tediously long parkway, I saw an ad listing a small house for rent. When I called the number, the woman who answered told me the house was located in the little horseshoe-shaped town I had observed from the bus window. She was an Italian expat named Paola who spoke no English. Her one-acre parcel of land lay along the Río Agujas, a stream that flowed from the hills behind the village of Quebrada Ganado to the ocean, less than four kilometers away. Her residence faced the main road, and as she led us on a tour, we passed through a gate where two smaller cottages stood on a well-groomed lot dotted with cashew, guanabana, or soursop, and lemon trees. (The latter came in handy to throw at the possums that buckled our corrugated roof in the middle of the night.) Criminals were deterred as much by the strands of barbed wire and broken glass along the brick walls that contained the property as with the two pacing Weimaraners eyeing us warily.

In Spanish, she told us, "I have tangerine trees back here, near the river. Take as much fruit as you want." When she reached up to pick one for the girls, she stopped and said in a quiet voice, "Look." A pygmy owl, no more than six inches tall, gripped a branch by his talons, undisturbed by our presence. I could see Lloyd mentally perusing his pamphlet for that entry. A few minutes later, he pursed his lips when Paola introduced us to her caged parrot, Nixon, who laughed hysterically when we came near. He was incarcerated in a cage hanging from a large papaya tree, home to a clutch of bats.

Lloyd could not resist whispering to me, "Oh the irony—the free alongside the imprisoned."

The town was charming, albeit dry and dusty, and houses were constructed out of cinder block or painted stucco. Paola's house and cottages were built to European standards, right down to the bidets in the bathrooms.

"It's like a Swiss villa in the middle of small-town Central America," I said to Lloyd.

"But it's an ideal spot to learn Spanish," Lloyd said. "And it's only fifteen minutes from the school."

At least the village met our criteria. It was devoid of expats except for a retired American gentleman who lived a hermitic life across from the dilapidated bullfighting arena, and an American family headed by Bruno and

Ruth and their two children—Leah and Joel. They had moved to town so the kids could be near their tico grandpa.

So, we left the hotel in Jacó and moved to the village. Having brought the clothes on our backs, the tent, four air mattresses, and little else, we made quick work of unloading our belongings and setting up house. The villa was completely furnished. Jocelyn and Natalie slept on cots in an L-shaped loft, Lloyd and I took the double bed on the main floor. The villa was decorated with antique Mexican cupboards, too oversized, really, for the negligible amount of space. Into these, we deposited our lean supply of books, professional papers, passports, and clothes.

To stock the narrow, blue-tiled kitchen, I experimented with the bus routes. Orotina, to the north, was as close as Jacó, both about forty minutes away. The bus stopped kitty corner to Orotina's central market. Across the street, I noted a couple of large grocers and a discount department store where I bought lunch kits, a blender, and plastic containers. Then I went next door to pick up staples. I never shopped for food outside of Quebrada Ganado again. I felt it was important to support the local family-owned pulpería in town. The owner, Ricardo, had a booming voice and a friendly disposition. His wife, whose name we never remembered so we took to calling Mrs. Ricardo, was equally jovial, and both went out of their way to welcome us to their town. They were sweet to the girls; any time we sent them to buy milk, they spoke to them slowly in Spanish and gave them candies for the walk home.

Over the next few days, I primed everyone for impending transitions, preparing the girls to attend school for the first time and fussing about needlessly to avoid facing an identity crisis. For eight years I had been a full-time stay-at-home mom, committed to homeschooling. Now the opportunity Lloyd had so graciously offered me amounted to living a dream. Not many people indulge their interests full-time while their husband bankrolls the entire process.

We explained to the girls that their attendance at school was to drive the "field trip" agenda forward and repeated this confusing rhetoric whenever we could. "Remember, you're only there to learn the language," I said.

I accompanied the lot of them to school the first day. Natalie admonished me, "Don't kiss me or hug me or anything like that when you say goodbye."

I led her to her classroom. Her teacher indicated where to put their lunch kits (*loncheras*) and backpacks (*mochilas*). As I gave Natalie a surreptitious wave goodbye, the other mothers fell all over their children kissing and embracing them. Natalie, observing this display, rushed over and clutched me in a bear hug.

Next, I popped in to see Jocelyn. A mob of five or six girls circled her and she was observing them so intently she barely noticed me leaving. The next morning at the appointed hour, the girls, decked out in their uniforms and long hair pulled back into ponytails, set off with their dad. I blinked back the tears. Then, I was left alone to my laptop; its winking green eye gazed up at me from the plastic table I'd placed in my new "office"—a nook underneath the stairs. I took to a routine of writing like a duck to water, at the crack of 7:15, when the gang cleared out of the villa. I managed to accomplish a lot before the oppressive equatorial heat sweltered me slowly into incoherence. I complained to Lloyd who summed it up best by saying, "Canadian roasting in an adobe oven?"

After school, everyone was tired, hungry, and surly. It was a tremendously long day for Natalie, who was struggling to cope with hunger, heat, and fatigue. After supper, all three of them showered and went to bed, whereas I had barely exerted myself, so I passed the time watching TV. To avoid numbing my mind with the boob tube I watched English-language movies with the sound off, reading the Spanish subtitles. Other times, I watched Spanish-language movies but covered the English subtitles with a piece of cardboard.

I faithfully persisted in writing every morning, but apart from brief interactions with Ricardo and Mrs. Ricardo, I felt more lonesome than I'd ever felt in my life. Because the cottage stood behind Paola's house, far back from the main gate, I was cut off from the outside world. Many hours could pass without me seeing another human soul. It became apparent that of the four of us, I was failing the most at adapting to our new lives. I routinely walked out every day to the far end of the village to buy produce, and twice a week I rode the bus north to Orotina to check messages at the internet café, but I had made no friends in town. Maybe it was a mistake to veer from our goal to live like the locals by choosing to place security above authenticity. Locals had bars on their windows, but they were not isolated from each other like we were inside our compound. Now I was faced with another obstacle; the heat was making me ill. About every three weeks, I was overcome with nausea that kept me in bed all day. Back in Parismina I had suffered from this, and now, in the hot coastal sun, I was still having no success at acclimatizing to the heat.

One Friday I set off for Jacó to do some errands. I did not take care to hydrate properly and withered under a blistering sun. By the time we got the girls to bed that night I was writhing with abdominal pain. Lloyd paced back and forth fretting about my well-being. While he rifled through the health books, I gasped a few suggestions. "Make me some salty tea," I said, thinking my electrolytes were out of balance. Close to dawn, I fell asleep.

The next day Lloyd was punch-drunk after being up most of the night worrying about what to do with the girls while he took me to see a doctor. I had no insight into my physical and emotional struggles, and I spent little time even considering them because the girls and I were obligated to renew our visas. For the second time we prepared for a border run, this time without Lloyd.

He sat in a plastic chair on the terrace and spread out the map. "Nicaragua isn't necessarily closer, but maybe the roads are better than the route to Panama."

I was overly quiet, thinking only of how I was going to handle this journey on my own with the girls. In the end, we elected to mollify immigration by spending our seventy-two-hour mandatory break from Costa Rica in the small fishing village–cum–expat community called San Juan del Sur, just over the border in Nicaragua. This little cobblestoned town became our home away from home on four subsequent border runs. Even though we didn't know it at the time, Lloyd was compelled to exit as well. To live within the parameters of the law, Lloyd requested the school provide him with a legitimate work visa. The process cost $1500, a fee both parties agreed to share. Therefore, at "exit" day, just the girls and I packed up to leave. Lloyd rented a car and drove us five hundred kilometers north to the border town of Peñas Blancas.

A few kilometers from the border, police checks sprang up on the side of the road. Lloyd had not yet received his work visa, and I remarked to him, "When you come back to get us, you'll be past your ninety days. You'd better get a letter from the school stating the work visa is in process."

"Good idea," he said.

Arriving in a rental car at the border of a developing country with Canadian flags embroidered on our packs meant one thing: *wealth*. It didn't help that I was nervous about crossing into Nicaragua by myself without Lloyd. Our previous crossings into Panama were accomplished by partnership, one of us physically herding the girls through the mazes while the other handled the paperwork. Now I felt my stress levels rising as I faced the process on my own.

Immediately the money changers and *tramitadores* descended upon us. A tramitador is a paperwork processor, someone who helps to navigate the red tape of the border. I picked one out to help with the legwork Lloyd typically handled. This man hoisted all three packs onto his shoulders, and with sad faces we waved goodbye to Lloyd.

Our tramitador directed us to stand in a long line of people in the customs office. The airless room was muggy and the three of us wore sheens of sweat. I demanded the girls stay beside me during the tedious wait, thinking the officer would want to see their faces. There was also the matter of crossing without their father to address. Among the passports and customs declaration forms was a typed letter from Lloyd, giving me permission to leave Costa Rica with his children.

Without a word, we were stamped out. Our tramitador was waiting for us and together we faced a kilometer of dusty road, lined haphazardly by enormous flatbeds waiting for clearance in the no man's land between nations. We saw the entrepreneurial spirit alive and well, people selling souvenirs, hammocks, lottery tickets, and chopped fruit. I was a bundle of nerves worrying for the girls' safety.

"Stay close. Hang on to me. Pay attention!" I barked at them.

The transports rumbled by us slowly when they were given the green light. Pedestrians zigged and zagged across their lanes. I clutched the girls when we passed in front of them. When we entered passport control on the Nicaraguan side, I attempted to comprehend the instructions on my entry form, all the while attached to two bored kids, trying to block out the noise of loud engines, screeching brakes, and distractions from the vendors. After an hour we cleared passport control and the tramitador led us through a fence and into Nicaragua.

We immediately sought out a soda for a bathroom break and something to eat. Our tramitador began negotiations. "Veinte dólares." Twenty dollars.

I was appalled. "I can't give you that."

Jocelyn interrupted. "Can we get an ice cream?"

"Fine," I snapped.

I bought the girls ice cream but as soon as they sat down, I heard, "Señora! Bus?" from a fellow on the steps of the soda.

"Yes!" I shouted back.

I grabbed the girls and their packs, muscled my own onto my back, ignored our tramitador and walked to the bus. When we boarded, I told the girls to sit down. Our tramitador was right on our heels. By now the chicken bus was rolling out of the border terminus. He stood in front of me with his hand out. I was overcome by stress, trying to watch the girls, dealing with this guy, and wondering how to pay for our tickets. I searched for the girls but couldn't see them anywhere. "Jocelyn! Natalie!" I shouted. I saw them pop up over the large seat backs just enough to see the ice cream had dripped down their t-shirts.

I needed to take control of the situation. I turned to the tramitador. "Five dollars." He agreed instantly, making me question if I had offered too much. The bus lurched forward. "I only have a twenty, though."

He reached out to take the twenty-dollar bill. "I get change."

"No," I said, "you bring back change. I'll give you twenty dollars."

He dashed off the bus; I raked my head around to keep an eye on the girls.

The bus was fully on its way now. I could see our man running back to us, wads of money balled in his fist. He hopped up, deftly opened the back door and passed down the aisle to present me with fifteen dollars.

I sat down opposite the girls and snarled, "Don't ever ask me for ice cream again." They looked stunned and I felt guilty right away. I was unable to keep my cool in the chaos. I regret having said it especially because they were the sweetest girls any mother could want.

Unknown to me at the time was the strange set of circumstances Lloyd faced on his way back to Quebrada Ganado. We were scheduled to rendezvous south of the border at a roadside Burger King in three days' time. To keep in touch, we agreed to check emails frequently. He could go online at the school, and I was to check emails periodically at an internet café in San Juan del Sur.

He returned from his short jaunt to the border and spent Sunday puttering around the villa. The next day he drove the rental car to school and queried administration about a letter to appease the border police about overstaying his ninety days. During the discussion, Lloyd found out that the lawyer hired to process the work visa had not even begun to file the papers. The school administrators took Lloyd aside and assured him he would be back in Canada before the papers would be ready, putting his status in the country in jeopardy. In the end, they negotiated to acknowledge Lloyd as a volunteer, allowing him to receive an income for living expenses in exchange for a document attesting to his legitimacy at the school. At least we were saved several hundred dollars in a long, drawn-out process that would not have benefited us in any way. Lloyd, describing this to me later, railed, "You try to do the right thing!"

Then, it dawned on him that he needed to get out of the country. He fired off an email to me, raced back to the villa, packed a bag, jumped back in the car, and sped off to the highway. He was in a race against the clock now, to get to the border before it closed at 8:00 p.m. The girls and I were expecting to depart Nicaragua the following morning.

Meanwhile, at the Hotel Nicaragua hostel, the three of us hit it off with the owners, an American/Nicaraguan couple named Karen and Francisco with an adorable toddler named Daniela. The girls took to nurturing Daniela like mother ducks. Then an American family, one of only three traveling families we met in Central America, showed up with their homeschooled eight-year-old boy, Ian. The girls had hit the jackpot, having two other kids to play with, and didn't notice when I asked the American mother to supervise them so I could check messages. I nipped out to the internet café, loaded my email account, and discovered that Lloyd was prowling the town looking for us at that very moment.

In the previous hours, Lloyd had dropped off the rental car in Liberia, a city south of the border, and one of the employees had ferried him to the bus station so he could catch the last bus to the border. They skidded into the station in the nick of time. The bus driver, though, had no intention of going all the way to the frontier. Along the route, passengers dismounted, and when there remained only four souls destined for Peñas Blancas, the driver refused to go any farther. In the confusion, Lloyd squeezed himself into a taxi with three strangers and sped to the checkpoint. With minutes to spare, he had cleared customs and proceeded to San Juan del Sur, rolling in at nightfall. Lloyd was panicking now, not knowing where we were and fearing that we would leave the next day to rendezvous with him at Burger King. He immediately went to an internet café to see if I'd received his earlier message, which I, in my shock, was just reading.

As I stitched together the details of the last few days of Lloyd's life, I realized he was in town. I fired off an email, letting him know our whereabouts and guessed that he would turn up at the hostel within the half hour. I revealed nothing to the girls. True to form, he knocked on our dorm door thirty minutes later.

Whereas Jocelyn was completely speechless, Natalie sputtered, "Daddy, how did you . . . ?" before both tackled him with hugs.

Lloyd was obligated to remain for seventy-two hours before reentering Costa Rica, so we took full advantage of the opportunity. "Like a vacation within a vacation," I said.

He tipped a mouthful of cold *Toña*, a Nicaraguan lager, into his mouth. "Oh, by the way, the boss felt so bad about the work visa, he told me to save all my receipts. He's going to reimburse me when I get back."

At that, I drank a mouthful of cold beer myself and grinned.

San Juan del Sur is a small fishing village overlooking a cookie-cutter shaped bay where wrinkled old fishermen bob in weathered boats and cobblestoned streets lead to pastel-colored clapboard buildings. Walking along the streets hand in hand with Jocelyn and Natalie, I peered into unlit homes occasionally, observing old men and women rocking away on the classic Nicaraguan rocking chair.

The village attracts expats, bringing with them amenities that are an outright luxury in Nicaragua: hotels, coffee shops, bookstores, bars, restaurants, and shockingly, a library!

Jane Mirandette, a local business owner, founded a stupendously successful lending library for locals and foreigners alike, complete with

English-language reading materials, a children's craft period every afternoon, and a mobile unit, dispatched three times a week to deliver reading material to remote enclaves. Lending libraries are all but nonexistent in Central America. The popularity of the Biblioteca de San Juan del Sur proves that there is need and desire. You can support the library's efforts here: http://www.sjdsbiblioteca.org/donations/.

While Lloyd and I relaxed in the English reading room, the next room was overrun by children (ours included) reading aloud, coloring, or doing crafts.

One block from the library, boutiques and ice cream shops flanked the central market. Entrepreneurs took advantage of the abundance of dollars by erecting stalls and kiosks on the streets to sell their wares. The vendors at the small mercado were predominantly old women, so we did our best to spread the money around, buying papaya from this one, tomatoes from that one. What we couldn't get from them we purchased at the small grocers along the main street. We stocked up on Cheerios and large jars of peanut butter, both of which were unavailable at Ricardo's in Quebrada Ganado.

Shopkeepers showered affection on the girls. In the corner store closest to the hostel, the owner dropped everything in the middle of my transaction when she saw the girls and called her husband over to admire the "Princessas."

That afternoon Lloyd and I drank rum at a beachfront bar, watching the girls run amok in the surf. The Gipsy Kings played softly over the loudspeaker, and I can scarcely hear that music even now, it tugs at my heartstrings so. The week afforded our family a valuable connection of souls. We were in a cocoon of beauty and sweetness. I was still feeling sorry about how I'd yelled at the girls on the bus and needed family time to mend some fences.

At the end of the week, little round-faced Daniela cried when she saw her playmates depart.

"We'll be back," Jocelyn said, giving her a hug.

Karen and Francisco waved goodbye from the stoop of the hostel. We humped down the cobblestoned street to the mercado, where we would catch a chicken bus to the border.

"Get off in front of the pulpería at the intersection before the bus turns left to go to Rivas," Francisco called out. "Stand in front of the statue of the Virgin Mary on the other side of the street. A bus will come along and take you to the border."

The route, which spans the narrow strip of land between the Pacific Ocean and the enormous Lago Nicaragua, was a common one and almost all the seats were taken by the time we boarded.

The girls giggled at the driver honking at intervals to alert passengers of his arrival. Ramshackle houses stood dark and barren on threadbare land. Corrugated metal roofs rusted on top of cinder block walls. Skeletal remains of cars pockmarked the landscape. We'd noticed none of this before, all of us having arrived in the dark. "San Juan del Sur is different from the rest of Nicaragua," some had warned. "Poverty is everywhere."

Loud music, tinged with accordion and trumpet, boomed out of speakers above the driver's seat. Coming down over a rise, the driver stopped for a passenger waiting on the side of the desolate road. A neatly dressed, elderly man with pop bottle glasses climbed the stairs, walked slowly down the aisle, and sat in the empty space beside Natalie. When he looked down on to the seat next to him, her paler, smoother face was looking up into his. His wrinkled face broke into a peaceful, friendly grin. He raised his gnarled hand with difficulty and gave her a gentle pat on the head.

SEMANA SANTA ADVENTURES

At dusk, we dragged ourselves through the cumbrous iron gate surrounding the villa after weathering the journey from San Juan del Sur that went as follows:

San Juan del Sur chicken bus to La Virgen (thirty minutes), chicken bus to the border (thirty minutes), customs proceedings at Peñas Blancas (one hour), waiting for chicken bus to Liberia (one hour), chicken bus to Liberia (one hour), chicken bus to la Cruz de Barranca (three hours), waiting at soda (thirty minutes), then chicken bus to Quebrada Ganado (ninety minutes).

It seemed overly complicated, but locals traveled this way, and that was the point. Plus, I'd adopted sneaky tricks. When I'd depleted the inventory in my pack's side pocket, I brought out little paper bags, one for each hour in transit. Into these, I'd plunked a little bauble. It could be the cheesiest piece of crap from the discount stores, called *chunches*, but presenting these gifts to the girls transformed them for two reasons. First, the gifts were a novelty, even if it wore off after an hour. Second, we shamelessly exploited Jocelyn's creative mind. All we had to do was hand over the bags, and their imaginations took over. They particularly liked the ornaments destined for the tops of wedding cakes. Teeny, plastic men in tuxedos and elegant brides sometimes bought us two hours. So, as frustrating as it was to act as Jocelyn's eyes and ears with chaos all around us, I totally relied on her in these circumstances.

Paola hurried out of her house to inspect our well-being; she'd been dead set against us going to Nicaragua in the first place and horrified that we'd attempted it alone, us females. In fact, I hadn't once thought about potential danger the entire time we were in San Juan del Sur, forgetting all the dire warnings we had received from the ticos who were appalled that we'd even think of taking children there. In effect, those who had cruised through it already, backpackers and others who did border runs, told a much different story than the residents of our village, most of whom had never been there.

Of course, we'd never even dreamed of being so irresponsible as to take the girls there, or so we'd explained to friends back home. No, we'd give Nicaragua a wide berth. We'd only felt comfortable exploring Costa Rica and using the border towns of Panama as visa run destinations. If we'd done any amount of additional research, we would have learned how appealing and accessible Nicaragua has become. If we had closed our minds to what other backpackers were telling us about their travels, we never would have dreamed of expanding our journey.

As we fell back into our routine, I resolved to appreciate life a little more. I had been refreshed from the break in my routine, enjoying my time reading books and magazines, having peers to talk to, developing a friendship with Karen, the American owner of the hostel in San Juan del Sur. At the villa, I was deprived of these stimuli, wallowing in isolation, becoming achingly lonely sitting by the window overlooking the lemon and cashew trees, listening to kiskadees sing and watching scarlet macaws soar above me, trailing their brilliant plumage. Now, waiting for the bus to take me into Jacó, I waved to dozens of people riding by on their bikes shouting "Hola" and had an epiphany that we weren't in Kansas anymore and I'd better learn to get something out of it.

One Saturday afternoon, Lloyd came in the door and announced, "I've just bought four bikes. Let's go pick them up."

Though Natalie had only just gotten the knack of riding without training wheels, everyone in town traveled by bike, so we would, too. On weekends we peddled to nearby Playa Agujas, across the highway on the Pacific Coast. The beach was rugged and clean, perfect for exploring tide pools and digging in the chocolate sand. As a bonus, the water was safe to swim in.

On the way to and from the beach, our bikes often broke down. Mateo, the bicycle mechanic and busiest man in town, worked out of a shed attached to his parents' home. He hung bikes by their front wheels from a single hook like slabs of beef to work on them.

One afternoon, Lloyd got a flat, so he went over to Mateo's, but the shop was closed. He limped the bike back to the villa and ran into a young man who offered to take it to his home to patch the flat and fill it with air. He introduced himself as Felipe. In his early twenties, he had a shock of frizzy black hair and an infectious smile. He led Lloyd to the home of his father, Axel, who set about immediately repairing Lloyd's bike with a clap on the shoulder and a chuckle. The two were originally from Limón, on the Caribbean side, which explained the darker complexion and coarser hair.

Axel was round and jolly, like Santa Claus. He and Felipe worked in construction with an uncle. When Lloyd returned to the villa, he introduced me to Felipe, who greeted me with a polite handshake and a warm smile. Felipe and Axel became great friends to us over the months. Such interactions made me realize we were beginning to fulfill more of our goals to understand new cultures and learn the language. However, for me, these occasional moments of interpersonal contact were too sparse.

A few days later, Paola knocked on my door. "Do you have time to teach me English?" she asked.

I resisted the temptation. I was committed to writing and wanted to make that a priority. But people in town heard that the gringos living behind the red gate were teachers from Canada. Then, I reasoned, if Professor Mullins had gone to all that trouble training me for an international teaching career, I might as well make good on it.

The local community center seemed as good a place as any to hold classes. That year, the municipal council had reconfigured the hall to double as a high school. In halting Spanish, I pitched the idea of teaching English a couple of nights a week, using the community center–cum–high school to run classes. Initially, they misunderstood; they thought I was asking for a job. Once I assured them that I would teach the lessons for free, the director suggested charging a small fee to fundraise for the school. I agreed.

The school secretary handled all the administrative details—the advertising, collecting of money, and answering phone calls. I offered to teach the classes and provide the community with two necessary things: funds and English-language skills. We decided to begin lessons after Semana Santa, or Holy Week as Catholics refer to it, the period running from Palm Sunday to Easter. I spent a few weeks developing lesson plans and spreading the word around town. Now I was out on the street, talking to people, having no choice but to speak Spanish and get to know my community. Their warmth transformed my spirits. Their naturally hospitable temperament made me feel an instant rapport with them. "They're so friendly," I told Lloyd. "How could I have stayed locked up for so long?"

"This place is starting to grow on you," he said. "Maybe we should stay?"

"Maybe." *Could we make a go of it here?* I wondered, watching him gather clothes and roll them into his pack. We were about to go back on the road, taking advantage of Lloyd's time off to coordinate some excursions. I'd organized them with one thing in mind: cooler temperatures. The entire week would be spent in the hills and mountains of the Central Valley.

Weaving slowly through foothills leading to San José, Jocelyn looked ashen as we twisted from the coast to the Central Valley. Finally, she surrendered and vomited out the bus window. As gross as that sounds, it was preferable to barfing in a plastic bag, as others did, and letting it fester. Our mini-adventure brought us back around to Parque Nacional Volcán Poás, which Lloyd had been pining for ever since we'd arrived in the country.

After a brief pit stop to pull on sweaters (Imagine! Due to the altitude we were chilly!), Jocelyn and Natalie ran to the crater and peered down into the roiling cauldron of Volcán Poás.

"Whoa!" Natalie cried.

Usually turquoise, the lake now sent up fumaroles in plumes. Lloyd, ever the armchair geologist, butted in between the girls at the barricade. "Do you see the scars going up the side?"

"You mean those ruts?" Jocelyn asked.

"Yes, every time the volcano erupts, it cools and leaves a new layer." He was bent low, to match their sight line, motioning to the layered creases along the edge of the basin.

"Kind of like the rings of a tree, Daddy?" Natalie asked.

"In a way." Lloyd looked serene. If there was a laminated pamphlet listing geological formations, he would be the first to buy it.

We hiked along a winding path that led to an extinct lake. "These trees look very familiar," I said. I pointed to pine trees bordering the water and felt a twinge of homesickness. Back on the narrow trail, the shade of the trees darkened our path, and each time we rounded a corner, a puff of mysterious smoke drifted skyward. This otherworldly setting lent a creepy air to the place. The lingering fear that we would be buried alive by lava at any moment made us duck for cover when we heard the roar of airplanes overhead.

We spent a full cloudless day on Poás and rolled back down the mountain, blistered and dizzy with fatigue, into Alajuela. The next morning at breakfast Lloyd leaned back with his mug of coffee, waiting to eat leftover food when the girls complained of fullness. "We're gonna walk off this food at Zoo Ave," he said, stabbing at a cube of papaya on Natalie's plate.

I consulted my notes. "Bus leaves in thirty minutes."

Zoo Ave (pronounced "Zoo Avay"), an animal rehabilitation center on the outskirts of town, is a misnomer. It's essentially a sanctuary for injured, orphaned, or abandoned animals. The more vulnerable animals, such as parrots, are bred right on the premises and released. For a comprehensive sighting of most birds, reptiles, and mammals that inhabit Costa Rica, there's no better place than Zoo Ave. We wanted to support this site instead of the traditional Simón Bolívar Zoo in San José (you wouldn't catch Lloyd dead in a zoo) because of Zoo Ave's mandate to drive home the message that endangered animals must not be caught and sold as pets. Nixon came to mind.

Lloyd, having left his pamphlet at the villa, relied on placards to identify creatures. "Girls, do you see that monkey?" He pointed to a one-armed monkey swinging on a vine. "He is a white-faced capuchin."

"Awww, what happened to him?" Natalie tugged on her dad's sleeve, prodding him for an explanation.

"Maybe he had an accident, got hit by a car or was attacked by another animal," he said. "What do you think would happen to that little guy if he lived in the wild?"

"I think he wouldn't be fast enough to get away from predators, or maybe he would fall and hurt himself," Natalie replied.

"That's right."

"How did he get here?" Jocelyn asked.

"People rescue them and bring them here."

Lloyd steered us to the bird enclosure to explain the process of breeding macaws to increase their numbers. Like at Volcán Poás, he was in his element, sharing his enthusiasm for the outdoors with the girls. It wasn't a tough sell, for all children cherish animals, and they were getting their fill at Zoo Ave.

At the end of the tour, we hurried back to the hostel, collected our gear, and hustled to the bus station. We were aiming for Sarapiquí, a canton near the Tirimbina Rainforest. We rolled in to the small, wet town at dusk, after plying the highway in a driving rainstorm. Our taxi took us to a woodsy cabin that overlooked the Río Sarapiquí. The owners had cleverly designed the rooms to face the river. That night we fell asleep, serenaded by an orchestra of frogs, crickets, and . . . chickens who had crossed the road from neighboring homes to cluck at us, after dodging bananas, I can only assume.

The next day we signed up for the mouth-watering "Chocolate Tour." Although the girls were fit and well-prepared to hike the rainforest, they were overwhelmingly motivated by the chocolate. The gods of guides were looking down on us again when we met our guide, Juan Esteban, none other than the director of the Tirimbina Rainforest itself. Like Tomas in Tortuguero and Fernando who patrolled with us in Parismina, this highly knowledgeable English-speaking gentleman knew the rainforest like his backyard.

Juan Esteban led us across Costa Rica's longest suspension bridge into the canopy of the rainforest. The three-hour hike was punctuated by Juan Esteban's explanations of how important chocolate was to the region. "Before Europeans showed up, the Maya used the cacao beans as currency." He picked an orange-yellow cacao pod, shaped like a football, and handed it to Jocelyn. He took a small knife from his pocket and cut the fruit down the middle to show the girls the cacao beans resting in a bed of pale-yellow flesh. "The meat of the fruit is delicious." He sliced a chunk of flesh for each of the girls. "Servants prepared a bitter drink, known as *xocoatl*, by mixing together crushed cacao beans and water. They served it to their masters as soon as they exited the temples.

"Back then the people drank their xocoatl unsweetened." Then he said with a sly smile, "Perhaps the only contribution the Europeans ever made to the Indigenous communities of Central America was sugar."

On we walked, pausing to peer into the brush, hoping to see sloths or monkeys, but Juan Esteban reminded us, "The forest is teeming with life." He demonstrated how the path of the leaf cutter ant could be sabotaged by merely wiping a wet finger across their path. He showed us the trail of a bullet ant colony, so named for the pain caused by one innocuous bite, and pointed out two of the gigantic insects crawling on my shoe and pant leg.

Panic!

"Tranquila," he said, and he had me wait patiently until they walked off my shoe and back into the jungle.

We finished up our tour under a thatched-roof pavilion where two members of the Rainforest Alliance Women's Collective were waiting to begin the chocolate-making tutorial. Jocelyn and Natalie rolled up their sleeves and got busy. First, they were shown how to harvest the cacao plant, split open the shell, and scoop out the beans. One of the matronly ladies showed them how to dry the beans in the hot sun, then grind them to a powder. After that, the girls were led to a counter where they were instructed to pour the cacao powder and hot water into a large goblet and stir it with a whisk. They tried the original unsweetened concoction first, but it will come as no surprise to learn that they preferred the European recipe. Then the entire group profited from the fruits of their labor. We all agreed that the tour was a success, indeed, how could it be otherwise with such a treat at the end?

The following morning, we backtracked to San José and checked in at Costa Rica Backpackers when we bumped right into Eric and Jennifer. We had last seen them at the hostel in David, and now they had come to the end of a six-month Central American tour and were booked to fly home to Chicago the next day. Coincidence?

Natalie stretched out on the couch in the common room next to Jennifer. At this point, Lloyd and I were ruminating about making our way back to Canada (if we were, indeed, going back) overland to Cancún. It was out of the question before we left. However, the more travelers we ran into, the more we realized that we had judged the other countries from outdated, media-hyped stories. Our small trip to Nicaragua left us feeling confident that we could kick back with the girls all the way to Mexico.

"Did you ever feel unsafe?" I asked Jennifer.

"Not really," she admitted. "There is always the threat of banditos, but we didn't see any."

I picked Jennifer's brain about where they had stayed and sights they had seen. Afterwards, we exchanged follow-up emails. Thanks to Eric and Jennifer, we felt reassured that our trek with the girls was plausible.

The next morning, I proposed going to "Fossil Land," a theme park dedicated to geology education and environmental protection. How could Lloyd say no to that?

We'll never spend a better ninety dollars in one shot. The property owner had created an interactive program for school children to teach them about the natural environment and the importance of preserving it. Except, he does it in character as "Capitán Tula," outfitted in blue coveralls, superhero cape, face mask, and baseball cap. The girls were riveted by this jumping, shouting masked man while Lloyd and I bit our tongues to keep from laughing out loud.

During the orientation exercises, Capitán Tula demanded we give ourselves a name to inspire us to work together during the tour.

"C'mon! What is your name?" he asked us encouragingly. "Yes? Yes! What is it?"

Jocelyn stammered, "Ummm . . ."

"Okay! Your team name is Ummm! Yes?"

The girls burst out laughing. Natalie tentatively offered, "Travel Team?"

"Yes! Y . . . E . . . S!" he shouted, "You are the Travel Team! Go! Go!"

His student guide, Isabel, who spoke nearly perfect English, led us to a trail ascending through rock and brush. I craned my neck to study the plateau and noticed that the guide rope climbed thirty feet, close to perpendicular, and passed through a small waterfall. I was skeptical about this plan, but the girls had fallen in love with Capitán Tula and would have agreed to anything he suggested.

Isabel led the way, gaining a foothold on jutting rock and hoisting herself up, swaying in and out of the water. At the top, she swung her legs up and over the ledge. "Now your turn," she called down to Jocelyn.

All the walking, hiking, and bike riding had made my legs fit, but my upper body strength could be described as doubtful, so when Jocelyn began her ascent I hastily stowed my camera in a plastic bag, shoved it to the bottom of my day pack, and remarked to Lloyd, "Stay close in case you have to haul me up."

I'm proud to say I accomplished this first task independently, even if the park dogs ran circles around me a few times and even lay down to rest, watching me grunt through maneuvers.

At intervals, we heard Capitán Tula in the distance shout "Matanga!" to which the girls shouted "Matanga!" back to him. Then, after deducing our whereabouts, he whizzed to us in his jeep, cape flapping out the side. He sprayed stones when he braked and then jumped out to offer drinks and cookies.

At the peak of the trail, Isabel fastened the girls into harnesses, and they ziplined across a shallow gorge, screaming with a mixture of fear and joy. Capitán Tula casually mentioned, "Some people are too nervous for this."

"How do they cross the gorge?" I asked him.

"I drive them around to the other side in my truck."

I could see the gang through the jungle foliage shouting encouragements and waving me over. Capitán Tula buckled me in. I wondered how long the ride in the truck would take. I had no time to contemplate the answer. I was on my way, screaming bloody murder before crashing into Isabel's outstretched arms.

On and on we hiked, over hardened mud track and into a clearing. "Millions of years ago, this mountain top was submersed in the sea." Capitán Tula was explaining this to a rapt audience of three: Lloyd, Jocelyn, and Natalie. I sat and rested my forty-one years on a rock. "All that is left behind are thousands of silvery fossils in the shape of shells." He motioned to a wall of rock, imprinted with the ancient remains of sea creatures. He handed Lloyd and the girls gloves, safety goggles and a pickaxe to chip away at the fossils, which they then studied in minute detail.

Next, we hiked downhill to the caves to examine stalactites and stalagmites. Lloyd could hardly contain himself. We made our way to a gaping hole in the earth's crust and, led by the intrepid Isabel, spelunked our way into the inky black. In the silence of the airless cavern, I could see that all three of my family members wore looks of contentment. Me, I couldn't breathe.

"There is a lower level," Isabel explained when we had descended to the third circle of Dante's *Inferno*, "but is forbidden for children."

I glanced at Natalie, who was visibly upset at being restricted to the first three levels.

When we surfaced, the light of the afternoon sun was waning and our connecting bus to Orosí was leaving. All in all, we had spent a grueling, hilarious, and educational day atop that mountain. Today, from time to time, we still shout "Matanga!" to one another.

The final stage of our Central Valley tour terminated in Orosí, a region rife with verdant, rolling hills and fertile coffee plantations sprawling downward to bubbling rivers. At that elevation, the evenings were cool. As a nocturnal urinator, I didn't dare get out of bed to go to the bathroom with bare feet on the icy tile floor. But we had a plan to warm up; it was why we had come all this way.

Two things characterize Orosí: hot springs and coffee. Lloyd, especially, was looking forward to relaxing in the heated pools after straining his muscles piggybacking Natalie when her little legs had had enough. We hiked out of town on a sunny Good Friday. Jocelyn and Natalie stopped to pick ripe coffee beans that hung over the side of the road. We passed streets carpeted with petals in vibrant colors. The carpets led to shrines decorated with candles to commemorate the Lord's resurrection. We carried on past the coffee farms, turned off the road, and accessed a trail hemmed in by enormous palms. The track sloped downward, becoming rock; rocks gave way to water. We dropped our bottled water and snacks and stripped down to our bathing suits. Alas, we were disappointed to see dozens of tico families picnicking at the edge of the river, loud music blaring and empty beer cans scattered about. As I waded into the pool, I stepped over a soiled diaper lying on the ground.

On our return to Quebrada Ganado we felt heat seeping into the bus little by little during the descent, reducing us to limp dish rags, like frogs being gradually boiled in water. We were worn out and had spent way too much money. We collapsed on the bed and slept fitfully, having been acclimated to the cooler temperatures for a short time. For now, life returned to normal.

ESL

I resumed my writing routine huddled under the stairs, interrupted by a sojourn beyond the gates of Fort Knox to confer with the high school about the number of students registered in the ESL classes. As it turned out, the school had put up a poster in the community center but neglected to announce the classes to the community at large. I didn't realize this until the morning of the first class. Fearing only three people would show up, I hurriedly prepared dozens of poorly worded Spanish notices, written in faded marker in lopsided, left-handed script.

At the southern end of the horseshoe, I got permission from the owner of the fruit and veggie market to tape a poster above the piles of enormous papayas and watermelons stacked like logs under the awning. I pressed on to the center of town, dodging roving pick-up trucks selling fruit on the go, waving away the driver as he shouted through his megaphone, "Señora! Piña, quiniento la una!" Laaaaady! Pineapple, one for a dollar!

The kindly gentleman who operated the local chunches store allowed a poster in his window. Then I jogged up and down the main street, taping up posters at the perpetually closed internet café, Ricardo's grocery store, and then the bakery, the recreation center, the discoteca, and the restaurant at the far end of town. Random people were curious about my efforts and took flyers with keen interest. My efforts paid off. More than thirty people attended the first class. Axel and Felipe waved at me from the back of the room.

The enthusiasm in the room was palpable. I started by introducing myself in both languages. Then I bumbled through a summary of what I hoped to teach. They nodded politely, giving me confidence that my Spanish was understandable. I asked them for their preference of class time, and the next day I sat down with the school secretary to organize a timetable for the classes. I held them four nights a week, in some cases, teaching two classes a night. The principal and I decided that every six weeks, students would cough up two thousand colones (about four dollars) for the classes.

The interest in the classes was due to the town's proximity to Jacó, one of the most visited regions of Costa Rica. Scads of people flowed in and out of the area; some came for week-long surfing holidays, and thousands more relocated to the area from colder and more expensive countries.

I tried my best to accommodate everyone's busy schedule. Some rode the bus seventeen kilometers to Jacó every day to work at the Masxmenos grocery store or at one of the hotels. After work, they hopped off the bus right outside the doors of the community center, came in, and sat down, ready to learn. For them, English meant improved employment opportunities.

I absolutely loved it. I slowly introduced the basics of conversational English to students ranging in age from ten to sixty-seven (including Paola). The jovial and smiling students were sweet to each other, helping each other with difficult exercises, chuckling at themselves over slight mistakes in pronunciation, furiously copying notes from a classmate due to a missed lesson.

I was steeped in their world, culturally speaking. I came to learn how dedicated these people were to their community. Filtering into class, they discussed community concerns and arranged committee meetings. These were salt-of-the-earth types; many of them worked two and three jobs, some were students from the high school, and several were teachers themselves.

My best lessons occurred when Jocelyn and Natalie attended as teacher's helpers. The pupils were so enthusiastic that I needed tutors to help lighten the pressure on me during the constant demands ("Teacher? Here Teacher!"). With Jocelyn and Natalie, I could break up the class into three groups and have the girls lead exercises by example: "Hi, my name is Natalie. It's nice to meet you." (We were tackling the basics in the early days.) Once the students became comfortable, I had them present themselves in English to the rest of the class.

Eduardo, who worked next door to the villa at the video store, rose from his desk and introduced himself in English. "Hello, mya name ees Eduardo, Ima esstudent."

I corrected him. "*I'm a student.*"

He nodded. "Ima esstudent."

"*I'm. A. Student.*"

"Sí, Ima esstudent."

I puzzled for a bit then wrote on the board: *I'm student*. "Please say this."

"Ok. I'm esstudent."

Perfect.

Jocelyn proved especially helpful because by then, after eight months, she was so strong in Spanish that she could understand and respond to students' questions. I was surprised that she was a good listener; she was so often on another planet, but in class I was seeing her in a different light. She was attentive to others and diplomatic with her corrections.

The girls helped me in other ways, too. Some students brought their babies or small children with them because to leave them at home wouldn't have crossed their minds. "Why would it matter if you brought your kids to a night school class anyway?" I told Lloyd. Jocelyn and Natalie acted as babysitters, playing with the children in the hallway while their mothers studied English inside my classroom.

I cherished the presence of the girls at my classes. I missed them terribly during the day. We had forged a solid connection long ago, and I missed the 24/7 interaction. The students sensed that I was happy with this arrangement. Though I had a university education, economic privilege, and spoke English fluently, all things that could act as a wedge between people of different worlds, we shared an ideology about family life. My acceptance of other mothers and their children breached the culture barrier in a way that nothing else could have. If ever there was a compelling argument for traveling with kids, this was it.

While my life relaxed into a productive and pleasant routine, Lloyd felt pressured to keep up with the mounting expenses related to sending the girls to a private school.

"You have done remarkably well," he congratulated me. "Spending like the locals has allowed us to stay on budget."

I had ten dollars per day to spend on food and toiletries. I managed it scrupulously, adding and subtracting every colón to stay within budget. My daily walks to the market at the end of town produced lettuce, cauliflower, pineapple, mangoes, tomatoes, a small papaya, grenadines, and potatoes for about three dollars. From time to time oatmeal, milk, pasta, cheese, plantains, bananas, apple juice, lentils, chickpeas, bread, and yogurt rounded out my list and even then, I was under budget. When we needed toilet paper, shampoo, or sunscreen, we were forced to eat bland staples like rice and plantain for a couple of days until Lloyd was paid.

Like the locals with limited cash flow, I bought items in small quantities. The shelves at Ricardo's store held dozens of products available in singles: a single diaper, acetaminophen in single packets, even a single egg. Milk was sold in five-hundred-milliliter bags (larger volumes spoiled lightning quick). Smokers could buy one cigarette. People, such as Lloyd, looking to quench their thirst, could buy one bottle of beer. And then later, another, etc.

Lloyd went on, "The fees for the school are eating away at our reserves. For the sake of learning Spanish, we are dipping into too much of our garage sale money. It's time to think about coming up with a few hundred dollars per month to have something left over for side trips and emergencies."

Not at all like the locals, I thought.

Coincidentally, no less than one week after commencing the ESL classes at the community center, the principal of the high school offered me the job of English teacher if she could obtain permission from immigration.

Then I received phone calls from two of Lloyd's colleagues who had asked me to fill in for them during their absences. I learned that they were leaving at the summer break, creating two employment possibilities for me. I mulled this over sadly. Any of these positions would likely mean I would be forced to give up my beloved night school ESL classes. I didn't feel it would be workable given the responsibilities to my family and my writing routine.

As the summer break loomed, my students requested the sign-up sheet to get a leg up on the rest of the community who were already registering for future classes. Finally, I admitted to them that I was unsure I could continue. The room grew quiet. I looked out into the crowd of faces. *I've never been happier in my career than I am now*, I thought, *interacting with these people* and thinking that maybe I'm making a difference in their lives. They surely had made a difference in mine.

Being out in the community was like a balm to my soul. The economic divide separating our family from others was immense. Some in town were dirt poor. The lady we hired to do little sewing repairs lived in a tumbledown house in an alleyway behind the bullring. Her home was propped in a dark corner behind two others and was riddled with mildew. When I called, I could plainly see her son passed out drunk on a ratty sofa while she was hunched over her ancient sewing machine. Others in town lived in more desperate conditions. Coming back by bus from Orotina I saw a man living in a ditch beside a swamp. With no running water or electricity, corrugated metal slats leaned like a precarious deck of cards against each other.

However, people in town were resourceful and industrious. Cars were not plentiful. Poorly scheduled and ridiculously overcrowded buses could carry you anywhere in the country. The town was so small, villagers either walked or rode their bikes. Businesses in town employed young boys who made deliveries by bike, one with a large basket on the front. Once I even saw a lady balance a large cake easily with one hand, steering a bike with the other as she rode down the street.

I took every opportunity to learn about the differences in culture, after having felt imprisoned behind the red gate for months, including accepting an invitation from Felipe, who approached me after class one evening. "Teacher, tonight is ladies' night at the discoteca. You and Lloyd will come?"

"Only one of us can go. One has to stay with the girls," I said, packing up my papers. "I'll go with you."

Felipe hesitated. "For Lloyd, it's okay to come with us?"

I was about to explain that I didn't need permission from my husband to go out with friends, but I was in the middle of a cultural moment and just went with it. "I will drop off my things and ask."

I strolled home in the twilight with Felipe and Axel. They waited for me at the gate and I went in and wasted a few minutes, making like Lloyd was giving me his consent to go dancing with them. In reality, I let myself into the villa, whispered into a sleeping husband's ear, "I'm going out with Felipe and Axel," then went up to the loft to kiss the girls goodnight and hooked up with my posse back on the street.

Approximately 75 percent of Quebrada Ganado was at the discoteca, and possibly 100 percent of my students. It took me some minutes to make my way to the table Felipe's cousin, Manuel, had reserved for us. "Hello teacher!" rang out above earsplitting decibels. It was clear that this was the most fun you could have on two legs in Quebrada Ganado on a Thursday night.

We were four at the table—Manuel, Axel, Felipe, and me. Felipe ordered the first round. I looked forward to a cold beer after working up a sweat teaching English for two hours in a dank classroom.

I'd adopted the local dress by now: tank top, A-line skirt, ponytail, and flip-flops. I fit in well; only a smattering of freckles gave away the Irish ancestry in my blood. Sadly, my dancing ability revealed an utter incompetence that guaranteed I could, in no way, be misconstrued for a tica. It didn't deter Felipe from urging me to have another dance. Beer after beer I rose to go to the dance floor, shoes slapping. Flip. Flop. Flop. Flip.

I sat down hard and asked Manuel what he was drinking. Surely it was my round by now?

"I don't drink," he said. "This is Coke."

"What about you, Axel? What are you having?"

"I'm on antibiotics. I can't drink tonight."

"Oh. Felipe, can I get you a drink?"

"No, I have to get up early tomorrow."

"*You mean I'm the only one drinking?*" I wailed.

At that, Felipe grabbed my arm again, and we cut another rug to the pumping percussion typical of popular Latino music, played at a volume no human should tolerate. Flip. Flop. Flop. Flip.

The next day, dehydrated and achy, I confided to Lloyd about how I was feeling. "Even though we're struggling, I can't imagine not teaching those classes."

He set a mug of coffee down in front of me. "I know. When you come in the door at night you're beaming."

Time ticked by, but I heard nothing from the local high school about the teaching position. Summer break was just weeks away and I felt an obligation to tell my students what my plans were. Then Lloyd came home and revealed that administration at his school had not even begun thinking about hiring anyone.

"I think it's time to have a family meeting," I said.

We explained to the girls that our financial circumstances due to the tuition of the private school placed a strain on our budget. We brainstormed for solutions.

"My teacher is too strict," admitted Natalie. "She gets mad when the kids fart in class."

"Well, I like my teachers, but I have nothing in common with my classmates," Jocelyn added. "They're all rich."

"What about the public school across the street?" Lloyd said. "It would be totally free, and no one speaks English there."

We sat for a moment, pondering, then Lloyd said, "And think of how much they will be learning about the culture, surrounded by all the village kids."

"Girls, what do you think?"

"I'd like to make some friends here in town," Jocelyn said.

"I think kids should be able to fart without getting in trouble," Natalie added.

The solution was unexpected. The relief from having to pay the exorbitant fee at the private school was the answer. We didn't need an influx of several hundred dollars if we could *save* several hundred dollars. The only question remaining was whether they would allow us, as non-nationals, to enroll our children in the school. We would never have considered it if we hadn't met the fine people of the community at my English classes.

I sent Lloyd over to speak with the director, who scoffed at his worries. "Of course they can attend." How could she refuse when many of her staff were attending my classes for virtually nothing?

I wandered around the school squelching doubts about our decision. The school was like others we had seen in Parismina and Puerto Viejo, real throwbacks to the fifties. Square wooden desks with tilt-top openings lined up in rows facing the blackboard. The dim classrooms were desolate and open air. Mosquitoes buzzed in hordes. Save for the desks, there was nothing else, no books, no pencils, no paper, no light bulbs, no chalk.

No books.

The only luxury they allowed was the electricity to circulate some air via the dirty fans on the ceiling. The kindergarten area was a little more pleasant. The teacher, Alma, one of my own students, gasped to learn that our Natalie would be attending. She dug out three powder blue uniforms for her to try on.

The next evening, I unlocked the community center and prepared the classroom. I waited until everyone had trickled in and said their hellos. They sat waiting for me to begin. I explained the lesson for the evening and then said in Spanish, "Oh, by the way, I will be teaching classes after the summer break."

The classroom erupted in cheers. I sputtered, not having a clue what to say next.

"Teacher, we must have a party!"

So, we did. Felipe and Axel offered to bring the rice and beans, Manuel the pizza, Paola, drinks (a bottle of rum), Cataleya, salads, and so on. Lloyd and the girls dressed up to join us. I presented certificates of achievement to each student and suggested we begin supper. Axel and Felipe had not yet arrived. It was getting late, and we were all starving and full of too much rum.

Lloyd leaned over to me. "They won't start eating until the rice and beans turn up."

"Why?"

"It's like having no pasta at an Italian potluck."

That, I understood.

I encouraged people to begin. There was more than enough food, but they held back. At last, father and son burst through the doors. Axel plunked a vat of beans and rice onto the makeshift buffet table and the class swarmed it. Without this incident, how would we ever have come to know the cultural importance of rice and beans?

Fully stuffed, we moved the tables and chairs aside to dance away the humid night under a rickety ceiling, lit by one, flickering fluorescent bulb.

The girls finished out two final weeks at the private school, said quiet goodbyes to their friends and teachers, and began their new school the first week of June. The cultural divide was profound. At 7:00 a.m., we crossed the street, and merged with hundreds of mothers and older siblings dropping off children at their classrooms. An older gentleman acted as a security guard, helping children park their bikes in the racks and surveying everyone who came and went.

Whereas private drivers delivered their former classmates in shiny, black, air-conditioned, window-tinted SUVs, we were now awash with mothers yammering last minute instructions to their children. Screams of hello were nearly deafening. The World Cup soccer tournament had gotten underway, and the main office was full of staff and parent volunteers watching the game on the old set the principal had turned on for that purpose. She even convened a staff meeting with others wandering in and out to catch the score.

Natalie loved it immediately. Her teacher, Alma—called Señora by her pupils—encouraged imaginary play. She had arranged stations around the classroom—a puppet theater, a toy kitchen, a puzzle corner, and a small library. At recess, they had exclusive access to a small covered playground. Each day the children were invited to visit any of the centers, provided they informed the Señora, who recorded their preference in a notebook. Alma didn't mind that Natalie was a year older than the other children, and Lloyd and I didn't care either. In fact, I was tickled about it. She was free to play with the Spanish-speaking children following a method Professor Mullins put forward: learning a language through movement.

Natty had a little anglophone to talk to in her own language because Bruno and Ruth's daughter, Leah, was also in Alma's class. Alma used their attendance to her advantage. She pulled them aside for a few minutes every day to help translate Spanish words into English, which she recorded in her ESL notebook.

Jocelyn's transition was more challenging because she was enrolled in one of those dreary, bare classrooms. She accepted her new environment, though, because she was longing to establish friends in her own neighborhood. As my sweet little homebody, she could come home for lunch and a little hug from mom, change out of her uniform, and then meet up with friends back on the street. But she took her studies very seriously, more so than I was comfortable with.

"I've got to learn the countries of South America by Monday," she announced on a Friday afternoon. "I have a test."

I stopped myself from suggesting she be absent Monday and instead went down to the chunches and bought a roll of yellow paper, brought it home, and wallpapered my office with it. Lloyd drew the continent of South America in outline and had Jocelyn label the countries. Then, as any good unschooling mom would do, I made her learn each nation by rote memorization, covering the labels and testing her repeatedly throughout the weekend.

She came home Monday afternoon and handed over her paper with a look of pride. One hundred percent. Having no prior school experience in her life, I was amazed how quickly she picked up on the concept of pleasing her teacher.

During exam week, I reminded her, "You are only there to learn Spanish, you don't need to write those exams if you don't want to."

She rolled her eyes. "Mom, I'm gonna ace them."

That afternoon she flew in the door, slammed her math exam on the table and yelled, "I only got 86 percent!"

Considering the test was written in Spanish, I'd say it was an outstanding mark.

She disagreed. "I don't get 86 percent on exams!"

"Let me see it."

She handed it to me and looked over my shoulder as I went through each question. "Wait a minute, what does this mean? Hand me the dictionary." It took me a couple of minutes, but I deduced that question number five, worth twelve marks, asked students to write out the numbers that followed the examples. Jocelyn wrote "46, 47, 48, 49," after the example "42, 43, 44, 45." However, the Spanish instructions indicated that the students were to write out the numbers in *words*.

"I can write the words!" She took the paper from me, scribbled out the answers and handed it back. All correct. Spelling and everything.

"Let's go over to the school and talk to the teacher."

The teacher met us at the classroom door.

"Excuse me profesora," I said in Spanish, "Jocelyn misunderstood the instructions for number five." I showed her the exam.

She looked at it, smiled, took a pen, wrote something and handed it back without a word. Ninety-eight percent. Just like that. Jocelyn clutched the paper like it was a precious piece of gold and my heart fluttered at how something so insignificant to me could render her so emotional.

The student body was twice the capacity the school could handle. Sometimes the girls attended in the early morning, other times class began late and ended at 5:30. Because of the staggered schedules, both girls spent only a few hours each day at school and were free to do as they pleased for the remainder of the day. I admit I was content with this arrangement. It offered me the best of both worlds. I still had a few hours every day to devote to writing. I spent the rest of the day outside the compound, looking in at the girls playing video games at Eduardo's store or wandering off to play bingo at the seniors' center.

Then we heard sad news from Axel and Felipe. After trying to make it work in Quebrada Ganado, they decided to return to Limón where their large family lived. I felt their positive attitude directly impacted the atmosphere of my classroom. One afternoon, Lloyd and I left Ricardo's store and strolled home along the main *avenida* to the villa. A pick-up truck bumped by us stacked to the heavens with furniture. Felipe and Axel leaned out the windows shouting, "Teacher! Oye!" and waving goodbye.

Chapter 10

Summer Vacation—Back to Panama

The school year in Costa Rica is divided into two chunks: January to July, then August to December. With summer approaching, my writing nook became covered with maps and notes scrawled on scratch pads, outlining ideas for a detour south through a couple of National Parks. "How would you feel about going back to Panama?" I asked the Travel Team as we ate supper on the terrace.

"To see the canal again?" Jocelyn asked.

"We won't go as far as Panama City, but I think we need to spend a few days in David to do some shopping."

"Is it farther than San Juan del Sur?" Lloyd asked. "We have to do a visa run."

"Yes, it is. We can take it slow, stopping at a few places on our way to the border."

"I hope we can see some monkeys this time," Natalie said through a mouthful of beans and rice.

I brought out my notes and presented some options: Parque Nacional Manuel Antonio, one of Costa Rica's most popular attractions, then Wilson Botanical Gardens. "From there, we can cross at an obscure border post I've read about."

"It means we'll have to endure that stretch between Quepos and Dominical," Lloyd warned.

He was right; the route was agony, but I countered brightly. "We can hack it. Right girls?"

They agreed; everything was still a novelty for them, even bus rides. Back home, they'd rarely ever done anything more than ride around in the back of the minivan.

We struck out for Manuel Antonio National Park following lumpy roads in a hard, humid rain. I looked out the window, angling my head down to see road beneath our wheels, but I couldn't. The bus driver had aligned his wheels at the very edge of a narrow bridge. I shut my eyes tight and sweated it out.

We gained access to the park by a rowboat crossing high tide rivulets. For a few minutes, Jocelyn took Natalie to an imaginary medieval land as we approached the entrance on the far side. "Natalie, this is what you call a moat."

We went ashore and walked into the jungle. The rain had cleared. We wound our way up the forested trail, dodging red crabs that lived in the sandy loam. We came across a troupe of howler monkeys that roared at us from the treetops. A raccoon-type creature called a *pizote* startled Natalie as it sauntered by her on the main trail, heedless of her gaping at the sight of him.

Now and then, the azure waters of the Pacific were visible through gaps in the vegetation at strategic lookout points. We took a break from hiking to peer out over the ocean. Others jostled us to rubberneck the scene. Jocelyn, age eight, summarizes what happened next:

> One day we were at Manuel Antonio National Park. We were walking on a trail when we saw some bees. We didn't think that they were bees, we thought that they were flies, so we walked right past them. Then they started stinging us! We screamed, and Mommy had to get the bug spray that was buried twenty feet under other stuff that was in the backpack. She sprayed our legs, our clothes, and even our hair. We ran like the wind and soon enough we were at the beach. I sighed a great sigh of relief as we got into the cool water. The End.

We spent a relaxing afternoon on the beach among hundreds of vacationers. The girls were forbidden to wade into the ocean deeper than their ankles, as the previous night's storm was churning the surf into malevolent waves. A tour guide screamed at a group of young people from the United States, "Up to your knees only!"

Eight days earlier, an excursion turned tragic when four young Americans had drowned in a strong rip tide. According to the World Health Organization,[4] vehicle accidents and drowning are two of the most common

---

4. World Health Organization, "Injuries and Violence," https://www.who.int/ith/other_health_risks/injuries_violence/en/.

causes of accidental death among vacationers, while *La Nación* reported that many vehicle fatalities in Costa Rica involved cars hitting pedestrians or cyclists on the sides of those winding, dark, and rutted highways.[5] Thank goodness the girls only had to walk out the front gate of the villa and across the quiet street to school. As for the water, we were much more likely to admire the ocean from the safety of the beach rather than risk battling riptides and strong waves.

When we arrived back at the hostel with sand wedged in delicate places, Lloyd's expression brightened when he heard that the town had shut down the water. "No showers right now guys, there's no water." He tapped me on the shoulder and pointed to the lobby TV, broadcasting the ongoing World Cup tournament. "There's a game on; let's go watch it."

Lloyd and I had little in common with our children who'd been steeped in the arts since toddlerhood. Jocelyn was more interested in singing show tunes or designing dresses. Natalie, as athletic as she was, preferred to channel her energy into dance. Watching sports was probably the one thing we did together as a couple. Lloyd and I missed it. The girls, uninterested in something as frivolous as sports, passed the time watching sheets of rain careen down the street in front of the hostel. Lloyd and I took turns checking on the girls; every fifteen minutes, one of us would get up and look in on them.

"I think this place is about to be flooded," Lloyd reported to me after his shift.

"Mmm hmmm," I muttered. *Didn't he realize the score was 1–1 with five minutes to go?* I thought. *This is an important game. Why is he talking to me right now? Wait. What?*

The owner of the hostel, named Javier, leaned his squat, bulky frame against the entranceway, chuckling at the girls. Water flowed like a river down the street; the girls watched in amazement as it rose quickly, breaching the banks of the sidewalk, and spilled over.

"It's coming right for us, Mom!" Natalie exclaimed.

Lloyd looked around at the electrical outlets and shrugged. "Well Javier seems indifferent."

"That's because it's old hat." I pointed down the street. Javier and other business owners merely slid a piece of wood into the bottom of the door frame to keep the water out.

---

5. Recio, "Atropellos."

LONG DURATION AND URINATION

The next leg was the one we dreaded most. Sixty kilometers of road lay ahead of us. Did I say road? Sorry, I meant rocky, lunar surface passing under two washed out bridges. We possessed enough brains to buy two large garbage bags to protect our packs from getting wet in the hold of the bus. The next morning as we were waiting in line for the bus to shuttle us to Dominical, a British traveler asked us, "Why have you got your packs in bin bags?"

"There's a washed out bridge up ahead, and the bus has to barrel right through the river," we explained. "The level of the water can be high enough to flood the hold."

"Uh . . . can you hold my spot? I'm going to bring my pack on the bus."

He walked over to retrieve his pack and as he did so, Lloyd said with a smug smile on his face, "It's feels good to mentor the younger generation, doesn't it?"

We clattered toward Dominical at a mind-numbing twenty-four kilometers per hour. "At this rate the journey should take up half the day," Lloyd muttered. He looked at me, expecting a response. "Why are you leaning to the side?"

"I have to pee," I said with a grimace, then, "Why on such a bumpy road?" And therein lay all my future travel dilemmas. Reduce hydration to prevent normal bladder function and risk electrolyte imbalance or hydrate and contort myself into a pretzel to avoid an accident? Costa Rican buses are saunas on eight wheels—no air conditioning, no bathrooms, standing room only, and the windows don't open. When selectively dehydrating, these are not ideal conditions. I was agonizing over peeing my pants or risking kidney infection.

I'd learned my lesson about dehydration and electrolyte imbalance. On three more occasions I had endured nights of unbearable abdominal pain, always preceded by me not taking care to hydrate and reestablish my electrolytes properly. At the villa, Lloyd had expropriated the machete from Paola and was chopping down coconuts and draining the fluid into a bottle for me to drink. When the pain hit, he vacillated between waking the girls and bringing them with us to the clinic in Jacó, or just letting me sweat it out. My intestinal tract throbbed, feeling as though a string of gravel was wending its way through. "Don't wake them," I grunted. This gravel, upon egress, left me weak, sweaty and drained.

Before leaving for Panama, I had packed a device cleverly designed with openings and receptacles and a cap, designed for use "on the road," literally "in motion." On the bus to Dominical, I would have relied on that contraption, but it's good for only one go-round and we had a long way to go.

I "made it" to the surfers' haven of Dominical where we stopped for a bite and use of the baño before ascending through the coastal mountains. It became blessedly cool, and even though the ride buffeted us left and right, we closed our eyes and savored the breeze. We stopped off for one night at a town called Buenos Aires. Jocelyn impressed me with her retention of rote-memorized South American capitals. "Argentina already? That was fast."

Actually, it was a small city with few tourist amenities. We rented a room at a nondescript cinder block establishment with a TV shackled to a metal shelf waaaay up in the corner. Lloyd and I ignored discomfort from cricked necks to follow the World Cup from prone positions on saggy beds.

After the match, I slipped out to find an internet café, and when I located one, I wasted an hour listening to the hard drive grind to a halt trying to load my email account. I gave up and ambled through the Parque Central on the way back to the cinder block. Workers were transforming it into an amusement park in celebration of some festival.

Lloyd had resorted to desperate measures and looked up at me pathetically from his hand of Go Fish when I walked through the door.

I bent over and whispered in his ear. "There's a fair at the park tonight. At least it will get us out of the motel and give us something to do in this town."

Relieved, he threw in his hand. "I'm out."

Of course, at the fair the girls were elated and skipped and ran among the vendors and flashing lights. Lloyd and I negotiated over who would accompany them on the rides. Well, "negotiated" is a word, "argued" is a better one. Both of us had weak stomachs when it came to midway rides, so we compromised. In the end, both of us went on the spinning teacups, sandwiching the girls between us. I only laughed because I felt it would be culturally inappropriate to cry. When the ride came to an end, the two of us adults staggered down the metal ramp and clutched each other like two sad drunks weaving in and out of the crowds. The girls, convulsing with laughter, skipped away hand in hand.

SAN VITO . . . EL SITIO BARRILES

San Vito—a hilly town eponymously named after Italian soldier Vito Sansonetti—was colonized with a purpose: to live a life of peace after World War II. To complete our tour of Panama, we could cross the border at Río Sereno, a mere eleven kilometers from San Vito.

As the crow flies, we were due south of Puerto Viejo; the only thing separating the two communities was the impenetrable vastness of Parque Nacional La Amistad. In town we saw the Indigenous Ngobe in traditional clothing like the petite family on the bus to David when we were last in Panama, wearing long, solid-colored dresses called *naguas*, trimmed in contrasting hues.

We split up to find accommodations. One cabbie loaded all the packs along with Lloyd and Natalie and drove off while Jocelyn and I hit the street to scope out what was available on the main drag.

When we were shown a lovely peach-colored room Jocelyn breathed, "Oh Mom, can we stay here?"

"It's too expensive," I told her. "And we have to find a place with a kitchen."

We met up with the others later, piled into their cab, compared notes, took the driver's advice, and rented a cabina overlooking an orange orchard. Two double beds took up the bulk of the space. The owner had imaginatively wired the suicide shower and television set by rigging a secondary connection, stealing current directly from the wires on the street. Turning on the shower dimmed the TV.

Despite its questionable electrical safety, the cabina had three things going for it: the price, the lookout onto the orchard, and the large laundry sink we could use to wash vegetables to prepare a cold supper. Using the five adventure-by-chicken-bus essential items—a knife, a can opener, a grater, a garlic press, and a peeler—we could prepare a cold stew of chopped avocado, corn niblets, chick peas, grated cheese, diced carrots, chopped tomatoes, and cucumber. Add to large Ziploc bag, add crushed garlic, juice of a freshly squeezed lime, and salt. Shake and serve. Delicious.

I confess, I had no intention of using that laundry sink for its intended purpose. There were just some things I could not adapt to. I tolerated cold showers, but hand-washing our dirty clothes required super-human strength in the wrists to wring them out. Lloyd and I tackled this task together back in Parismina before Don Rodrigo took pity on the foreigners and let us use his washing machine.

We'd been on the road several days, and we were down to our last pair, so after we dumped our gear, I approached the owner. "Do you know of a laundry service in town?"

"No, but you can use our washing machine," he said, pointing to his back porch. "You'll have to wait until my daughter is finished."

Lloyd commenced his usual routine of crisscrossing clotheslines back and forth, fastening the ends to miscellaneous protrusions in the wall to hang up towels. The girls fiddled with the TV, looking for their favorite

Spanish-language programs. Lloyd insisted they switch on the soccer tournament first.

Natalie was exasperated. "Can't we find out the score when we go to the pulpería?"

He *could* have. No matter where we were, we could walk down the street in any town and pick up the trail of the World Cup at any shop. Business owners had resorted to propping their television sets on counters to face the street. It was total soccer immersion. Costa Rica's elimination did nothing to dampen ticos' enthusiasm for the tournament.

"Look," I said. "We need ingredients for supper. You go shopping and pick up the score. The girls and I will work on the laundry."

"Okay." He high-fived me on the way out the door.

When it came time to use the washer, Jocelyn and I lugged over our festering pile. The owner's daughter, a university student, was surprised that I didn't bother to scrub the girls' grungy socks to their original whiteness. She insisted on showing me how to wash them properly. I couldn't have cared less. Jocelyn, though, got interested in it and spent the afternoon with the girl, soaking and scrubbing all our socks.

In snippets, between me muttering to myself about the washer ("Which word means drain again?"), I listened to Jocelyn chattering to the girl as they scrubbed the socks against a cement washboard built into the laundry sink that seemed ubiquitous in every home I'd seen.

The girl called over her shoulder, "She speaks Spanish very well."

Indeed, maybe because she started talking at an early age or maybe because she heard me speaking Spanish or maybe a million other reasons, she had surpassed my expectations. That afternoon, after we'd hung our wet laundry, we taxied to the children's library and beautiful estate of Finca Cántaros, overlooking the majestic Valle de Coto Brus and Panama beyond. Birders, gardeners, and ardent nature lovers throng to the Valley, Lloyd among them. We wandered along the pathways before getting caught in a downpour and retreating inside. A young receptionist showed us into the library and brought the girls paper and crayons.

We waited out the deluge reading, chatting, and drawing pictures. The young woman came in and out, stocking shelves and cleaning up. Natalie asked me, "Can you get me some more paper?"

"No," I said. "But you can."

Without missing a beat, she stood up and said to the young woman, "Permiso, hay más papel?" The woman, who had heard us speaking English, stood for a moment with her mouth hanging open, then smiled and went off to find her some.

I kidded to Lloyd. "We can go home now; we got what we wanted out of this trip."

Later that night, we watched *Toy Story 2* in Spanish back at the cabina. In a crucial scene, the arch nemesis of Buzz Lightyear leans over to him and in a menacing tone, says, "Yo . . . soy . . . tu . . . padre." The three of us females burst into laughter.

Lloyd, still bumbling through Spanish like Tarzan, looked confused, so the girls jumped on their dad, the planet's biggest *Star Wars* fan, tickling him with sharp fingers digging into his armpits and yelled in unison, "I am your father!"

The Coto Brus Valley is one of the few zones in Costa Rica where the Indigenous population is recognizable by their clothing. When an Ngobe couple crossed our path one afternoon as we strolled through San Vito, Lloyd pointed out, "They have lived here for a long time, before there was even a Costa Rica or a Panama. They can pass back and forth freely between the two countries without a passport."

"We have to use passports, right?" Natalie said.

Lloyd nodded. It's hard to say if a child as young as Natalie could comprehend the importance of ancestral land rights; we were more concerned with demonstrating respect for their way of life so that our girls would grow up to honor all aboriginal people, including the ones in our own country.

After we packed up and left the cabina, we plastered our faces against the cool windows of the bus. The road to Panama was the prettiest scenery I'd seen in my life. The border post at Río Sereno was deserted and aptly named, as it turned out. No vendors, no hawkers, no money changers, no chaos. At the window, Lloyd was told to walk down the hill, enter Panama, go into the grocery store, buy four tourist cards, walk back up the hill, enter back into Costa Rica, and present these cards to the official.

As we crossed into Panama, I turned back and looked at the road we had just traveled.

"Give me your camera," I said to Lloyd. "This is the only way people will see the difference.

I snapped off a shot of the dilapidated Costa Rican road leading right up to the demarcation line, where it flattened out wide and smooth.

An hour later, we rolled up to a little town called Volcán, and trudged the few blocks to the El Cubano hostel. The owner, an older woman named Lucía, was happy to see us, especially because of the children. Lucía had a large collection of brochures spread out on the dining room table. "I recommend El Sitio Barriles," Lucía said in Spanish. The brochure described El Sitio Barriles as a privately run, interactive archaeological site, funded solely by private donors. "It is located on the Landau farm. The land has been handed down from grandfather to son to daughter."

Señor Landau's daughter, Edna, stepped from the veranda to greet us in English the moment we arrived. She smiled at the girls and initiated the tour at the clearing in front of the farmhouse. "Our family began cultivating the land for coffee, but right away we found artifacts that archaeologists have dated back to 1500 BC." The lawn was riddled with large stone carvings, mostly oblong in shape. They stood in clusters alongside bushes of vibrant reds, yellows, and greens. Indicating a large boulder, she said, "This is an accurate, to-scale topographical map of the area." She ran her hand over the smooth surface. We were confused; all we saw was a huge stone. Then, she took a hose and doused the rock. Markings appeared on its surface, like the invisible ink notes we used to write to each other as kids.

The girls lost interest in its historical significance and spent a few minutes playing with the water. Edna turned her attention to us. "Some pieces have been taken to Museo Nacional de Antropología Reina Torres in Panama City."

"Has the government helped in any way?" Lloyd asked.

"Not much," she admitted. "Everything that was not taken to the museum is here, as you see it. The smallest items are in a shed in the backyard."

The girls were drawn to her calm disposition and fell in step with her as we walked on.

"Do you know what this is?" Edna asked them.

They huddled around a smooth, large, oval table shaped like a small granite surfboard, with four stubby legs and concaved slightly at the center, where an egg-shaped rock was resting.

Edna instructed Natalie, "Roll the rock to one end and let go."

Natalie did as she was told. The egg-rock rolled back and forth, climbing up one side of the tray and back down the other.

"What is it for?" Jocelyn asked.

"It's an automatic maize grinder called a *metate*," she explained.

The history of El Sitio Barriles was as interesting as the site was beautiful. Streams and pathways, adorned with heliconia and concealing chirping geckos, shadowed us as we proceeded with the tour.

"My father tried to cultivate a small area for our family's needs, but he was forced to stop to prevent damage to the artifacts." You can still see intact urns, tools, and dishes as they found them, jutting out of the earth in a pit on their property.

"Thank God he had enough foresight to preserve them," Lloyd remarked. "What must these items be worth?"

"You can read *National Geographic*'s article about the site in the February 1950 edition," Edna said proudly.

In her shed on dusty shelves, Styrofoam blocks held carvings and artifacts dating back thousands of years. Out front, a semi-excavated pit stretched from the back shed to the farmhouse. We'd come full circle. Three archaeologists from a US university, salivating impatiently, intercepted us at the shed, unable to contain their excitement, and walked with us to the front porch where they would begin their tour.

"I have to admit, I'm blown away by the whole thing," I said to Lloyd while we waited for a taxi to take us back to El Cubano.

"To think how many undiscovered civilizations are lying under the earth because no one has funded a dig," Lloyd said.

The girls were only six and eight; I assumed their inability to comprehend the concept of time would render the history lessons irrelevant. I pointed out, "Edna was so good with them. They got more out of it than I would have expected."

"The hands-on stuff helped make it interesting, I suppose," Lloyd said.

We dallied in the front yard playing with Edna's Dalmatian. The girls took pity on him; he had been run down by a car and hobbled on three good legs, the fourth jutted out to the side at a ninety-degree angle.

"Mommy, why don't they get his leg fixed?" Natalie asked.

As much as I cherished the opportunity to provide lessons in history and archaeology by visiting places like El Sitio Barriles, I hoped the girls would come to understand the difference between a privileged life and the life of the Majority World. Here was my chance. "Taking a dog to the vet probably costs more than this family can afford."

Something must have clicked, because out of the blue Jocelyn asked, "Does Santa come to these houses?"

So perhaps things were sinking in. They had only been at the public school in Quebrada Ganado a few weeks, but their enrollment generated interactions with local kids, many of whom they visited at their simple homes. Homes without screens, doors, much furniture, or toys.

I did not answer her. A taxi came along, distracting us all from the hapless pooch.

TRANSPORTATION WOES

In Boquete, an expat community not far from Volcán, we rented a room at a chocolate-paneled, homey pension after Lloyd plodded through the streets looking for a vacancy. We waited for him in the leafy Parque Central, under a gazebo where Jocelyn reenacted "Sixteen Going on Seventeen" from *The Sound of Music* and Natalie bounded from railing to railing. I could observe the town clearly from there. Unlike lonely, barren Volcán, who hosted four tourists when we visited (i.e., us), Boquete appeared to profit from foreigners stocking up on booze at the grocery store.

We wasted no time organizing an outing to the hot springs of Los Pozos, just outside of Boquete near a village called Caldera. Steve and Derek, our American buddies from Rocking J's who had kept in touch, emailed us at this juncture, asking us for directions to the hot springs. I emailed back explaining that it seemed tricky at first, but after shambling down a steep hill for twenty minutes, crossing a wobbly rope bridge, slipping and sliding uphill over muddy terrain for about fifty meters, crossing a stream by way of a log, then turning left at the goat, they shouldn't have any trouble finding it.

After shambling, wobbling, slipping, and sliding all the way to Los Pozos, I relaxed for as long as five minutes in the pool; the rest of the time I stewed about convincing two children to walk back to Caldera the way we had come. Lloyd was content to soldier on, to get the walk over with, but I knew it would be a chore. There was zero chance to get a ride back. We'd passed a couple of *campesinos*, or farmers, on horseback, leading buffalo to pasture, but no vehicles.

"Lloyd," I said as we peeled off wet bathing suits, "I have an idea to make the walk back more tolerable for the girls. Give me everything you have to eat."

He dug into his pack and unearthed a half-eaten granola bar and a soft banana. I had about four mouthfuls of Gatorade.

"Okay, that won't work. We haven't even got enough to bribe them with treats."

"What if we stop every fifteen minutes and play a game?"

"You got any ideas for games?"

"I Spy? Either that or desperate measures."

"I Spy *is* desperate measures," I pointed out. "How did we get so disorganized?"

He didn't hear me. He was rounding up the girls, making sure shoes were on feet, and rolling up wet towels. He led the way, back over the mud, the stream, and the bridge. Then we leaned into the incline, calf muscles straining in the humid air and ascended, nodding hola to farmers piled into the back of a pick-up truck, bouncing down the hill.

I Spy worked, as did the promise of a treat upon our return. When we surfaced at Caldera, we discovered that buses had stopped running; we were stranded in the hamlet with no way back to Boquete. This must have been the highlight of the sleepy village's year because by the time we had stopped to buy water and treats the entire town knew about our predicament. People wheeled by on their bicycles to offer suggestions. A few pointed to a house across the street and insisted the fellow who lived there would drive us back to town. They were right. All Lloyd had to do was walk up to his front door and ask him.

The next day I packed granola bars, yogurt, water, and fruit into Lloyd's day pack for a picnic beside the Quetzal Trail, at the base of Volcán Barú. On our way to the bus stop, we crossed over from the wealthy section of Boquete—where lodgings are in abundance and little old ladies charge seven dollars to wash your clothes—to the area the locals frequent—where grocery stores are powered down to save money on electricity and shuttle vans are rusty and falling apart.

The pedestrian Quetzal Trail runs between Boquete and Guadalupe, a village on the west side of Volcán Barú, and the only direct route linking the communities. By public transport, one must divert all the way to David, and change buses. Sequestered within Volcán Barú National Park, the trail takes as much as nine hours to complete. Steve and Derek would hike the Quetzal Trail in October. We were unwilling to take the girls on such a rigorous trek. (Steve and Derek told me later they'd had a harrowing time trying to negotiate the poorly marked trail in pelting rain. By the time they'd conquered it, on the outskirts of Boquete, they were drenched. A pick-up truck full of onions pulled up, found them looking like drowned rats, and hauled them to town in the back with the harvest.)

When we disembarked near the trailhead, the bus driver assured us that he would be by every half hour on the hour, giving us false confidence that we would easily find our way back to town. We walked along the roadway looking for somewhere to eat our lunch.

"Look at those gardens," Natalie said, pointing to the terraced plots sprouting rows of coffee, beans, peas, and lettuce. Hues of green imbued the eye. The air hung still, saturated with moisture.

"What secret breed of spider people could work on those hills, Jocelyn, do you think?" I said.

"Don't say spider!" she said, as we sat down beside the bank of a rushing river to eat a few sandwiches. We were becoming accustomed to keeping hands and feet protected. From biting ants to scorpions, snakes to spiders, the potential for something to harm you from the undergrowth weighed heavy on our minds. Whenever we hiked, we kept to abandoned roadways or well-worn paths, for safety.

When lunch was over, we strolled back to the main road to wait for our bus. After ninety minutes Lloyd admitted, "It's time to stick out our thumbs."

We walked by a construction site where an older fellow was having no luck getting his truck started. "Too bad it's kaput," I lamented. "We could have jumped in the back." We walked down the hill further, crossing a river topped by a narrow stone bridge. "Let's sit by the side of the road here and rest," I suggested.

The girls threw stones into the river and Lloyd scratched his head at our dilemma. Boquete, visible below us, was still too far away. "It's not that no buses have passed," he said, "No vehicles whatsoever are on the roads today."

The older fellow must have fixed his truck because a few minutes later, it was farting down the hill, but it gasped and died, smack dab in the middle of that bridge. He got out of the truck looking a little sheepish, walked over to us and said in Spanish, "There's no something something today, wouldn't you like to something something?"

What the heck is he saying?

Jocelyn piped up immediately. "He said there's no tow trucks today. Wouldn't you like to help him push it?"

Oh.

The four of us heaved the truck off the bridge and onto the side of the road. The bridge was a little precarious, too, since one side had no rail—it was wide open to the rushing water. Just another day in the life of the Travel Team.

The old guy muttered gracias, got back into the truck, and managed to start her up again. He lurched off down the road a speck, but the engine died near an Indigenous family that lived on the banks of the river. We saw him stop and speak to them for a few minutes. At last, a taxi came up over the rise in our direction, and Lloyd flagged him down. The driver stopped, and a group of people got out. Now our turn. Except that the people were now getting in the front seat. The four of us got in the back, and we coasted down the road to pick up our fellow with the bad truck. He tipped his hat as he squeezed in the back with us.

"That makes nine people in this taxi," Natalie said. "Four in the front and five in the back."

By now some of our clothes were in such bad shape they could only be thrown out. Plus, the girls were growing, and we hadn't shopped for new clothing in a year. So, back to David, city of bargains. The pension we found had a lounge and a small kitchen with a fridge. Because there was no stove, we stopped in at the colossal grocery store to stock up on essentials for our cold Ziploc stew. If I added sandwiches, it made for a filling meal. On our daily excursions, we usually packed a lunch, which typically consisted of yogurt, bananas, apples, and granola bars. Cereal with milk, and peanut butter on bread made up breakfast. In the morning Lloyd found take-out coffee at comedors, decanted in recycled pop bottles or glass tumblers that we returned later. The deals we were getting on accommodations and eating in this way amounted to huge savings.

And the bargains didn't end there. We paid outrageously low prices at the downtown shopping district. Twenty-five cents to two dollars for a t-shirt, forty-nine cents for underwear or three for a dollar. Flip-flops, bathing suits, souvenirs, watches, all for a buck or less. We relaxed a bit on our budget and had supper at an excellent Chinese restaurant so we could idle in the air conditioning watching the quarter finals. We saw movies, went to malls, bought huge jars of peanut butter, and paid less than forty cents for a bottle of beer (the price of which indicates the true cost of living, *verdad*?). We bought new travel speakers for our mp3 player, flashlight bulbs, and new backpacks for the girls. We bought books for my English classes, magazines, lipstick for dress-up—things we had no hope of finding in Costa Rica.

At this point, the underwear situation in our family was in such tatters, that we threw out the old to start anew. For the girls and Lloyd, this was a simple matter of submitting to any one of the dozens of discount stores on David's main street to pick out a few pairs and fait accompli. Not so for the larger sized female of the family. I only mention this to explain why I bought men's underwear.

It confounded me that the women of Central America wore thongs. Market stalls overflowed with huge baskets of them, trimmed with lace in hundreds of shades. Who could bring themselves to wear these sections of dental floss? In the unbearable heat of the tropics, how could anyone be willing to wedge a scratchy piece of lace between the butt cheeks of life? I searched in vain for cotton, large, soft undies that fit from stem to stern—sometimes over the belt line—but nonetheless, the type that enclosed the butt cheeks, not exposed them. Therefore, I was forced to purchase cottony, soft men's underwear in such feminine colors as mustard, grey, charcoal, black, and navy.

The process of buying undergarments had only just begun. I still had bras to buy. I left everybody back at the pension for the day so I could concentrate. Some department stores were reluctant to allow me to try on potential purchases because when I queried the clerks, they shook their heads, no. At one store the bras and undies were displayed adjacent to the bargain bins at street level. Nearby, two workmen stood on a ladder repairing something in the ceiling. I was peering up at them when a sales lady floated over to me.

"Can I try these on?" I showed her the boxes of bras.

She furrowed her brow, then called over to a fellow employee, and together they nodded their approval. I dumbly waited for them to show me the way to the change room, but one snuck around behind me, and the other emptied one of the boxes. Before I knew what was happening, they had a bra around me, trying to hook it up. Repairmen fiddled with wires overhead and the busy street thrummed with shoppers just a few feet away. They assured me that the item fit perfectly, snapping straps into place and wedging parts of my body into cups with me dying of mortification right in the middle of the store. To paint the picture, I was now wearing a bra *over top of my clothes*, standing helplessly, stunned at what had just taken place.

How I managed to get out of there with my self-esteem still intact is a mystery. It made for a great story later over cold stew. I managed to complete my purchases at a nearby department store. The saleslady nodded affirmatively to me when I asked her if I could use the change room. "Cómo no!" Certainly!

THE ROAD TO MONO FELIZ

During our stay in Boquete, Lloyd and I glued ourselves to the TV in the pension's salon to follow the World Cup. The girls, avoiding the miserable owner, who chain smoked in the lounge and shushed them unnecessarily, created an imaginary travel agency near the entrance using glossy brochures from local businesses as props. Once the game was over, we resumed our role as attentive parents.

As I helped the girls in tidying up, I spied a leaflet advertising a monkey sanctuary called Mono Feliz that offered accommodations right on the shores of the Pacific Ocean. My curiosity piqued, I sought out some more information on this mysterious place. However, other than the flyer, which provided little information, only a handful of internet blogs mentioned Mono Feliz. In hindsight, it was just as well. If I had known how difficult it was to get there, I would have vetoed the idea altogether.

Translated to mean "Happy Monkey," we made the classic parental error of showing the children the leaflet.

Natalie gasped, "We will get to see monkeys after all!"

Could I then turn around and say, "Look, we don't know very much about this place so let's just forget it"? No.

On a leap of faith, we decided to take a bus to the nearest town to the sanctuary, called Puerto Armuelles, and figure out from the locals how to get to Mono Feliz.

We barreled down the highway from David at a good clip. Near town, the driver slowed. We were distressed to see dozens of soldiers milling about beside their vehicles at various points along the road. Then, the driver stopped, and a soldier got on to check identification. A man sitting next to Lloyd explained that there was a transit protest up ahead, and the military had been called in.

Gulp.

At the next major intersection, we were instructed to disembark.

The driver explained, "Go to that van across the road."

We wound our way through factions of taxistas, military personnel, and ordinary folk and saw a driver motioning to us. We were aghast at the condition of his van. It was literally falling apart. He loaded us in one by one. Gone were the air conditioning, comfy seats, and legroom. When it was full, still more people were made to pile in, and they did so without complaint. By the end, I was in the worst possible spot, directly in the center of the van. Lloyd was to my left, next to the window. Both girls were in our laps, and their backpacks were in *their* laps. I don't know how many people were behind me because I couldn't turn around. Beside me was a mother with her two children in her lap and another woman sharing her seat. Ahead of us, same thing.

After what seemed like hours, they slid closed the doors to what I hoped would not be the capsule of our deaths. I was overcome. It was intolerably hot, and I could barely see. My breathing became shallow, and I felt the pangs of nausea.

I turned to Lloyd in a panic. "I don't think I can do this."

I sought the door to escape, which was about three feet away but seemed to be separated from me by a chasm of miles. Unbelievably, all the windows on that side of the van were closed. My throat constricted, and I imagined myself making everybody get out.

"Let's get out, then," Lloyd said, reading my mind.

I focused on his open window and breathed in deeply. Jocelyn, who probably wasn't looking forward to getting barfed on, leaned forward. I squeezed my eyes shut to block out the crowd. *If only the driver would get going.*

"I'll be okay once I feel some breeze." I turned to the woman next to me. "How far away is Puerto Armuelles?"

"A few kilometers."

"Okay, I can do this, I think."

People had begun looking at me with raised eyebrows by then, so I said, to break the tension, "For God's sake somebody count the number of people in here, so we can tell everyone back home about it."

Here is the tally: twenty-five people in a fifteen-seater van.

"I'm being generous with the number of actual seats," Lloyd said after craning his neck around. "I counted the hump over the gear shift as one seat. There *is* a guy sitting on it."

The driver put the van into gear and advanced. To my great relief, people disembarked one by one as we passed through villages on our way to Puerto Armuelles. When we arrived, we headed straight for a comedor, and here I cracked, breaking down into tears while the girls fluttered around me, giving me neck rubs and hugs to make me feel better.

After a time, I composed myself and suggested we figure out how to get to Mono Feliz. A police officer told us, "The truck with the blue tarp over it goes to Mono Feliz."

The truck sat idle on a side street for six hours. Every few minutes, I'd drift over to ask people what time it left. I always got the same answer: 3:00 p.m.

I returned to the comedor where I had left Lloyd and the girls playing with the salt and pepper shakers and a few Lego pieces. "Apparently, trucks leave for the villages along the coast depending on the tide."

At around 2:45 we saw some activity at the truck. The Travel Team bulked up with packs and walked over. Two ladies and their children sat on benches underneath the tarp holding onto loads of produce. Two planks had been propped the length of the truck bed so that we could sit down. They weren't fastened to anything, so Lloyd adjusted them forward for more cotton-undied butt room.

In fact, three separate trucks departed Puerto Armuelles together and I saw the wisdom in it. It was a convoy of safety and convenience. If anyone broke down along the way, another driver was right behind. These were not pick-up trucks but rather large roofless delivery trucks with steel frames extending vertically about three feet and a tarp stretched between them. The driver had attached ropes and wooden bars across the frames to secure the bags of produce the ladies had filled with purchases from the market. The sole reason for securing the bags in this way, we found out later, was to free up your hands to hang on for dear life.

The trucks clicked along at a moderate pace for several kilometers, past painted cement homes topped with rusty, corrugated metal, before coming to a track that ran parallel to the shore. A length of petroleum pipeline emerged from the ocean, coiling its way to the Caribbean. If anyone had told me that we were on another planet at that point, I would have believed them, so weird was the landscape with enormous pipes coming out of the water. Jocelyn must have felt the same way because she said, "Daddy, it looks like the pipes are sucking the water out of the ocean! What are they?"

"The bane of our existence," muttered Lloyd.

Immediately after that, the driver took an abrupt left and drove down a steep embankment directly onto the beach. We zipped along at high speed. The girls, whose ponytails were whipping their faces, were screaming with laughter. We stood up, clinging to a bar and took in the rest of the trip Leonardo DiCaprio style, aboard the stern of the Titanic. At times, the sand turned to rock, and the driver slowed to traverse the bumps. We yelled out "Teeth!" to warn the girls to shut their mouths tight against the looming metal bar banging in front of them.

We were heading to the farthest point in southwestern Panama, where we could go no farther without encroaching into Costa Rica, and yet all three trucks disgorged dozens and dozens of passengers, including the ladies on our truck, at unseen villages along the way.

By now the other trucks had completed their course, but our driver had agreed to take us all the way to Mono Feliz. We will forever be grateful to him for making that harrowing journey through rushing rivers, steep embankments, and heaps of mud. A time or two, when we thought, "That's it, we'll have to walk the rest of the way," he'd gun it, and we'd go another few hundred meters.

When he finally turned inland, we changed our warning shouts to "Tree!" to duck from the branches that came whipping into the back of the truck. Once, I mistimed it, and a branch caught me on the nostril. I snorted it away. Now, we were crouching in the bed of the truck. The ride was so jarring the planks flew off their props and lay askew, slapping against the floor. At Mono Feliz, Lloyd paid the driver an exorbitant amount, knowing we never could have made it without him.

MONO FELIZ

Natalie was greeted the instant she jumped from the truck by a red squirrel monkey who launched himself onto her neck. John, the owner of Mono Feliz, welcomed us and introduced us to Mickey, who had been adopted by John as a baby after he was orphaned. The girls studied every inch of him as he clamored over their arms and necks. He possessed human-like characteristics, right down to the tiny hands, dirty fingernails, and thumb sucking. He sat on Natalie's shoulder and clamped one hand around her neck. With the other, he snatched a dragonfly from the air in midflight and bit down on it, ripping its head off with one chomp as if it were a piece of celery.

John led us from the rocky beach into the jungle, explaining the genesis of Mono Feliz. "It used to be a pig farm, but I'm slowly reverting the land back to its wild state." He had designed it so well that each outbuilding was cleverly hidden by foliage. Neatly groomed dirt paths, stained only by splotches of banana poop, linked the outdoor kitchen to the bathroom.

"You've got your choice of two cabinas. One here, close to the bathroom, or the other, overlooking the ocean."

Overlooking the ocean sounded exquisite on paper but walking to the bathroom from the beach through a jungle trail in the middle of the night was out of the question. The girls flung their backpacks on their beds and were about to tear off running along the paths to explore all the nooks and crannies, but Lloyd halted them instantly. He stressed that they were to go nowhere by themselves. "Girls, this area is full of critters. We have to be careful."

John must be congratulated for returning the area to its natural splendor. For a family with two children, however, Mono Feliz was an accident waiting to happen. The bathrooms were a constant source of fear for the three of us females. As a substitute for showers, the girls swam in a pool that John had carved out of rocky outcroppings and was fed by freshwater streaming down from the mountain.

At night, the girls were warned to stay in the cabina and under no circumstances was anyone to leave without an adult until sunup. Thankfully, we had the pee pee device.

"It's exhausting," Lloyd said. "It's like they're two years old again. We have to follow them everywhere."

We accidentally discovered our nearness to nature the next day when we decided to do some laundry by hand. John supplied wash buckets for guests to use and as I picked one up, Lloyd said sharply, "Drop the bucket and back away!"

A giant red tarantula with long, thin hairy legs was clinging to the underside. Lloyd slid the pail over to the jungle with his foot and flicked the spider off with a leaf. It reared up on its haunches in attack position.

"Lloyd!" I cried. "Get a stick!"

He came back with the proverbial ten-foot pole and, in keeping with his Canadian upbringing, slapshotted that monster into the wild. As much as the girls loved it there, Lloyd and I wanted to cut and run. I challenge *you* to try and convince young monkey lovers to leave.

Three species of primate stopped by habitually, coming down from the trees to forage for food or snatch bananas or mangoes that John had left out for them. "This property is on their route. Every morning they pass by here as they have done for a long time," he explained. "I've replanted trees that would have been natural to the area before the pig farm."

The most tenacious were the white-faced capuchins, most well known as organ-grinder monkeys. Mickey's counterparts, the squirrel monkeys, came by in packs of up to thirty, perching on low branches to eat their fruit. Perhaps the saddest was the lone howler monkey that never came closer than the top of the smallest tree, looking at us from his black face.

Admiring wildlife this close was fascinating, but coping day to day with a domesticated monkey like Mickey was aggravating. He snatched objects like the caps of our water bottles right out of our hands and not all that gently. We instructed the girls to place their hands underneath their armpits to protect them from Mickey's scratches. When we packed up to leave, he sat on the half-wall enclosing our cabina and studied our movements. Whenever one of us folded an article of clothing and placed it in our backpack, he'd jump off the wall and reach into the pack with his tiny hand and yank it out. He tore open every Ziploc bag, ripped the lids off the girls' markers, and flung toys all over the cabina. Animal lover to the core, it was all Lloyd could do to refrain from throttling him.

Finally, I said, "Okay, here's what we're gonna do. I'll distract him out on the path with this water bottle. You guys pack fast!"

The girls and Lloyd stood poised over their packs while I lured Mickey out of the cabina. "Hey Mickey! What's this?" I said, shaking the bottle. Then, they all flew around the room, shoving clothes into the bags and zipping them up before Mickey caught on.

Mickey was not the only force of nature to stymie our departure. Because of the tide, we were restricted to hiking out at 4:45 a.m. to catch the vegetable truck at 6:00 a.m. in the upper village of Bella Vista. It was impossible to hire the same driver to carry us back to Puerto Armuelles; I think he was still muttering "Gracias a Dios" that we had made it in the first place. John suggested we hike out with a couple of local youths who were coming by the property for some work. "You could sleep overnight in their village and catch the veggie truck to Puerto Armuelles the following morning. If you give them a little money, they will carry your packs for you, too."

The alternative was to walk in the dark and hope to catch the truck as it passed by, something I refused to do. John's comment tipped the scale for me. "You might come across a few snakes, that's the only thing."

At around 11:00 the next day the boys had finished up their work for John and were ready to go. They were handsome, robust young men who had no trouble carrying our adult packs over muddy cow tracks and uphill for fifty minutes. The hike was not at all difficult, especially for Natalie who ran almost the whole way, in sheer ecstasy at being in nature.

We chatted with the boys about the final of the World Cup, the progress of which we had been following from town to town all the way from Quebrada Ganado to our next destination, the sequestered hamlet of Bella Vista.

I nudged Lloyd when I overheard Natalie ask them, "Where can we watch the game?"

They responded, "You'll see."

Bella Vista was like Parismina, the Costa Rican town on the Caribbean coast where we had begun our adventure on those late-night turtle patrols. It sat up from the ocean along with several other cloistered villages. There was one vehicle in town, the very truck that conveyed people to these backwaters after having completed their shopping at the bustling mercado of Puerto Armuelles.

The boys delivered us to our accommodation, which was, as it turned out, their grandmother's house. She showed us to our room and told us lunch would be ready in a few minutes. We thanked her and peeled off our sweaty clothes and went to find the bathroom and shower. Unlike Parismina, Bella Vista existed with less public works, if that was possible. Here we were to use an outhouse and outdoor shower, constructed out of four uneven, corrugated metal sheets leaning on one another like a house of cards. Water came out of a hose wired to a board.

"Fill this pail with water," I explained to the girls, "and dump it over your body." I'm proud to say the girls took this in stride and got the knack of using this rudimentary system to clean up before changing into fresh clothes and finding a television.

The one guy in town with a TV was the owner of a crumbling snack bar, directly across the dirt track from Grandma's. He propped the TV on his counter facing out for the community to take in the game. We will forever remember watching the finals, settled on picnic tables and benches with the townsfolk of Bella Vista.

We were in a festive mood because it was also our wedding anniversary that day. We dined together later, the whole family and Grandma, in her kitchen, eating a simple meal of beans and rice. Lloyd and I clinked our cold cans of beer together and reveled in how far we had come as a family. We had been on the road for almost a year, the girls were thriving, learning, and speaking the language; Lloyd and I were backpacking as we had done when we were younger. There was a lot to celebrate.

By nightfall, people of the village had heard about the newcomers, and our presence became a novelty. "Foreigners are rare in Bella Vista," John had told us. "Only a few intrepid souls have made the trek up there."

Children and their mothers swarmed the girls, and Jocelyn, weary of all the attention, told me in frustration, "There's one lady out there bossing me around. She keeps throwing words at me to translate into English."

Later, as I was washing clothes in the outdoor laundry sink, I heard Lloyd speaking with a man. After a few minutes they shook hands, and the man walked off.

"I prefer talking to men," Lloyd said. "I can understand them better."

"Why?"

"They don't use as many words as women do."

"I should email Professor Mullins that nugget of wisdom."

Before dusk, we took a stroll around the village. We passed a run-down park and waited while the girls tried it out for a few minutes. Around the park, a fine sand path meandered in an oval, and occupying the center stood the village's soccer pitch, as omnipresent in Latin America as hockey arenas back home. Circumnavigating the town took all of three and a half minutes.

"At least we know where the 'bus stop' is," Lloyd said, using air quotes.

The truck (bus stop) was a thirty-second walk from Grandma's. Because of the tide, departure was scheduled for 6:00 a.m. The girls were accustomed to waking early, so we weren't worried about that. Lloyd, on the other hand, was concerned about the sleeping arrangements. The house consisted of a mix of concrete and dirt floors, a smattering of chairs, and a freezer propped up on wooden blocks. The entire building was open to the outdoors by unscreened windows and wide-open doors.

The bedroom contained one double "bed"—nothing more than a box spring with a grimy fabric covering. The sheets were laced with mothballs, but fortunately I had thought to bring the sleep sacks with us. Lloyd blew up the air mattresses, and I swept the room and removed the bedsheets in favor of our sleep sacks. For safety, Lloyd insisted on pairing up. Jocelyn and I took the bed (which was lucky or unlucky, depending on your point of view). Lloyd and Natalie slept on air mattresses on the floor. Lloyd had pushed the panic button after an experience in the outhouse. Before bedtime, he visited the privy with a flashlight. When he came back, he was pale.

"Can you take the girls to the bathroom now, before they go to bed?" I asked him.

"No," he said curtly. Instead, he led them to a grassy patch beyond the outdoor shower and made them squat.

I pestered him. "Did you see a creature? A scorpion?"

"Let's not talk about it right now, okay?"

When the girls were tucked in for the night, he whispered to me, "I shined the flashlight around the walls and seat to check for spiders and scorpions." He took a deep breath before continuing. "Then I shined that flashlight down into the hole and every inch of that space was crawling with insects. Cockroaches, millipedes, centipedes, wriggling worms." Because of the nature of nature's call, he was forced to sit upon that seat. "It took all my resolve to sit down." His voice quivered. "It was beyond *Fear Factor*."

I thanked our lucky stars that we had brought that urinator contraption all the way from Canada. His concern was justified. We were all suffering from bites and blisters from Mono Feliz. Small red markings stretched out over our skin like scars. They didn't itch, and they faded within a couple of days. Lloyd's feet were covered in pinprick red welts that itched him like crazy. He was concerned that spiders or scorpions would invade our room in the night and convinced the girls to wear long shirts and cargo pants. I also doused them with repellent to protect them from mosquitoes carrying malaria or dengue.

To say that we were awakened at 4:45 a.m. the next morning implies that we slept. Lights went off and on at all hours; people came and went. We heard our hostess whipping up food for people who stopped by in the middle of the night. The house buzzed with activity as she sold ice cream and cold drinks out of her freezer. At the ungodly hour, she poked her head into our room and told us that the truck was leaving at 5:30 instead of 6:00.

Rumpled and sweaty, we popped the plugs of the air mattresses, packed our things, and said goodbye to our hostess. In the dark, we bumbled to the truck and saw that it was already full of passengers and five gigantic bags of avocados.

"You get the kids seated, and I'll handle the packs," Lloyd said. We climbed into the truck bed and squeezed our way through the crowd to get closer to the front. Natalie burrowed onto a bench seat between two young women and Jocelyn draped herself over a sack of avocados. I stood the entire two hours, along with dozens of others clinging to the overhead bar. Lloyd was dangling out the back with the other men, riding firefighter style, gripping the external steel frame with his fingernails. Because so many passengers were clinging to the exterior as he was, he had only enough space on the bumper for one foot. He was right above the tailpipe, which caused him to choke from breathing in the black exhaust.

The truck inched its way down the rocky embankment to the beach. Stray dogs trotted along effortlessly beside us. The carriage groaned as it rocked back and forth. At the beach, it gradually got light. I had just enough space between noggins to see the magnificent sunrise over the east-facing peninsula protruding out of the Pacific Ocean. We rattled along the beach slowly, a noticeable change from a few days before when our driver channeled Mario Andretti in the Indy 500. This time, we were so loaded down that the shocks whined with every jolt. At the point where the rocky hills stretched right down into the water, the driver made the men get out and walk up the beach. Then he advanced slowly, rolling the tires carefully over these rocks, then picked up the walkers about half a mile down the beach.

Scores of villagers traveled the beach, the only thoroughfare to Puerto Armuelles, to transact business, shop at the mercado, or attend medical appointments. I noticed several school children, with the pants of their uniforms rolled up to the knees, walking barefoot to school in the surf. The presence of an Indigenous population was evident. In the truck, a toddler rode the full two hours clutching the brightly embroidered dress of his Ngobe mother.

After about an hour, Jocelyn jammed herself in next to Natalie and both fell asleep on the shoulders of the people next to them. Now and then, usually after a particularly hairy section of rocky beach (eliciting "Whoas" from the passengers), I'd crane my neck to search for Lloyd. If he could see me through all the bodies, he'd raise his eyebrows as if to ask, "Everything okay?" I'd nod "Yep."

On a straight stretch, the driver played chicken with the dogs lying on the sand. When he saw a pack of them still asleep, he gunned the engine, accelerating straight for them. From the back of the truck, I was never able to see the dogs jump up at the last minute to get out of the way. I wanted to bite my nails down to the quick waiting to feel the thud of a little body under the wheels of the truck.

We rolled into Puerto Armuelles at 7:30 a.m., grabbed a quick breakfast, and angled north to the border. The frenzied, congested border post of Paso Canoas marked the end of the Panama portion of our adventure. A couple of weeks later, back at the villa, I sat on the terrace sipping a cold beer with Lloyd. "If you had to do it all over again, would you go to Mono Feliz?"

He put his beer down on the plastic table. "I'm glad we went, but no, I wouldn't do it again." He hesitated. "Would you?"

"No," I said. "It was way outside of my comfort zone. We can't make decisions based on whims anymore."

On the other hand, one might argue, how else would we have experienced a hint of what life was like in a rural backwater in Panama but to have taken a leap of faith, trucked to Mono Feliz, and become forced to stay overnight in Bella Vista? If we were to tackle the other Central American countries, though, we'd have to restrict ourselves to places near clinics and markets. We agreed to strike isolated regions from the list.

After crossing back into Costa Rica, we hopscotched back to Quebrada Ganado, stopping along the way at a few towns to spend the night. Right away we were greeted with the deplorable roads and appalling condition of the buses—gaps in the floor opening straight down to the highway below and seats that were not fastened down.

We paused at Parque Nacional Marino Ballena to rest up and brace ourselves for the horrible Dominical to Quepos stretch. The entrance to the National Park was a short walk from the guest house, along a narrow, lonely dirt road. We spent long hours at the beach under the brazen rays of the sun. I spent half my time applying sunscreen to exposed shoulders and the other half staying hydrated.

A few days later, we faced our destiny. The only way back to the villa was lunging around giant potholes and plunging into rivers. Lloyd studied the budget and decided that we hadn't overspent that much. We hired a driver named Mario, who introduced himself by squashing Lloyd's hand and then helped us load the trunk. Mario was a friendly guy who laughed with us as we lunged and plunged to Quepos. The girls endured the ride, listening to music piping through the mp3 player and sipping juice.

Mario left us at Quepos with a huge smile and a painfully firm handshake for Lloyd. Another two hours brought us to Quebrada Ganado. When we stepped off the bus, we were tired, hot, and a little grouchy. It all melted away when we were greeted by "Hello Teachers!" from the townspeople who saw us return, a month later, with the girls. Ricardo boomed out from the pulpería across the street, "Welcome once again to Quebrada Ganado!"

We took no more than ten steps from the bus when Lloyd stopped dead in his tracks. "Where's the bum bag with the mp3 player in it?"

I wracked my brain and looked at him gravely. "In the back of Mario's car."

Mario, who had turned around in Quepos and receded over the wretched road to Dominical, was now the proud owner of all our music from Canada recorded on our mp3 player, the brand-new travel speakers we had bought in David, two headphones, new flashlight bulbs, and *the keys to the villa*.

Paola answered our cacophonous knocks at the gate and let us into the villa with her spare set of keys. The next day, Lloyd did laundry, the girls rode around on their bikes, and I returned to Quepos on the 12:30 bus. I got off the bus in Quepos at 2:30 and sprinted to the bus company's office to pick up our mislaid items that Mario had already sent up by bus from the depot in Dominical. I had only to introduce myself, ask for my *paquete*, then dash back to the terminal to catch the last bus departing for Quebrada Ganado at 3:00.

Chapter 11

Winding Down

WE RESUMED OUR REGULAR lives under rainy skies. The short, violent downpours in the evening produced an enormous racket on the metal roof of the community center but did nothing to cool things down. The sun rose in the morning and by 8:00 a.m. the land gave off plumes of steam until baked dry by the scorching heat.

The popularity of the English classes continued unabated. Some of the students implored Lloyd and me to stay and open a school. It was hard to say no. We kept asking ourselves, "Isn't it smarter to stay?" For all intents and purposes, we were going home. Lloyd notified the Board of Education of his intention to return to his post and I spent a little time every day looking at guidebooks and maps, figuring out a way to get home, venturing north through Nicaragua, El Salvador, Guatemala, and Mexico. The summer vacation acted as a rehearsal for a more complicated trip come January, once Lloyd's contract was up. For example, we learned how to safeguard our belongings (the most effective strategy was not forgetting them in someone's car) and decided we'd had enough of hardcore, off-the-beaten-path backpacking. Still, we kept an open mind.

Beatriz, one of my brightest students, was married to a savvy businessman named Luis. They owned a private transport company, mostly to shuttle tourists to and from the airport. Beatriz had enrolled in my classes to improve her ability to communicate with clients. Luis discussed with me, at length, the financial points of opening a school. "Look," he said, showing me his figures, "this is how much ticos will be able to pay for ESL lessons."

I turned the paper toward me. "Will it cost much to rent a space for the classes?" I asked.

"No, it won't, and you can always live and teach in the same building."

Economically speaking, it made no sense to return to Canada with its high cost of living and "working for the man" when we could live in the tropics for much less, work for ourselves, and avoid the harsh Canadian winter.

I often inspected the storefronts of an abandoned plaza across from Ricardo's grocer. "It would be perfect for a small English school," I said to Lloyd. "The bus stops directly in front. Talk about exposure." I envisioned us living in a cottage across from the villa that boasted a shaded yard and pastel blue walls. It was vacant the entire time we resided in Quebrada Ganado.

We had also heard rumors that Playa Agujas, our quiet beach across the highway, was poised to become the next resort destination. What better location for an English school than right in the very community in which employees would live? However, there were more factors to consider, and they came into play as we lived out the rest of the year in this little town.

After one year as expats we had fostered a strong core of friendships, compared to the early weeks I was so lonesome inside the villa missing Lloyd and the girls. Now we flitted here and there, kayaking at Playa Agujas with our friends Neil and Yasmin who owned Kayak Jacó, or strolling around town to see friends: Silvana, a retired teacher who offered to help the girls with penmanship, and Diana, a latecomer to my classes. She and I chatted over cold juice, reclining in plastic chairs in front of the pulpería near her home, located on a solitary side street I'd found on one of my cycling explorations, and Ruth, the only English-speaking mom in town (also the only person in town who had air conditioning in her bedroom). On brutally hot days, I'd pop in and we'd lie gossiping on her bed, looking up at the ceiling.

The girls integrated seamlessly into the community. They came home from school and spent the rest of the afternoon with Paola. Natalie helped care for the lame animals she had adopted when no one else would. Apart from the patrolling Weimaraners, she possessed five others that were either blind, deaf, or limbless. The two of them worked together to give the crippled dogs a bath, and afterwards they ate a light lunch together on her terrace.

When the girls weren't inside our fortress, they were out on the street riding their bikes with a wee classmate named Kevin or playing foosball at Eduardo's video store. But could we adapt to the 1950s lifestyle? Folks had few material possessions. Clothes were mended and handed down. Children rode oversized bikes. Mothers didn't work; they chitchatted over backyard fences and hung wet clothes to dry in the breezy tropical air. Children were seen everywhere in packs, roaming the paths along the decaying river or throwing rocks at horses until they were shooed away by an adult. Time would tell.

Near the end of the rainy season, Natalie developed recurrent fevers that waxed and waned for about ten days and that I initially dismissed as a simple virus. One night the heat radiating off her body felt excessive.

On a rush of adrenaline, I cried out, "Lloyd! Get a thermometer!"

I wet some towels to cool her down while he slid the thermometer under her armpit.

104.

Lloyd jumped on his bicycle to fetch the village doctor. After a brief examination, he expressed concern that the intermittent hot spells suggested dengue fever. Early the next morning, Bruno drove us to the clinic in Jacó and then we waited an agonizing twenty-four hours until the results came back. All through the night, we applied cold, wet towels. It did little to lower her temperature.

In the morning, the doctor called with worse news. "Ella tiene una infección muy seria." She has a very serious infection. "I've contacted the hospital in Quepos, they're expecting you."

I hung up and barked at Lloyd, "Get the passports and the credit card."

As the wheels of the medical community were being put into motion, I tried not to let the bile in my stomach burble up from worry. I had pleaded with the universe that it not be dengue, but she was worse off with a severe bacterial infection. In my paranoia, I could only think of flesh-eating disease or meningitis (she showed no symptoms of either). Now, she was sticky, sweaty, and weak, with a fluttering heart.

Luis immediately freed up one of his drivers, Javier, to take us down to Quepos. I paced the length of the villa waiting for him. Jocelyn huddled on the rocking chair, despondence shrouding her face. "I don't want Natalie to die."

My stomach clenched. *Oh God.*

Lloyd banged into the villa when Javier pulled up, cradled Natalie in his arms, and laid her down on the back seat of the van. At the hospital, I noticed with anxiety the conditions present. The waiting room was dingy and hot and full of voracious mosquitoes. Lloyd registered us while I tried to keep her cool *and* prevent the mosquitoes from biting her. She was a heap in my arms. Her hair was plastered to my skin. The doctor uttered no greetings. He simply scanned her test results and said, "She's dehydrated."

He turned, left the room and spoke to a nurse who directed us to the pediatric exam room. He inserted an IV, which caused a great deal of shrieking from the semi-conscious Natalie, and began a potassium drip. I had brought the thermometer with me and checked it frequently. After an hour, her temperature remained unchanged.

"Let's give her a cold shower," the nurse suggested.

I picked her up and staggered next door, put her under the suicide shower, and turned on the water. In a twist of perfect irony, the suicide shower functioned normally, producing a spray of hot water. I sat Natalie, now bawling, on the toilet and gingerly adjusted the settings. Nothing worked; I could not make cold water come out. I left Natalie sagging on the toilet and whipped out to ask Lloyd to adjust the settings. He fumbled for a few seconds himself until he pulled the breaker, recessed into the wall beside the shower.

These efforts did nothing to lower her fever. I was shattered from two sleepless nights. I sought out the doctor. "Should she be admitted?" I didn't think I could take care of her properly myself.

"No," he said without looking at me.

In the examination room, the IV came to an end. The doctor then recommended an injection to bring down the fever. The challenge? Convincing Natalie to agree to it.

"She must stay completely still," the nurse instructed me.

"Natalie, you're going to feel a little pinch in your . . . butt," I told her as she lay there.

"No!" she cried.

She relented when I promised her, "After this we can go home."

When the nurse stuck the needle into her derriere, she screamed a bloody murder that, despite the muffling of the pillow, could have been heard back in Canada.

After a few seconds, she raised her head and turned to screech at the nurse in Spanish, "Ya! Ya!" Enough! Enough! She wept pitifully into her pillow, and I thought long and hard about joining her.

Within minutes the doctor came in explaining the prescriptions he had written out and asking would we please leave. Even though Natalie had begun sitting up a bit, her fever wasn't any better, but somewhere along the slippery highway, her fever came down. Though my stomach is in knots to this day thinking of her being carried into that hospital in a heap of sweat, she walked out on her own two legs after four hours of rehydration and a shot in the bottom to bring down the fever.

Family back home hadn't been made aware of our circumstances until the worst had passed. When I could get word to my parents, I received this happy email from my mom:

"Hi. Sounds like you've had a stressful few days. Thankful to hear Natalie is okay. To make her feel even better tell her Mimi is coming on September 27th."

When "Mimi" arrived, the girls flew into her arms and crushed her with hugs. They went berserk chattering about all the minutiae of our everyday lives. She had timed her visit to coincide with a trip to Nicaragua for a border run, and because she was a seasoned traveler, I planned the excursion Travel Team style, by chicken bus.

Despite the brutal heat and humidity, she kept up with us on the maze to the border (chicken bus to la Cruz de Barranca, another to Liberia, and then another to the border, etc.). My mother got to witness firsthand what we took in stride: hawkers, money changers, masses of people, women selling drinks or gum, busloads on their way to Managua. Winding our way through lurching transports, we cleared the fence and reached the Nicaraguan side. I made the girls stand next to their grandmother under the "Bienvenidos a Nicaragua" sign so I could capture the moment on film. "How many people can say they've been to Nicaragua with their grandmother?" I said, beaming with pride.

Then she rubbernecked the scene under the incessant *honk honk* of the bus driver warning future passengers of his imminent arrival. To the right we pointed out the imposing sight of the twin volcanoes on Ometepe Island, to the left the dry hinterland of rural Nicaragua.

We disembarked at La Virgen at dusk, doubting we could catch a bus to San Juan del Sur at that hour. Fortunately, an enterprising cab driver, who must have thanked his lucky stars upon seeing five foreigners on the side of the road, stopped to pick us up.

In recent weeks, Nicaragua's public works had begun to crumble. For several hours every day the country suffered rolling blackouts and water outages. In the taxi, we bumped our way down the main road in complete darkness, save for our taxi's dim headlights.

Karen and Francisco were delighted to see us. Francisco looked strained this time, though. Karen checked us into two private rooms and confided to me, "Francisco is wringing his hands worrying whether our well will run dry." As it was, guests were using flashlights to navigate around town and staff at the hostel were ready to give out bottles of water. She handed me the key to our room. "We've had to invest in a generator to keep the business running."

I pointed to the candles set out in the lounge. "The new lighting gives off a nice atmosphere though."

"Well, I'm glad you're here. I could use the distraction."

The next night Francisco loaded both families into the back of his pickup and took us to the nesting site of the Olive Ridley sea turtle to observe the *arribada*—the mass arrival—of the turtles who come ashore in great numbers to lay their eggs on the beach.

Jocelyn pinpointed the turtles immediately upon stepping foot onto the beach. "There they are," she told Mimi, pointing to their heads bobbing in and out of the surf to see if the coast was clear.

We waited patiently at the edge of the beach. The Olive Ridleys moved much more quickly than their Caribbean counterparts that we had become familiar with the year before. The reason was obvious—the Olive Ridleys were nearly half the size. One bobbled awkwardly out of the ocean and commenced laying her eggs right in front of us. Then, she buried them. It was amusing to see her do a dance, looking like an overturned plate swiveling round and round until it came to a stop.

The next day we contacted an outfit called Da' Flying Frog who offered ziplining for a very reasonable rate. Lloyd had allowed for some relaxation in the expenditures column of the budget for these excursions with Mimi and not for a second did we regret it.

Harnessed into safety straps, we trundled up the mountain. Ziplines bisected the jungle downward in stages, some a short distance, others stretched as much as a hundred meters. Clearings in the canopy afforded stunning prospects of the bay. Mimi was the first to step off the roost.

"Make sure you look at the view!" I yelled.

The harnesses cut into fleshy pockets and even though we were safe, our instinct was to avoid plummeting to our deaths, so we tightened our back muscles or pulled down too hard with our brake hand. Once, my mother braked too early and was left dangling several hundred feet above the jungle floor. One of the guides zipped out to pull her in.

One of the highlights of returning to San Juan del Sur every three months was spending time with Karen and Francisco. Their gorgeous Daniela was mothered lovingly by Jocelyn and Natalie, giving me another avenue into the personalities of the girls I'd never noticed before. Jocelyn, in particular, was gentle and kind to her. Karen and I sat in the lounge of the hostel one morning drinking coffee together. "When your girls are here, I feel like it's one of the few times I get a break." Daniela, as an only child, relaxed her efforts at seeking attention from her parents and concentrated on playing with the girls. "What do you say we take advantage of the situation?"

"What did you have in mind?"

"Let's grab a bottle of wine and take your mother to the new Italian restaurant."

It wasn't a budget worthy activity, but I agreed without consulting Lloyd. He needed the male bonding time with Francisco as much as I needed girl time with Karen and my mother.

On the terrace of the restaurant, we pushed a few tables together. The three little girls sat at one end with small toys and coloring books while the adults chatted in the twilight at the other. I peered out into the dim streets at locals inside their colonial clapboard houses rocking away and wondered if Nicaragua knew how magical it was.

A few days after the trip to San Juan del Sur, incidents at the public school served to set off a chain of events that affected Jocelyn in an unexpected way. Her teacher had been absent for several weeks due to illness and classes were cancelled until a replacement was hired, so she was stuck passing the time at the villa.

Lloyd said, "She's been home more days than she's been at school."

Then the school hired a temporary teacher who had no control of the class. According to Jocelyn, her classmates, now with no adult guidance, pestered her about her absences. She had missed a week because of our summer trip to Panama (Lloyd's school year differed from hers), and then a day after returning from Natty's hospital episode. Then she was absent for a couple of days for a border run. As a homeschooled kid who spoke Spanish as a second language, she found it impossible to explain to them why it didn't matter a whit to us that she missed school at all. I listened to her complaints as best I could, but it was Natalie's health I was focused on and admittedly I dropped the ball. I tried to remedy it as best I could. I ordered a cake from the bakery and invited the class to her birthday party in the school cafeteria. Her classmates presented her with little gifts—hair clips and small toys. At the end of the party, as we were packing up to leave, a few kids asked me to teach them some conversational English. I considered it, to improve conditions, but I couldn't see how I could manage it with the little time I seemed to have now.

But things at school deteriorated. I resolved to find out why.

With Mimi set to collect Natalie after class, I parked myself outside Jocelyn's classroom on a bench reading and writing, to get a sense of what was going on. Don't ask me where the substitute teacher was. Her students behaved as any unsupervised children would. They threw crumpled paper around the room, screamed at each other, and later some urinated in the garbage can, so I was told. But the final straw was the look of sheer boredom on their faces. I saw Jocelyn in such a pose: head back, body flopped against the chair, eyes staring at the ceiling.

"I think she was getting very little out of school aside from the Spanish immersion," I explained to Lloyd. "I think we should pull her out."

He didn't need any convincing. We had been discussing that the country was experiencing something of an educational crisis at the time. Young kids were abandoning their studies to work on farms to alleviate the desperate conditions their families were living in. Opportunities for children (especially girls) were nonexistent. Lloyd and I became much more appreciative of our home country, where the girls could explore avenues of their own choosing (including whether to be homeschooled or not) and go on to post-secondary education, if they wanted to.

And so, we had a change of heart about staying. Apart from the state of the dismal Quepos hospital, the incident at the public school solidified our decision to return to Canada.

With Jocelyn no longer at school, I worried about her losing her Spanish. More than that, I cherished at least a few hours to myself. Without Natalie to play with, I worried that I would become her primary companion. I draped my arm around her shoulder and drew her to me, kissing the top of her head. "Honey, can you find something to do until Natalie gets home from school? What about helping out at the seniors' center?"

She replied quickly. "I think I'd like to work at the nursery school."

I stared at this child whom I was getting to know, it seemed, all over again. I'd seen her pick up the language much faster than I expected. Sometimes I was frustrated when I spoke to her because it seemed as if she didn't listen, but the ease with which she learned Spanish meant only one thing: there was nothing wrong with her listening skills. Now I noticed how nurturing she had become. I decided to take a hard look at my own communication style.

"Let's go over and ask the teacher if there's any way you can help out."

We waited politely for the teacher to detach herself from her charges and come over to us. In Spanish, I explained that Jocelyn was interested in volunteering at the nursery school and that we were asking permission for her to come in and help.

She smiled. "Well, we certainly love that attitude in young people." She consulted her schedule. "I think we can set aside two mornings a week for Jocelyn to come and teach the children English."

Jocelyn broke into a wide smile and nodded. Then we moved on to the seniors' center. The director immediately agreed that both Jocelyn and Natalie could attend the center twice a week to help the women with sewing if I consented to teach English there on Saturdays.

Now Jocelyn and I planned our ESL lessons together, but she proved much more conscientious than I. The night before her classes, she wrote out her objectives and slipped them into her teacher's bag, along with all the necessary pencils, markers, puppets, and other props.

She became well-known in the community; little ones called out to her in the street, "Hola, Teacher!" Parents, when they bumped into us at Ricardo's, asked if we were staying. They wanted their toddlers to take English from the little Canadian girl who lived in the red villa.

But no, we were definitely leaving.

Nonetheless, I felt content that we had chosen to settle in to this charming community for so long. How would we have ever known how Jocelyn possessed a natural talent for teaching small children? I can't imagine any nursery school back home agreeing to let her volunteer at nine years of age. Being an integral part of Quebrada Ganado illustrated to us that interdependence is the key to a strong community. The seniors' center agreed to allow the girls to volunteer because I was doing the same thing myself. We knew that settling in one community would offer us life experiences otherwise unavailable if we had just leapfrogged from town to town.

Mimi had only a few more days before her flight home, so we decided to hire a private driver for a weekend sojourn. Yes, reader, we fell off the chicken bus bandwagon at this point, for good reason, I'm sure you'll agree, when you remember the deplorable condition of Costa Rica's roads and the unworkable public bus schedule.

I arranged with Luis to dispatch a van to pick us up at the villa on a Thursday afternoon to take us up to Monteverde, where we would kick off our mini-adventure in the Santa Elena Cloud Forest Reserve. Right on time, our driver rolled up at the front gate to load our bags and secure the girls in their seatbelts for the taxing journey, first past the port town of Puntarenas, then north to the twin communities of Santa Elena and Monteverde.

Mimi balked as we swerved through the rises of the Tilarán Mountains and careened around hairpin bends and dodged giant potholes. Typifying the worst excuse for a road in the country notwithstanding the tourist attraction at its peak, we knew that between this pass and the Quepos to Dominical run, no one left Costa Rica with both kidneys. At least Jocelyn managed to keep everything down all the way up.

Santa Elena, the town proper, boasted a post office, a grocery store, several sodas, and a collection of churches and municipal buildings. Monteverde, the quarter that stretches from Santa Elena to the entrance of the famous Monteverde Cloud Forest Reserve contained a cheese factory, butterfly gardens, two private schools, a number of resorts, and a research institute. Initially, we had been heartbroken by the rejection from the Quaker school, but from a different perspective, we recognized that if we had been selected to teach here, we never would have visited Tortuguero or Parismina on the Caribbean coast nor any of Panama or Nicaragua. There also would have been no time to fit in the rest of Central America as we now planned to do. Contrasted to Tortuguero, Monteverde is almost as difficult to get to, but possesses modern installations. Surviving the treacherous journey meant enjoying lodges offering spectacular views, fine restaurants, bank machines, internet cafés, and gift shops.

At the crack of 6:00 a.m. the next day, tour participants gathered at the rendezvous point. "Let's try to get a guide just for our party of five." Lloyd was unveiling his *Wildlife of Costa Rica* pamphlet. "I don't want an exasperated foreigner waiting for the girls to admire ants on the trail."

Thanks to the gods of guides, we were assigned one that had lived in the area his whole life and spoke English well. He led us through the dense growth along footpaths that hid every manner of scary creature such as tarantulas, the main attraction of the twilight tour. My top lip curled in disgust when he said, "At night, they are easily seen all along the path at the entrances to their lairs."

Lairs.

Even though the girls had hiked many trails already, they were equally spellbound by the Santa Elena Cloud Forest, as was their grandmother. Lloyd wore a constant smile, pleased to see how a community was capitalizing on and preserving nature. My mother, inspired by Natalie's stories about Mono Feliz, wanted to see monkeys. Our guide was adept at leading us to them by following their calls and the trail of banana poops they had left behind on their flight through the jungle. However, whenever we would pinpoint their supposed location, we could only see the treetops swaying violently after they had flung themselves away. Our guide made sure to deflect us from the upper portion of the jungle to the lower where more creatures lived. But the higher up a critter lived, the cuter and fluffier it was, whereas, the lower inhabitants were usually multi-legged and exoskeletal.

The next morning, we detoured to La Fortuna to visit Volcán Arenal. Santa Elena and La Fortuna are only twenty-five kilometers apart, but in those twenty-five kilometers, a lot of geology is going on. Mountainous passes, steep drops to rushing rivers, dense forests, and Costa Rica's largest lake render road travel between the two communities almost impossible. By chicken bus? Eight hours door to door. Costa Rica's private transport system has sprung up in response to these geographic realities. A minivan collected us around the corner from the pension and sped off to Lake Arenal, some ninety minutes from Santa Elena.

On the opposite shore of the lake, Jocelyn was captivated by the sight of Volcán Arenal, standing tall and smoldering. Arenal's conical shape dominates the panorama in La Fortuna, a community on the far side of the volcano. Lloyd resorted to walking backwards to keep it in his sights when we went on a walkabout in town.

We bunked at Frank's Hostel, a rather funky place, run by a brash middle-aged man, who showed his softer side to the girls by reading to them from a Shel Silverstein book at a picnic table on the back terrace. Lloyd, accustomed to having attentive children listening to his geographic drivelings, settled for Mimi and me and began the lecture. "Volcán Arenal is an active andesitic stratovolcano, you see? It erupts regularly, spitting out red hot lava at intervals such that you can hear the eruption and subsequent thud of hot boulders on the mountainside." We sat politely on the divan waiting for him to finish. "On lucky evenings, when it isn't too cloudy, you may be able to see the lava flowing over the cone." With that, he clapped his hands together and declared, "Janet, this might be your lucky night!"

My mother and I looked at each other, trying not to laugh.

We only had time to stay one night in La Fortuna, so after building up our hopes with *that* prologue, we could only cross our fingers that it would be a cloudless evening. Pressing our faces against the window of the bus, we examined the sky for clouds. We were in luck; we could see straight to the top of Arenal. We alighted at a rather fancy restaurant and hotel whose extensive grounds sloped downwards at the back, permitting spectacular views of the volcano. Mimi and I ordered a glass of wine and watched the show on the patio next to the pool. Lloyd took Jocelyn and Natalie on a little tour.

When they came back, he said, "You've got to look at this place."

Natalie took me by the hand and led me down the sloping manicured pathways to the edge of the property. We passed others sitting on their private terraces sipping wine and gazing at the volcano. I peered inside some of the vacant rooms. The designer of the hotel had cleverly oriented them so that Arenal loomed large in the window as guests were lying on their beds.

I eased back into my patio chair beside the pool. "Lloyd, we've got to come back when we have enough money to actually stay at a place like this."

"Yes."

If there was one thing we never argued about . . .

Then we went home, bringing an end to Mimi's mini-adventure by chicken bus. The girls said tearful goodbyes to their grandmother on a hot morning in October. She was weighed down by several items including my laptop (my old friend those many months), Jocelyn's stuffed dog Pepper, and little mementos we'd collected. We were reducing our possessions to prepare for the strenuous trek north through Nicaragua, Honduras, El Salvador, Guatemala, and Mexico. Lloyd informed the private school that he would not be renewing his contract, and I said as much to my students at night school.

My class arranged a pizza party and Manuel, one of my students, who owned Discoteca Lucill and the adjacent recreation center, delegated his staff to make the food. He delivered it triumphantly, striding through the large double doors of the community center with pizza and a few cold beers. It was a bittersweet moment, leaving these wonderful people behind yet looking forward to another adventure.

I popped in to see one of my students, Valeria, and her chubby baby, Luis, who lived directly beside Kevin, the cherub in Natalie's class. Kevin rolled his trucks around in the dirt as I bounced Luis in my lap and described to Valeria our plans to travel through the rest of Central America.

Kevin, still wheeling his trucks around asked, "You're leaving?"

"Yes," I said.

He stopped and looked up at me. "When are you coming back?"

I fought back the tears and swallowed hard. "I don't know."

Lloyd arranged a raucous staff party for his colleagues at the recreation center (Manuel was getting a lot of business during those final weeks). In a heartwarming display of international conviviality, English-speaking North Americans and Spanish-speaking Latinos from Central and South America lounged around the billiard tables, caught up in a friendly game of eight-ball, laughing at each other, slapping Lloyd on the back, all of us speaking in both languages as the case fit. Natalie and Jocelyn also attended their class parties respectively, Natalie with her classmates, Jocelyn with her students.

To commit everything to memory, I roamed around the village on foot over many days to inhale the exotic landscape and wave hello (though in my mind it was goodbye) to the townspeople. I took photos of everything: the wild horses who flew by me, furious at being tied up, trapping me behind a fence; Eduardo's video store we frequented so often (where one of the workers, in keeping with his Colombian roots, slaughtered a shrieking pig on the front steps one afternoon); the stagnant river, full of sludge and muck, strewn with broken appliances around which children waded; the cops, who comically buzzed through town on a moped, holding their helmets in their hands; the dark interior of the community center where I held my classes; the skinny, stupid dogs, who wandered all over town, oblivious to cars advancing straight for them.

After Christmas break, we entered Nicaragua on the first leg of our trip home. In sixteen months we had backpacked along the Caribbean coast, spent several weeks in Panama, and the remaining months stationed in a small Costa Rican village not more than four kilometers from the Pacific Coast. In that time, we had hiked, swum, ziplined, sweated, trudged, kayaked, camped, spelunked, climbed mountains, and peered into bubbling volcanoes. We had made cheese and chocolate, saved sea turtles, studied monkeys in the wild, and watched scarlet macaws fly overhead every day at five o'clock. We had also weathered blisters from ant bites and bacterial infections.

We felt we were well-prepared for the rest of Central America.

Chapter 12

Nicaragua

The aroma of Argentinean samosas, wrapped in gingham cloth and cushioned in a basket, wafted through Hotel Nicaragua. I reposed lazily in a hammock with my novel, savoring the smell. For once the four of us were not pressed to hurry back to Costa Rica after seventy-two hours. We were resting up before the grand adventure which was about to commence. The slower pace infected me. Instead of charging to the market to buy food we couldn't find in Quebrada Ganado, I procrastinated. So what if supper wasn't prepared on the dot of 6:00? If the girls got peckish, I could beckon the Argentineans over and buy four samosas.

In the final week at the villa, we set up a mini-yard sale on the sidewalk outside the impenetrable front gate and out of range of the vicious Weimaraners. People ambled over to buy up our spare shoes and the little everyday items that one collects over time. Paola bought the girls' bikes and donated them immediately to a needy family. Lloyd and I wheeled over to the home of one of my students, a single mother, and gifted our own bikes to her and her sons.

Our packs were a shell of their former selves. Lloyd's contained most of the critical hardware: the tent, air mattresses, flashlights, and kitchen wares (the essential five). Mine held a few articles of clothing and various medicines, salves, vitamins, and the first aid kit. The girls had only their bathing suits, towels, and little else; Natalie had mostly air in hers.

Lloyd commissioned the sewing lady to stitch secret pockets into our clothing. We cached passports, credit cards and American dollars into flaps sewn into collars, waistbands and armpits of shirts. Lloyd calculated the daily amount of necessary cash and doled it out evenly among us; even the girls had money concealed in secret pockets.

This time, we left Costa Rica like most other foreigners do, on a coach. Eschewing a chicken bus in favor of comfort, we cruised to the familiar Peñas Blancas border post in style. Instead of dodging Mack trucks and hawkers, the driver collected all the passports, entered *la duana* (customs), and for some inexplicable reason, completed the stamping procedure all by himself. We collected our bags and proceeded through immigration. We were subjected to random luggage checks, only opening our bags for inspection when signaled to do so by a red light from a small console. If the console flashed green, you were free to pass. When Lloyd got to the front of the line, he pressed the button on the console and immediately broke the machine. That was good enough for the border guard, who laughed, slapped him on the back, and said, "Adelante." Go ahead.

What a joy to see Karen, Francisco, and Daniela again after three months. They had moved into their newly constructed apartment above the hostel, and Jocelyn and Natalie alleviated the burden on Daniela's nanny by introducing the three-year-old to the department of imagination, pooling all dolls and toys into one big civilization. Lloyd and I were free to spend some time together, strolling along the beach hand in hand, gazing at the boats bobbing under the romantic Nicaraguan sun.

In between the frenetic pace of running the hostel and the chaos of renovating major sections of it, Karen and Francisco still made time for us. "I've got a bottle of wine; meet us out front at 5:45," Karen said.

When we congregated on the street, Francisco loaded all of us into the truck and took off to a piece of land overlooking the Pacific. We made it in time to toast the friendship and admire the big red ball sinking into the bay. A few days later Karen took us out to Playa Majagual for the day so the kids could run around at the beach. On the path through the jungle, a troupe of howler monkeys swung low from the trees directly in front of us. They were showing off, the young ones hanging upside down by the tail to grab leaves.

We stayed for several hours, letting the kids blow off some steam. Before returning to town, I stopped in at a campsite to book in for a few nights. We needed respite. A month before we moved out of the villa, we had lived moments of great stress. Jocelyn had developed a cough that wouldn't go away, and she suffered unpleasant side effects from the medication she had been prescribed that included shaking, quivering, extreme anxiety, and nausea. Her ailment rendered her countenance chalk white, and she sported dark purple shiners under her eyes.

Six times I took her to the clinic to get to the bottom of it. The doctor finally ran out of ideas and suggested it could be allergies. As her mother,

I could barely look at her. She is such a beautiful, smooth-skinned girl that her ghoulish expression made my heart palpitate each time I looked at her.

On the last visit to the clinic, I overheard two doctors discussing her case in front of me, in Spanish. The words "fibrosis quística" came up.

I interrupted them. "You think she might have cystic fibrosis?"

The doctors looked stricken, having underestimated how much Spanish I could understand.

"I think we need to be referred to a pediatrician," I said.

The older, grandfatherly pediatrician insisted it was nothing more than allergies, even though a blood test came back positive for bacteria in her lungs.

Totally confused and anxious about the impending expiry of our visas, Lloyd zipped around, making tentative arrangements to fly us all home to get her proper treatment, if need be. I sought out a third opinion. As we said our goodbyes to friends, this mystery was hanging over our heads. Though we were sad to leave, I was eager to get to San José to seek out another physician.

The dry air of the capital hit me like a desert punch. The rainy season had turned my lungs wet, but I ignored my own health to solve this mystery about Jocelyn. I set out with Jocelyn in tow and found a doctor who reassured me that in no way could it be cystic fibrosis. When I mentioned the test results had detected pseudomonas bacteria in her lungs he stopped smiling. "Pseudomonas? She has pseudomonas in her lungs?" He scribbled something on a piece of paper. "She may fight the presence of the bacteria on her own. However, we need to culture her blood to confirm that her own defenses have eradicated it." He handed me directions to the lab.

"How long does that take?" I coughed into a tissue.

"Ten days."

I explained that we would be in Nicaragua by then, but he said, "I will email you the results." He was kind and sensed how worried I was. "She is a healthy girl; her immune system can handle it."

The results of the test were hanging over our heads while I sat on the steps of Hotel Nicaragua with Lloyd, drinking beer and watching the life of the town pass us by. We sifted through the options available to us and realized that despite the fear we felt, we counted our blessings. We had the financial resources to fly home immediately and access the Canadian health care system, Lloyd could return to his job to support his family, and we lived in a safe and secure country, all things that most people here did not possess. I held my head in shame.

The campground was already uncomfortably hot even in the early morning. The wind formed dust devils along the sand and the tent stayed in place only because our four bodies weighed it down. Sand burrowed into every crack and crevice, making us wipe our eyes and re-activating my wet lungs. The wind made it virtually impossible to enjoy ourselves; we couldn't spend any time on the beach, and I confess that my lungs were causing me real concern. I confided to Lloyd—after he grunted and struggled to put up the tent all by himself in the gale, saw to the kids' needs, and prepared supper—that I could barely breathe. We stayed only one night.

Back in San Juan del Sur, we waited for the results of Jocelyn's blood test and tried to stay positive. One morning I went out to the internet café and saw the email waiting for us from the doctor. "Señora Janet," he wrote, "your daughter is bacteria-free. There is no cause for worry. Please enjoy the rest of your trip."

Like a little kid, I skipped back to the hostel and gave Lloyd the news. I smashed Jocelyn with hugs and kisses. That afternoon we meandered out to the bay to sip iced tea at a restaurant overlooking the beach. Nothing else mattered at that moment; even though poverty lurked all around us, *my kid was okay*. Later, after the initial euphoria wore off, I felt a piercing sense of guilt. Anyone in my family could be plucked out of harm's way at a moment's notice by the powerful arm of money, but the inhabitants here were forced to remain, surviving day to day without those things that we, as Canadians, took for granted.

When it came time to leave, Karen and Francisco offered to take us as far as Rivas so we could catch a bus to Granada. We had spent our last night having dinner together on their terrace. After a few glasses of wine, Francisco shared some moving stories about living through the Contra War—stories that will not make the pages of this book—but hearing about what he went through put our small moments of strife even more painfully into perspective.

The next day we gathered up the three children and piled them into the back seat of the pick-up. Lloyd took an old hostel mattress and laid it out in the truck bed. He and I bounced around among the bags while Francisco motored away from Hotel Nicaragua. I watched it recede from view and knew I would likely never be here again in my lifetime. Lloyd wrapped an arm around my waist to steady me while I took photo after photo of the Nicaraguan countryside, including a perfect shot of something commonly seen here: a baby in a bicycle basket.

Some of the images are sobering. Beyond the village of San Juan del Sur, the poverty and miserable conditions we hadn't seen in Costa Rica assaulted us. We had seen some dire sights in Panama, where destitute families constructed ramshackle bathrooms at the ends of docks, depositing directly into the Caribbean. When we arrived in Rivas, the bus station was a complete shock. The din, the dinge, the dirt . . . and in the middle of this—dust flying, horns honking, vendors shouting—Karen and I met face to face to say goodbye. We bumbled a few words, but behind both pairs of sunglasses, we were fighting back the tears.

GRANADA

I turned my attention from the receding image of Karen and Francisco's pick-up that had brought us from our home away from home at Hotel Nicaragua to the tumbledown circumstances of the Rivas bus terminal. We were entering a new world. The infrastructure of Panama and Costa Rica disappeared. Instead, we witnessed destitute conditions where people eked out a living under an unforgiving sun. Garbage blew everywhere; chicken buses idled noxiously. Women and child vendors swarmed the bus when they saw us getting on, spotting the ever-present but invisible dollar signs tattooed on our foreheads.

We knew only one thing: that the bus was departing for Granada (confirmed by Cisco himself). We had no idea *when* it left because by now we understood that a driver's salary was directly impacted by the number of passengers. The longer he waited, the more people filled the bus, the more income he made.

The call of nature crept over me during the delay. I'd forgotten my dehydration routine. "Anyone else have to go to the bathroom?"

"I do." Natalie got up and followed me off the bus.

Knowing the driver wouldn't leave without me (after all, we hadn't paid yet), I hired one of the young boy vendors to take us to the bathroom. "Puedes llevarnos al baño?" The layout of the adjacent mercado was so confusing I knew I wouldn't have the luxury of losing my way with my driver preparing to leave.

The little boy led Natalie and me through the maze. Rusted, derelict sections of corrugated metal were propped precariously upon rickety stilts to protect the vendors from the sun. A few bare light bulbs hung from the ceiling, casting the aisles in hues of black and grey. Novelties were being sold at some stalls; freshly wrung necks of chickens were being sold at others. Actually, they weren't so fresh, judging by our sense of smell.

The boy delivered us right to the door of the loo and Natty looked for all her seven years as disgusted as if she had stumbled across an open sewer, and as I entered my stall, I had to admit she wasn't far wrong. We emerged to find our little boy patiently waiting to take us back to the bus. I handed him two dollars for his efforts.

Jocelyn and Lloyd looked uneasy because the driver had begun to depart. I laughed when I saw their faces. I could have outwalked the bus. It was advancing at a turtle's pace, crunching dirty gravel underfoot. Then, he lurched the rattletrap onto the roadway.

At the front, the *ayudante* leaned out of the open door, clapped his hands and rang out in a loud voice, "Granada, Granada!"

As we had seen in Limón, his objective was to attract attention (pateeee!). An ayudante is also responsible for settling passengers and storing cargo, then picking his way through the crowd to collect fares. I'd seen them hoist old ladies with their sacks of onions onto the bus, settling their burlap bags in the back, where a few seats had been permanently ripped from their moorings to allow for cargo.

In a nation as poor as Nicaragua, where vehicle ownership was out of reach, public buses were a lifeline. It was common to see the proprietor of a small pulpería travel with dozens of boxes of stock for their business. Ayudantes were experts at finding spaces to cram them in. In fact, human bodies, having more elasticity, say, than a box of motor oil, were expected to contort themselves into uncomfortable positions to accommodate the ballast.

Jocelyn's head swiveled off its axis gawking at the all the activity on the bus. We caused a few double takes ourselves; it's possible that we were the only backpacking family that some had ever seen in their lives.

I bought the girls small bags of dried plantain and reminded them, "We can only drink out of a bottle from now on." The potable water of the most southern zones of the isthmus was now a thing of the past. San Juan del Sur acted as a buffer between the more developed communities of Panama and Costa Rica and the next ones. In San Juan del Sur we enforced restrictions on what we could eat (cook it, peel it, boil it, or forget it).

In the evening, Lloyd handed the girls bottles of water. "Don't use the tap water to brush your teeth. Use this water and rinse your mouth with it, too." At Hotel Nicaragua, if any of these rules was forgotten, it was no big deal, just a way to familiarize the girls with the new system. I was in no mood to tamper with anyone's health. Sometime in the past few days, Jocelyn's pallor had returned to normal, and I intended for it to stay that way.

The driver swung off the main highway at the outskirts of Granada. Several of the men at the back pointed out landmarks to us through the grimy windows of the bus. We disembarked at what was presumably Granada's bus terminal. The lonely, dusty blob of land was nothing more than a landfill used to deposit passengers and pick up a few more. Lloyd, a skilled map-reader, was disoriented by Granada's colonial walls. At one time, these walls were used to protect inhabitants from marauders. But the walls and roads behaved like a labyrinth; we didn't realize we had made a wrong turn until we rounded a corner and came upon a dead end. In Granada, we were unable to see off into the distance unless we stood in the middle of an intersection. We abandoned all hope that we would find the hostel on foot and hailed a taxi to take us there. At first glance, the entrance from the street revealed a rather pleasant looking place. Inside, the perimeter was lined with hammocks, computer stations, and a bar laden with rum. The center held a courtyard, open to sunny skies. A large palm surrounded by silvery pebbles stretched skyward.

Our impression soon soured. Between the common kitchen and the bathroom block lay a gravelly wasteland that acted as a garbage dump. Young Nicaraguan teens came early every morning to wash dishes and fling the grey water onto the landfill. Not only did the hostel cat and her kittens use the space as a litter box, they also slept in the potato bin.

For giving up our ten hard-earned, garage sale dollars, each of us got a bed, use of the kitchen/garbage dump/kitty litter area, free breakfast (including lots of potatoes), and free high-speed internet. We weathered the conditions for a day or two only because the bartender served ice cold Cuba Libres for one American dollar. The drinks were so heavy on the rum and light on the coke that we fought with other guests over the weaker drink. "No, no, you take this one. I insist!"

Anesthetized by alcohol or not, my lungs could not tolerate the grimy conditions and poor air quality of the hostel. "After dinner tonight, we are going to look for another place to stay," I told Lloyd, shooing away the cats.

"Fine by me. Did you know the door to our room doesn't lock?"

"Better take the passports and all our cash with us when we go out, just in case."

"Okay. Can we try to find a place with less college students? We've been awakened by enough drunken partiers."

The gentle nightlife of the city pulsed along Calle la Calzada, pointing south from the Parque Central. People lingered over meals at restaurants, and residents dragged their rocking chairs out to the cobblestoned streets to chat in the moonlight. As we passed them, they waved hello and murmured some approval about the girls. At the same time, as the second poorest country in the Western Hemisphere, behind Haiti, poverty was inescapable. People begged us for money. The girls were shaken by the disabled who held out their hands to us pitifully as we walked by. Preteen boys pleaded for the bottles of Gatorade I was drinking. I readily gave them up. I was wrenched by the sight of a young boy of about twelve or thirteen who habitually pulled up a piece of cardboard at the entrance to our hostel.

I asked the staff, "Who is that boy who sleeps outside at night?"

"He is from Jinotega," they told me, "and comes down here to look for work." I'd seen poverty before, but as a mother, something primal percolates inside you when it strikes children.

One night Natalie asked, "Mom, do you have some coins I can give to the people?"

Lloyd and I collected loose change and put it in a baggy. I knew the girls were too young to understand how to effectively support people in the developing world, but they were becoming aware, and that was our goal as parents, to introduce them to the world outside of their privileged lives, where the luck of geography was the only thing separating them from the struggles these children were facing. What they did with that awareness, well, that was up to them. We felt obligated to show them, on this "field trip," what we had talked about so much back home, that our wallets have the most profound effect on people, even those who live far away.

Halfway down the *calle*, we stopped in to check the recommended Hospedaje Cocibolca. With gleaming bathrooms, comfortable beds, and a clean kitchen for fifteen dollars a night, we booked a room for the next day on the spot and started back.

We walked a few paces and stopped. "What's going on?" Jocelyn asked. A crowd had gathered on the street. We pushed our way to the front and saw ten young men in the throes of rhythmic drumming and dancing.

"We are from El Salvador," they sang. "If you want us to continue playing, you must dance with us!"

People shied back, but one confident soul broke away from the crowd to get the feet stomping again. Yes, seven-year-old Natalie joined hands with one of the young men and they cut a mean rug for a good fifteen minutes until *he* pooped out. And both Lloyd and I with no camera! She was famous for two days afterwards. People stuck their hands out of car windows to give her a thumbs up.

Every day we set out to explore the rich cultural heritage of the city, herding the girls to museums and cathedrals. We stumbled upon hidden treasures: Jocelyn spotted something mysterious at the Casa de los Tres Mundos, an institution created to initiate, support, and promote cultural projects in Nicaragua. When we wandered through, admiring the artwork, we ascended to the second floor almost by accident. Up there, Jocelyn noticed something. "Oh look, there's a face on the floor."

We leaned over the balcony and saw from that height a man's frizzled face depicted in the tile floor. It turned out that on his eightieth birthday, the face of the founder, Dietmar Schönher, was laid in as a mosaic.

That night, the girls burrowed under the covers, hair wet from showering and skin smelling like soap. I squeezed in beside them, *Harry Potter and the Goblet of Fire* opened to chapter 12. Lloyd was propped up on our bed, flipping through the guidebook. "There is so much to do here. We won't have time to see it all."

I shrugged. "Why don't we do two excursions a day? One after breakfast and one after lunch?"

"It's the only way," he said, then added, "A week in Granada must be worth a year of history lessons."

We made a list of must-sees: youth orchestral performances, cigar rolling workshops, fortress tours. Then the daypack was filled with standard fare: water, granola bars, yogurt. And then out the door. At times, we doubled back looking for a museum or an art gallery, caught in a life-sized maze. Then we oriented ourselves by using Granada's majestic orange cathedral called Catedral de Nuestra Señora de la Asunción in the center of town as a focal point.

A historical and architectural showpiece, the church sat directly in front of the shady Parque Central. Beyond the park, the Hotel Plaza Colón, floored with red and white Moorish tiles, stood proud and regal. Dozens of horse-drawn carriages jockeyed to take newcomers on tours of the city. The plaza swelled with ice cream vendors, merchants selling handicrafts, or people simply loitering by the fountain. It was enough for a body to shout their enthusiasm to the skies, so I thought, what the hell. I belted out the words to the classic "Eres Tu" as it played over a loudspeaker while the girls, in total mortification, pretended not to know me.

Despite Granada's eye candy, the city's deteriorating infrastructure was impossible to ignore. In every bathroom from museums to restaurants, hostels to private homes, locals filled garbage pails with water in the morning in anticipation of a daily outage. I expected the girls to understand this aspect of everyday life, so I insisted they do the washing up after supper using the Nicaraguan method. "Watch how the women wash the dishes," I said. "Fill up this small bucket with water from the garbage pail and pour it into the sink."

"Do you notice how the Nicaraguans take it all in stride?" Lloyd asked as we cleared the table after supper. Restaurants sold lukewarm drinks and cooked food with fire. Museums, churches, and hotels placed large garbage pails filled with water in their bathrooms. Patrons were expected to use a bucket to scoop out water and flush the toilet with it. Some people were not getting the hang of it, though. They fumbled their way through the procedure, soaking the floor, using too much water (or not enough). When Lloyd went to the bathroom that night, he found the toilet in foul condition. He reached up to flush and discovered that the tank held no water. He exited the bathroom and came face to face with the previous occupant who had returned in embarrassed haste with her bucket of flush water.

The girls caught on, to a certain extent, but Lloyd drew me aside one night. "The girls are swimming in the hand-wash water."

Evidently, when they had gone to wash up as part of their usual bedtime routine, they found a large garbage pail of water in the shower stall, perfect for swimming and splashing around in. When Lloyd discovered them, he saw Natalie's torso submersed in the water with her legs bent over the sides, thereby using the system as her own personal cold-water Jacuzzi.

The next day, refreshed from our garbage pail sponge baths, we walked past a bookstore and coffee shop. "Whoa, whoa." I whistled everyone back. "Bookstore. Coffee."

The café was owned by Laura, a Canadian expat. We struck up a conversation and I described how we planned to journey north through Honduras, El Salvador, and Guatemala. "We're taking one of those long-distance coaches that leaves Managua at 4:00 a.m. and arrives in San Salvador sometime the following day. From there it's a short hop to Guatemala City," I told her. The girls had gravitated to Laura's living quarters, separated from the café by a floor-to-ceiling chain link fence, where her three children were playing. "I'm not looking forward to catching a bus at that hour," I said, taking a sip of coffee.

Laura scrunched up her face. "Ummm, is taking a night bus the best idea? They can be targets for robbers." Then she paused, looked at me gravely and said, "I went up to Tegucigalpa last year. In the middle of the night, when the bus crossed into Honduras, banditos burst from the jungle, shot up the bus and killed a passenger."

I felt sick.

"Look," she said, "why don't you leave the girls here tomorrow so you can figure things out. My kids would love some new faces to play with."

That night, at the *hospedaje*, I steeled myself to face the dire warnings from the Canadian Ministry of Foreign Affairs regarding travel through Honduras and El Salvador. I gulped hard and told Lloyd, "Prepare for a day of rearranging our route." The warnings were horrific. El Salvador was struck from the list. Long-distance coach, too.

Lloyd and I crisscrossed the whole of Granada the next day, going from one bus company office to another trying to glean information about schedules while the girls played with Laura's three children. Because of her helpful, if frightening, information, we opted to progress through Nicaragua by chicken bus and work our way through Honduras, skip Guatemala City and El Salvador altogether, and backpack through Belize, formerly not even on our short list. This way we would see more of Nicaragua and make ourselves less of a target, traveling in short hops by public bus instead of long-distance coach. This change made all the difference in our trip. Whereas we had not intended to travel entirely by chicken bus, this method was safer, more economical, more convenient, and more interesting.

There now remained two things to do in Granada: stalk the artisans' market of Masaya and hike its namesake, Volcán Masaya, both close enough to Granada for a day trip. The ride to the entrance of Masaya National Park was pleasant, and we hiked the short distance to the crater where Masaya was fuming. A sign warned asthmatics not to stay too long at the rim. My lungs spasmed in nervousness. Lloyd took the girls over to a placard to read safety tips to them. "If you feel tremors," he read, "hide under the car."

We looked around the empty parking lot. "Which one?" I asked aloud.

We circled the basin at the rim of Volcán Masaya, avoiding sections marked "Zona de Peligro" (Danger Zone). Though Masaya has not erupted since the 1700s, it discharges columns of sulfur dioxide continually. The Centro de Visitantes at the base displayed the formation of a volcano, explained in three languages. The girls, growing hungry, had to pull Lloyd away forcefully so we could eat a picnic lunch in the park's rest area.

"I would say Nicaragua's poised to become the next tourist destination," Lloyd commented as he crunched his granola bar. "The roads are smooth and paved; the distances are short . . ."

". . . And the rum is cheap," I interjected.

He laughed. "Which comes in handy during water and electrical outages."

"I think the misconception people have that it's a dangerous place is a big deterrent," I said. "Especially for families."

Lloyd agreed. "We were guilty of the same prejudice. Just think how we insisted we would never bring the girls to a 'dangerous' country like this." He used air quotes again.

For us, minor dangers bubbled up in unexpected places. On the way to Masaya's market, Natalie walked right into the rusted corner of a metal sign. As soon as I heard her screams, I knew she was injured. With blood streaming from her forehead, I dragged her into the closest pharmacy (the very one the sign was advertising). The stricken staff, upon seeing an injured child, and a foreign one at that, ripped open packages of gauze and brought us ice to bring down the goose egg.

Lloyd's efforts at first aid brought the bleeding under control, but he shot me a look that meant he thought she required stitches. Around the corner at the local hospital an armed guard halted us. I lifted Natalie's matted hair to reveal the gash in her forehead. The guard shouted something in Spanish and led the way to an adjoining room, removing obstacles like an offensive lineman protecting the quarterback.

For people who are curious about a developing country's health system, I can tell you that this little clinic was clean and professionally run. The physician came in and examined Natalie's forehead. After all the jabs she had received in Costa Rica, I was hoping beyond hope that she wouldn't need stitches. The doctor disinfected the wound and wiped and wiped at the gash, trying to pull the skin apart. I worried that the blow had caused a mild concussion; Natty was acting so unlike herself, laying placid, no screaming or screeching.

After a few minutes, the doctor stood upright and announced, "No, no necesita sutura." No stitches needed.

Later, Natalie told me that the doctor had whispered in her ear, "If you lie perfectly still and quiet while I examine your head, you won't need to get stitches."

My mind boggles at the audacity of the statement. If she had required stitches, how in the world would the doctor have convinced her to lie still as she stuck a needle into her head?

LEÓN

The change in itinerary—made after listening to the dire warnings from our fellow Canadian—rendered us at the mercy of the chicken bus system. This method was hotter, to the point of unbearable at times, more uncomfortable, to the point of unbearable at times, slower, to the point of unbearable at times, louder, to the point . . . okay, you get the idea. But it was also cheaper, and in our opinion, safer.

From Granada onwards, therefore, the overriding theme of the remainder of the trip became how to minimize risks. The added focus on health and safety included circuitous routes to avoid major metropolises. Whereas San José, Panama City, and Granada were benign, we intended to avoid the next four major cities: Managua, Tegucigalpa, San Pedro Sula, and Guatemala City. Thousands of young backpackers travel unharmed through these cities, but with two children, we wanted to err on the side of caution.

If nothing else, we learned a valuable lesson through the girls' illnesses. Although I had initially proposed following the "gringo trail" up to Mexico, passing through El Salvador and Antigua in Guatemala as the guidebooks suggested, the bouts of ill health served to rein in my enthusiasm. The bottom line now consisted of two things: that we remain close to medical attention and that we avoid risk as much as possible. Lloyd and I vowed to each other that we would be flexible about changing plans at the last minute if either one of us felt uncomfortable with anything, as we had done by deciding to avoid El Salvador altogether.

The conversation with Laura was timely. One could argue that from Panama City to Granada, an individual's level of personal safety could be assured. Don't misunderstand; it's not as safe as much of Canada. Costa Rica, in particular, was suffering from a swell of violent crime when we left. In general, it is safe. At points north of Granada, beginning with Managua, I would suggest a more "heads up" approach. From the weeks of research and the anecdotal stories from travelers, we knew skirting urban centers would be prudent.

So here we were in Granada, making decisions we had never had to make before. Health and safety were transferred from the back of our minds (as we reminisced about the good old days—turtle conservation projects, dilapidated bridges, vegetable truck rides, kayaking on the Pacific) to the forefront as we parsed the route down to the kilometer for the sake of safety.

At the terminal in Granada, vendors hounded us to buy packs of gum and Gatorade. I motioned to a thin, greying man with a face full of wrinkles covered by stubble. "Lloyd, look at the ayudante." He was the oldest we had seen but he had no problem climbing up and down the side of the mini-bus with a cigarette dangling out of the side of his mouth to affix baggage.

"As soon as he gives us the okay, get in the van to make sure we get a seat," Lloyd insisted. "It's a three-hour trip."

Worried about a repeat performance of a nervous breakdown, I lingered outside in the marginally cooler air instead of roasting alive inside the vehicle. Lloyd was proved correct in his assumption that the ayudante would cram the van full, and if I wanted to get a seat, I'd have to wait in oven-like temperatures for upwards of forty-five minutes.

Decisions, decisions.

After an hour, the ayudante, also our driver, it turned out, announced he was leaving, and I was left with enough space to wedge half a butt cheek between the window and the seat. I could feel my claustrophobia bubbling to the surface, but he drove with patience, cigarette dangling, along a poker-straight stretch of road. We arrived in one piece, tired and a little dehydrated, to the scenic, cobblestoned city of León.

Unlodging my buns (well, one of them) from the gap, I stumbled from the van and into blistering heat. It felt as though we were just west of the sun, which served to bore a hole in my head. It took me two full days to recuperate. The hostel sat on a quiet side street, and apart from the four of us, was completely vacant, so we were given a large dorm to ourselves, with attached bathroom and cold-water garbage pail Jacuzzi.

I lay in bed underneath the swirling fan the next day rehydrating and grousing at anyone who came within five feet. "You've got another parent, ask him for a drink."

The next day I felt well enough to park myself in the open-air lounge perusing four or five guidebooks from the hostel's library. The Moon *Nicaragua* travel guide wisely suggested staying out of the sun's rays between noon and 2:00. Sweating, they said, occurred at twice the rate of northern countries. "I'm sweating just sitting here," I announced to an empty lounge. I read on. "Probably the single most effective item in your medical kit are these packets of salt and sugar known as *suero orál*."[6]

I exerted myself for the first time in thirty-six hours and sat up, absorbed by what I read next. The author stated that electrolyte imbalance was a common problem here. Suero, dissolved in one liter of water, replaced lost minerals and salts from sweating, vomiting, and hangovers. The road to my recovery, it appeared, began with suero. I hefted my bulk out of the chair and went out immediately to find some.

At the very first pulpería, no more than ten square feet in size and selling mostly chips and pop, I approached the counter. "Se vende suero?"

"Yes, what flavor would you like, señora?"

"Flavor? It comes in different flavors?"

"Sí, naranja, fresa, o coco." Orange, strawberry, or coconut.

How could it be so easy? I bought all three flavors, returned to the hostel, and mixed the potion. Thereafter I always had a bottle of the seawater-tasting concoction with me wherever I went. Why I hadn't stumbled across this key piece of information before, I'll never know.

By day three in León, I felt ready to renew my efforts at parenting and apologized to the girls for being so grumpy.

"That's okay mommy. We knew you were sick." That was Natalie looking up at me with her baby face. I cupped her chin in my hand and thought, *Could you be any cuter?*

Lloyd whispered, "We haven't been doing much. The girls have been playing with their toys and swimming in the Jacuzzi for two days. Is it the hottest place on earth, or what?"

I had to agree. The heat closed tourist offices and museums every afternoon, a fact we kept forgetting. Luckily, Our Lady of Grace Cathedral, undergoing major renovations, remained open all day. The young woman at the ticket counter perked up when she saw us. Eager to show off her English, she told us we would have to wait a few minutes because, "The lady? She is sweeping the floor." She used her two arms to make full circles as if churning

---

6. Wood and Berman, *Nicaragua*, 426.

butter. She gave us strict instructions to avoid the delicate domes of the church, admonishing us with a wagging finger and an impressive elongation of rolling "r"s. "But rrrrrememberrrrr. Do not walk on the domes."

It was difficult not to laugh, so we took an absorbing interest in the architecture of the doorway.

Jocelyn muttered, "I think we should just speak in Spanish from now on."

Before long, we got the green light to ascend to the rooftop. It was a cloudless day; the Cordillera de los Maribios, a collection of eleven volcanoes, formed a spine down the middle of the country. From the roof, we could see highways braiding through their valleys. Lloyd went off half-cocked, unloading his encyclopedic knowledge of geology as we appraised the countryside under a sapphire sky.

"Beautiful," I murmured.

After a time, I could feel the sun working its magic, so I pointed to the street below. "Let's get something to drink at that café."

On the way to the stairs, Jocelyn grabbed her sister's arm. "Natalie, rrrrememberrrr, do not walk on the domes."

León was disappointing. Some museums no longer existed, and there were no parks for the girls to burn off their energy. It lacked the charm of Granada, and the heat was brutal. We were just passing through anyway. We aimed to see only four or five more sites, the pinnacle of which would be the Mayan pyramids of Tikal in Guatemala. We consulted the library's guidebooks and decided to advance north out of León, cutting through the valleys on our way to Estelí.

ESTELÍ

Back in Granada, the interlocking stone streets in the city center gave way to tarmac after a few blocks. The tarmac supported homes made of deteriorating metal slats, grey cinderblock, and dirt floors. Leaving León, we witnessed a parallel poverty among the dwellings that lead to the highway. Dingy, black interior walls were barely standing. "What happens to these people during an earthquake?" I asked Lloyd.

"Nothing good."

We joined dozens of laborers aboard a chicken bus traversing a lonely stretch of highway bisecting Volcán Telica Rota Natural Reserve. We passed people seeming to lead lives of desperation, eking out a meager income on the parched land. The shoulders were baked dry, and tumbleweeds blew at the mercy of the scorching breeze. Boys on horseback rounded up a few head of skinny cattle. We were slack jawed at people riding on top of tractor trailers, holding down tarps and eating their lunch as the truck hurtled down the highway.

"I thought the ride to Mono Feliz was bad," said Jocelyn.

In Estelí, our rustic motel was designed in the form of a square with rooms emptying into the courtyard rather than the busy street. The girls commenced their routine of arranging their toys into kingdoms on a small outdoor patio table. Lloyd went for a nap with the door open to keep one eye on them. I went out for provisions. After circling the town twice, I concluded that I was out of luck; Estelí appeared to have rolled up the sidewalks early.

"I think we might have to cave in and find a restaurant," I said to Lloyd when I returned. We were continuing to follow our self-imposed guidelines regarding the consumption of food and water. In Panama and Costa Rica, we could eat anything, anywhere. Now we were protecting foreign intestines from local bacteria.

"Can we get pizza tonight?" Natalie asked.

"Well, there is a pizza joint recommended here in *Lonely Planet*," Lloyd said, skimming the pages.

The girls looked at each other, buoyed with hope. I rarely allowed pizza, even back home, being what some would call a "crunchy" mom.

"There are no pulperías open anywhere. I can't think what else to do."

So, we went for pizza.

Later that evening, I tried in vain to get the girls settled into bed. Natalie squirmed and complained. "My stomach hurts."

At that moment, Lloyd emerged from the bathroom and announced, "I've got diarrhea."

Spasms were beginning in my own gut, and I suppose that on the face of it, we were lucky to have a private bathroom, but upon deeper reflection, we did only have *one* toilet for the four of us, three of whom now had compromised digestive tracts.

A fitful night's sleep was interrupted by a siren that went off at 6:00 a.m.

"What is that?" Lloyd cried. "Is it an earthquake warning?"

We waited, lying still in our beds, clutching the sheets. Nothing. There was nothing to do but get up. "We should stay close to home today, in case anyone needs to use the bathroom," I said to Lloyd, who was leaving for coffee. "The problem is breakfast. See if there are any pulperías open."

Within thirty minutes he was back with coffee and four take-out containers of gallo pinto. "I didn't think there was much harm in beans and rice," he explained. "Besides, I couldn't find any grocery stores."

"Who is up at this hour?" I asked.

"The whole town. I guess that siren wakes everybody up." The girls were filtering in and out of the bathroom. I brushed Natalie's hair up into a ponytail. "Are you feeling better?" She nodded and took her breakfast outside to the table next to Jocelyn.

"If she's hungry it can't be all that bad. I'm feeling a bit better myself," Lloyd remarked.

"Me, too." I sat on the edge of the bed, digging into my serving. "There's an art gallery across the street. I think I'll take the girls there after breakfast. If our stomachs hold out maybe we can visit the museum this afternoon."

"It's not my stomach I'm worried about," he said, pointing to his derriere.

The gallery did not open until 9:00. Lloyd and I passed the time reading. The girls played at the table, using singsong voices in their make-believe world.

At 9:00, I asked the girls to gather up their toys so we could go out. They plunked their pieces, one by one, into cloth, zip up pouches the sewing lady had made for us back in Quebrada Ganado. By now the sacks were fuller with the addition of little doodads picked up along the way, like the bride and groom, fuzzy caps from the ends of pens, and cheap, funky key chains sold at market stalls everywhere. There was no end to what they could conjure using the cheesiest props.

I left Lloyd sleeping back at the motel to rest a bit more and, hand in hand, the three of us girls went to the art gallery. Immediately they loved it. Mounted on mantelpieces sat exquisite urns, and richly colored artwork hung on the walls. Jocelyn reached out to touch an iguana, sculpted into a handle, on a hand-painted pitcher.

I gently took her hand. "They're beautiful, aren't they?"

She nodded.

"They're for sale, we mustn't touch them."

Natalie, on the other side of the room, called out to me. "Mommy, what does this say?"

I walked over, gazing at a large portrait of a young woman, rifle slung over her shoulder, beaming at the camera, baby attached to her breast. "I've seen this image everywhere." I bent down to read the caption. "La Miliciana de Waswalito."

Later, after naps, I said to Lloyd, "I bet the Gallery of Martyrs and Heroes has more information."

He was zipping up his daypack. "I've even seen t-shirts with that image on it."

Now that we had an objective, our history class for the day, provided by the Galería de Héroes y Mártires de Estelí, didn't feel so random. The girls, Natalie especially, were determined to find out about this woman breastfeeding her baby in the middle of a war.

The gallery was sobering and its subject matter hard to comprehend for young children who had never experienced national conflict. I was floored by the descriptions of the young militants, some in their early teens, who were willing to die for their freedom.

A blown-up photographic version of La Miliciana looked down on us from high up on the wall. "She was fighting with her baby?" Natalie asked.

"I'm not sure," I admitted. "Maybe the grandmother took care of it while she was fighting."

"What if the mother died?"

"I think lots of mothers and fathers died."

Jocelyn came over to us. "Did any children die?"

"Most likely."

From the look on her face, I think, at that moment, she matured by ten years.

We were quiet as we left the gallery, baffled by a nation of tender, kindhearted people who had been through so much turmoil. Estelí was decimated in the conflict, we learned, and suffered heavy losses.

"We did right by history today, don't you think?" Lloyd said, taking my hand. He recognized my mood and looked as distraught as I felt, picturing parents losing their children.

In our present state of mind, we were glad to come across the small, leafy Parque Central, hosting a fair when we strolled through. The girls rocketed around the tarmac on motorized mini-cars while Lloyd and I sat together under a broad-leafed tree.

"Did you know that the woman in that photo of La Miliciana was only fifteen years old?" I said.

"Pretty young to be in combat," Lloyd said.

"Pretty young to be a mother, too. And breastfeeding in public like it was nothing." I remembered how women in my mommies' groups back home shared tips on how to discretely nurse a baby. "She was even comfortable enough to have her picture taken doing it."

Lloyd touched my arm to add emphasis. "I saw girls in Quebrada Ganado that young nursing babies."

"Where?"

"When I caught the bus. The stop was in front of the high school, remember?"

"Were they nursing the babies in front of the boys?"

Lloyd nodded. "Not only that, they carried on conversations with them at the same time."

I was bowled over, thinking about young girls feeling more comfortable exposing themselves to feed their babies compared to grown women back home who were ashamed of it.

I turned to Lloyd with raised eyebrows. "Who knew one painting could reveal so much?"

We mistakenly decided to leave Estelí at the same time school let out on a Tuesday. Chicken buses were full to bursting with children in their navy and white uniforms, heading home for the day. The girls clammed up; they'd caused a few heads to turn at the sound of their English. Towns like Estelí were passed over by backpackers; locals had likely met few foreign children in their lives.

Lloyd nudged me. "Do you realize the irony? Kids in North America get transported to school for free, then when the buses are close to falling apart, like this one, they are sold to these countries where families have to *pay* to use them?"

We puttered along and from time to time, young children alighted onto the shoulder of the busy highway. The driver or ayudante paid attention to them after collecting them from their seats if they had nodded off and watched them until they were greeted by their mothers.

Chapter 13

Honduras

THE MOMENT WE CROSSED into Honduras, Lloyd and I both felt an unidentifiable creepiness permeate the air. We stood with our backs against the wall of the terminal like criminals on the lam and scolded the girls when they wandered too far away. Jocelyn distracted Natalie with an illusory scene using small, gritty boulders and the wall we were holding up to penetrate an imaginary world forever inaccessible to my adult mind. Lloyd and I guarded the girls fiercely, scrutinizing people coming and going, mostly laborers who were returning to Honduras. We felt cold eyes on us. People glared in our direction.

We escaped this unwanted attention when a bus bound for Danlí showed up. The driver, not one to waste time, put the pedal to the metal when we were barely seated. I worried about Jocelyn's stomach as we swayed violently to the left and right. A few minutes later, he came to a back breaking stop in a dusty village and bolted off the bus.

"Probably has to go to the bathroom," Lloyd reasoned, but after passengers filed back on the bus, our driver returned, gunned down hard on the accelerator and sped off. Then we caught sight of a printed sign behind his seat that read, roughly translated: *If you wish to vomit, please request a bag from the driver.*

Where Nicaragua was bone dry and split in two by an active volcanic range, Honduras was riddled with lush green valleys and rolling hills. We couldn't believe our eyes: *pine trees.*

Tourism in southern Honduras was still relatively uncommon; most people flew into San Pedro Sula then transferred north to the Caribbean or entered via Guatemala to see the Mayan ruins of Copán. People on the bus were taken aback to see Lloyd, with his reddish-brown hair, freckles, and tall, slender frame. One boy stood in the aisle, facing backwards about four feet away to stare at him until we disembarked in Danlí. The girls and I, with our fewer freckles and Mediterranean heritage, blended in. Most of the time, we could pass ourselves off as locals, which we deliberately tried to do, dressing like they did in skirts, tank tops, and flip-flops and wearing our long, dark hair in buns. If I didn't speak too loudly, they were unable to detect an accent. By then I don't think the girls even had an accent. Lloyd, on the other hand, was a walking circus act.

In Danlí, we dumped our packs at a bland hotel in the center of town and set out to stock up on food and water. We again decided to lift our ban on eating out and selected a small café on the main street. Jocelyn went off to find the bathroom and came back, saying offhandedly, "That bathroom was disgusting."

My ears pricked up immediately. I went to check for myself, and I recoiled in revulsion at what I saw, thinking only of taking Jocelyn back to the hotel and making her take a shower.

I hurried back to the table and hissed, "We're leaving."

"I've just ordered two cold cervezas," Lloyd said. To get out of there quickly, we guzzled our beers, acting as if we always took our young children drinking with us.

Only one store was open on the streets of Danlí that evening, a discount department store that sold bric-a-brac imported from China. The girls fondled the packages of cheaply made toys; Lloyd and I mulled over the choices available to feed our children. If we had our way, we would have bought two bottles of Gatorade and gone to bed early. With Natalie, it was simply impossible.

I was close to giving up when I spotted a microwave behind the cash register. I took two bottles of water from the fridge and gave them to the clerk, instructing her to open them, pour them into the cups of instant noodles they sold and microwave the mixture. For good measure, I gave her a bag of popcorn to pop, too. For dessert. We carted the whole lot back to the hotel in a cardboard box, and as the girls took a shower, I prepared a lovely meal of noodles and popcorn for the family.

Danlí was a layover, nothing more. We had serious reservations about traveling through Honduras, and we were meticulously plotting our course now, with our main goal: safety. At our hotel, Lloyd made a great friend in the night watchman. The two of them pored over maps until they came up with a reasonable strategy to get to Comayagua, bypassing the capital, Tegucigalpa, altogether. When Lloyd came in from his conference with the night watchman, he said, "We would do well to get through this country as fast as possible."

In the morning, I went out early to find an internet café and detected an eeriness in the air. Many months later Lloyd confided to me that he had gone out even earlier to fetch coffee and had discovered a young man lying in the street, severely beaten and left bloody and helpless not more than twenty-five meters from our hotel.

COMAYAGUA

It turned out that the night watchman had a toddler himself and understood Lloyd's concerns that we all arrive in Comayagua as we had arrived in Danlí—safe and sound. After hours of brainstorming and several phone calls, the two of them decided we should hire a private driver to take us north past Tegucigalpa and right to the door of our hotel in Comayagua.

The task of securing a driver wasn't difficult. In fact, half the town showed up at our hotel in the morning asking if they could chauffeur us. The presence of gringos had naturally caused the rumor mill to turn. The hard part was finding a vehicle with three seatbelts in the back seat.

Lloyd must have sent seven drivers away. "No, *three* seatbelts. Not *two*, *three*." One driver offered a creative solution, suggesting we tie one restraint around the three of us females in the back seat.

We decided to hire Pedro, an affable man with large teeth, who shuttled us in a brand-new, air-conditioned van, each passenger having their own functioning seatbelt. Before we left the city, Pedro stopped in to kiss his wife goodbye, then drove maniacally down the highway. He swerved inexplicably at times and rarely kept his eyes on the road because he was so busy chatting to Lloyd. I thought of saying, "I wish to vomit. May I request a bag from you, driver?"

Pedro drove no differently than all the others on the freeway. We wound through majestic stands of pine, slowing behind a fleet of freighters. Drivers, seeming to be at the snapping point in their impatience to get to their destination, crowded the vehicle ahead, almost bumping. Then, five cars fanned out behind the transports, accelerating and swerving, in a dangerous contest to be the first one to pass. Hills and curves did not discourage this practice in any way. At the rest stop, Lloyd and I looked at each other, dumbfounded. The girls had been preoccupied, playing with each other and listening to music. Sure, Pedro was a nice guy, but I could barely look at him. On the last leg to Comayagua, Lloyd pretended to doze off so that Pedro would refrain from talking to him and watch the road. It made no difference.

Pedro dropped us at the door of our hotel in Comayagua, another colonial style town. Kitty corner to the hotel was a saloon, of all things, painted deep carnelian red. Short cowboys with tall white Stetsons sauntered in, ostensibly for a cold Imperial, and staggered out after a few too many. On the opposite corner, a woman had set up a cart of snacks and drinks—a common way for women to make a bit of income, I noticed. All day long, workers stopped by for a bite and a drink. She saw me on the balcony and waved. I gestured to ask her if I could take her picture. She gave me the okay.

That afternoon, I went out to send messages to friends and family. By the time I began my walk back to the hotel it was getting dark. For the first time since we had left Canada, I felt intimidated by my surroundings. Here I was, a foreign woman, walking alone in a strange town at dusk. I was breaking lots of common-sense rules. As I rounded the corner, I saw Lloyd standing on the balcony craning his neck to see if I was coming. When he saw me, he visibly relaxed.

The next day I made the rounds to find laundry services and was directed to a mom-and-pop outfit where I inadvertently caused an argument when I asked the couple to recommend a seamstress. I winced when the husband shouted down his wife in front of me. From what I could discern as I slipped out, a woman who lived directly across the narrow lane behind a shadowy doorway took in sewing to make a little money.

I knocked hesitantly on the flimsy door. A quiet, bony woman ushered me in to the main room which contained a rotten couch, a table, four chairs, and a broken-down wall unit that propped up a TV. Threadbare curtains hung down from the ceiling to act as a room divider. A few toys were scattered about, and the only light piercing the gloom came from the door through which I had entered, but most of the sunlight was obliterated by a board to safeguard against break-ins.

Lloyd had asked me to have another shirt outfitted with secret pockets. He left Quebrada Ganado with one shirt expertly redesigned by our sewing lady. With the heat wrenching open his sweat glands though, he needed another to wear while the original was being washed. He doubted that he could effectively explain all this in Tarzanese, so I took the original shirt to use as a template.

The seamstress was so poor she did not even have enough fabric to make hidden pockets. I told her to cut a few inches off the bottom of Lloyd's shirt for that purpose. I also asked her to mend my backpack, which had started to unravel after a year and a half of being thrown on top of buses and used as a seat cushion at crowded bus terminals. For all of this, she charged me one dollar when I came by to pick up the items the next day. I countered by offering her about three dollars. She hesitated to accept that amount of money and did not look at me. From what I saw of her standard of living and the domestic dispute I'd witnessed the day before, I couldn't help but wonder if these two women had been conditioned to undervalue themselves.

The next day, freshly laundered, patched up, Lloyd sporting an almost midriff-baring shirt, we set out on a *rapidito* to the lake town of Peña Blanca for wildlife spotting. You would think that by now, our command of Spanish would have thrown up a few red flags when we heard the term "rapidito." The word means roughly "quickie." We careened down the freeway in this fashion—a little too quickie. Our van was driven by a young man in his early twenties in such a careless fashion that I assumed he had no regard for human life.

Lloyd and I were speechless by the time we dismounted at our transfer point to change buses. "We are so close to the lake now," he said. "Maybe we could take a taxi from here?"

We had no time to think about it further; an ayudante was shouting at us to get on his bus, a surprisingly modern vehicle driven by a man in his sixties.

I had the girls by the hand. "Maybe this grandpa is the driver for us? His bus *is* in good condition."

No. He was worse than all the others. He didn't drive a little too quickie, he drove recklessly fast. He stopped short, jarring all the standing passengers, including Lloyd, to the front of the bus, then stomped on the accelerator so hard they lurched to the back. He wound his way in this manner in and out of traffic on the highway. I hung my head and wanted to cry. One false move, and we would all be dead.

He had also lied to us about the route. What does it possibly matter as long as we get on the bus? When a driver's income is derived from fees collected, this explains, in part, why they drive so fast (to get to their destination and fill more seats) and why they lie to those who are not familiar with this system.

In a state of emotional shock and Jocelyn a little green, we disembarked a few kilometers from the lake. Several people, mostly drivers and ayudantes, swung by to solicit our business. They insisted they were going "right by the lake."

"Let's take a taxi," Lloyd suggested, but we were so far off the beaten path that there weren't any. In the end, we asked several people how to get to Peña Blanca and then cobbled the responses together. "Looks like we have to take one of these buses," I said. "By nightfall, God willing, we will be there."

LAGO DE YOJOA

The little T-shaped town of Peña Blanca, north of Lago de Yojoa ("yo-HO-a"), the largest lake in Honduras, was bustling as folks made their way to market. Modern Peugeot taxis wiggled in and out of traffic. We observed the same drivers pass us several times as they dropped off shoppers up the hill and brought others back down again. We made the acquaintance of Ivan, a quiet, sweet-natured Peugeot driver who took us to our hostel on the edge of town. He became our knight in shining armor, that Ivan. I was still shaking from a near nervous breakdown, precipitated by the perilous driving when we pulled into D&D Lodge and Microbrewery—not more than walking distance from the beautiful Parque Eco-arqueológico Los Naranjos.

Tranquility sank into my bones once Ivan turned down the country lane to the lodge. The grounds were exquisite, featuring a swimming pool fringed with heliconia, bougainvillea, and hibiscus. The main reception, kitchen, and dining room were set among grand trees whose branches bowed under the weight of the dangling teardrop-shaped nests of the oropendola. Hummingbirds buzzed in and out. It was impossible not to feel relaxed. (The homemade mango and apricot beer helped some.) Lloyd appreciated how Bob, the owner and American expat, had designed the hotel in tune with nature, taking care to clear only a few trees. So basically, we were sipping cold, homemade beer in the jungle.

They ran a nice meal service as well. We were so starved after a few days of popcorn and instant noodles that we ordered nearly everything on D&D's menu. The girls were torn between eating their first decent supper in weeks and jumping into the pool.

Later in our cabin Lloyd said, "Bob told me he cleared this area by himself. And the water is purified because of the microbrewery, including the water coming out of our taps." To emphasize the point, he turned on the suicide shower and placed his upright palm under the spray. "Oh!" he shouted.

The three of us looked at him in alarm. "Electrocution?" I asked.

"No," he laughed. "Scalding hot."

I scooped the girls up into my arms and jumped up and down. "Hot water!" I cried, tossing them on the bed. I dove in between them, covering my ears to their shrieks of laughter.

Natalie turned over and pointed at the ceiling. "Wow, that's a big spider."

"Lloyd! Tarantula!"

"Oh, I forgot to mention. That was the other thing Bob told me." He pushed a chair up against the bed. "When he was clearing the land, he uncovered a massive tarantula colony."

My top lip curled in revulsion, and I knew there was only one thing to do. "I'll meet you at the restaurant. I need beer."

In the morning, we prepared to hike Parque Eco-arqueológico Los Naranjos. "There's a back entrance down the road," Bob said. "It's unmarked, but you can't miss it."

The trails of the national park skirted tall, conical grassy lumps concealing unexcavated pyramids and temples of pre-Columbian societies. We followed the paths until the incessant drone of lawn mowers driven by the men maintaining the park ruined the atmosphere. To escape the noise, we changed course toward the lake and stood on the bridge spanning a narrow section and drank in the sight.

The next day we traveled a short hop by chicken bus to the spectacular Pulhapanzak Falls. Trundling along, I saw campesinos toiling on farms terraced against the rolling green countryside. I felt like I had stepped back in time. Young boys straddled burros, looking like Huckleberry Finn in threadbare trousers cinched at the waist with rope and wearing straw hats. We stopped occasionally to pick up passengers and in one town, at the very cusp of the main road, a woman, illustrating expertly the concept of "location, location, location," sold beer and gallo pinto from a stall erected from cinder block and corrugated metal. The bus honked its arrival and three men swigged the last of their beers, paid up, and hopped on the bus.

Pulhapanzak Falls attracts tour groups who flow in by coach and compete for purchase on the hard-packed trail that runs parallel to the falls. The trail ascended, breaking from time to time at observation platforms. The girls ran ahead, protected from plunging into Río Blanco by a barrier. A fine spray of water infused the air and floated down onto our skin in beads. The falls seemed to erupt out of nowhere, as if a giant faucet was turned on full blast from behind the jungle foliage. Shouts and whistles rang out from a group of American college students who had made the daring trek to the top and lined up to fling their bodies out and over the falls, plunging into the river below.

Natalie turned to me. "Can I try that?" She turned away when she saw the scowl on my face. I steered the family away from this sight and back down the trail. I could not face witnessing an accident and doubted that the mothers and fathers of those young people knew what their kids were up to. We enjoyed the rest of the day eating a picnic lunch at the adjoining park and knew it was time to leave when Natalie sustained another injury when she fell off the swing at the playground. I saw the whole thing happen before my eyes. She fell forward, flipping the seat up and it swung down, striking her ear. Her wailing made it difficult to assess the damage, but it left an angry red welt.

D&D's was flooded with new guests by the time we returned. The area is a well-known birders' paradise, and Lloyd was heartened again, as he was in Tortuguero, to learn that naturalists would make the journey all the way out here to hoist their binoculars for a peek at motmots, the elusive, resplendent quetzal, and oropendolas with their distinctive "booble ooble oop" call.

He and I sat back drinking cold mango beers beside the pool watching the girls. The amateur ornithologists, likely for the first time in their lives, impressed a rapt audience of two and flipped through digital photos, identifying each species of bird one by one. Natalie, especially, had developed a keen interest in anything to do with nature, and the birders passing through D&D's only reinforced this.

"I don't see a reason to leave anytime soon," I said to Lloyd, and we raised a glass, clinked them together, and drank.

Now, for the first time since Granada, I allowed myself to relax. Sitting there with Lloyd enjoying his company, I was, at least for a moment, able to let go of obsessing over the girls' safety and appreciate the science lesson that had taken over their lives in Lago de Yojoa. However, angst is hardly absent; it lies in wait for the right time to resurface and by the time we finished our meal, I was suffering full blown anxiety about our next leg.

We intended to traverse a small portion of the Caribbean, called the Bay of Omoa, by boat, rather than risk life and limb further on the roads, and enter Belize through the settlement of Dangriga. Getting to the port required a transfer in San Pedro Sula, a city we anxiously wanted to avoid.

"The other day when I was shopping in town, I made the mistake of reading a local newspaper," I said to Lloyd. "The headlines reported that hundreds of people were dying in the rapiditos that depart San Pedro Sula for the coast."

"Because of busjackers and the crime at the terminal?" he asked.

"No. The culprit is the age of the drivers. Some are as young as eighteen or nineteen."

That night, I lay down beside Natalie and looked at her cherubic face and almost burst into tears over the stress of it all. But my angst washed away, and rainbows appeared when Lloyd took me aside the next day. "Look, I've spoken to Ivan. He'd be happy to drive us all the way to the coast. He can take us in that brand-new Peugeot, and there are three functioning seatbelts in the back seat."

Other than the sense of relief I felt upon the removal of nine-and-a-half-pound Natalie from my birth canal, I have never felt a sense of relief to the depth I felt it that day. If I weren't careful, I'd be singing "Eres Tu." Out loud.

We rose late the following morning and dawdled, me reading in a hammock, the girls poking around the edge of the pool.

Jocelyn came over to me. "There's another family here with kids."

Mauricio and Jenny, a US/Honduran couple, had heard about the food and the pool and had stopped in to have lunch. They had a daughter, Lisa, about eight years old and a little boy, Justin, three. They were spending the weekend at the lake on vacation from San Pedro Sula where Mauricio worked. Anxious for Lisa to have kids her own age to play with, Jenny invited us to get together later that afternoon at their hotel so that they could play together at the hotel's water park.

This sounded like a fantastic idea at the time but by the end of the day we recognized that our family did not mix well with vacationing families. A long-term backpacking family on a maximum budget of fifty dollars per day does not go to water parks.

We called Ivan to pick us up and take us to their hotel instead of hopping on a chicken bus. Despite the shrieks of laughter from the kids, Lloyd and I could not fully enjoy ourselves. The company was lovely, but the entrance fee to the park combined with the taxi fee to and from the lodge made for an expensive day.

"We have a free swimming pool at the lodge," I whispered to Lloyd.

Vacationing families would have no way of knowing how little we lived on. In some cases, for instance, in Nicaragua, we could get by on as little as twenty to twenty-five dollars daily, including accommodations. The use of a kitchen was essential. As vegetarians, we could penny pinch a food budget of about five to ten dollars a day. I can't tell you how many people we met who could not wrap their minds around our ability to travel for so long without an income. Lloyd's meager wages in Costa Rica kept us in mangoes. We only dipped into savings for excursions or border runs. Now, on our journey home, we were delving into garage sale earnings entirely.

More than once, young backpackers asked us outright if we were wealthy. I wanted to ask them if they thought my saggy discount-store cargo pants looked like I was wealthy. And would we be staying in youth hostels eating beans and rice if we were wealthy? And who takes chicken buses unless they are skimping? Instead, I explained to them that if they took stock of their personal inventory after a period of ten years, they too would have the basis for great liquid wealth. Selling our cars alone was a huge financial boon to our travel fund.

We had made financial mistakes on the trip, but we had learned from them. We vowed never to give in to the excitement of participating in an expensive activity unless it was worth it, as this trip to the water park was not. I was thinking of Fossil Land by comparison. The girls were never put off by our refusal to take part in some frivolous activity; in fact, they found traditional children's activities a bit babyish. They preferred that we hire a guide and hike into the jungle to see animals in the wild. They loved museums and talking to young backpackers at the hostels, playing cards or chess, or answering the million questions that naturally flowed from their appearance with little backpacks on their backs.

After two more days, we decided to leave D&D's to catch the ferry from Puerto Cortés to Dangriga, Belize. Lloyd contacted Ivan and arranged a ride. The unique make up of D&D's, apart from the excellent atmosphere, the fruity beer, the hot water, and jungle setting, was the billing system. Bob used the American style tab system, which can be risky, if you don't keep track of your spending. I left most of that to Lloyd. When he returned from settling the bill, I asked him, "How much?"

"Oh, about $800."

My mind struggled to remember all that we had eaten, factoring in the nightly accommodation fee (around thirty-two dollars). I couldn't make it work. For five days had we eaten and drunk $640 worth?

"Uh . . ." I stammered. "Really? That's a lot, isn't it?"

Lloyd, who was on his way to fetch Ivan, called over his shoulder, "No, I figured on that much."

Our maximum budget per day was around fifty dollars and Lloyd had just pronounced that our expenditures for the five days amounted to $160 per day, an unforgivable breach. However, I trusted Lloyd so much that my mind couldn't accept that a) he would allow so much overspending and b) he was so blasé about it. I sat down on my newly sewn backpack and rested my chin in my hand to think about it. The girls skipped all around me, tossing rocks.

Later, when we laughed about the whole thing, he channeled the Grinch. "Your puzzler was sore?"

Evidently one of us may have misunderstood, but the other admitted to using the word dollars instead of *lempiras*. Eight hundred *lempiras*. Per day. He had already done the conversion by the time I questioned him. Around forty-three dollars per day.

Phew.

TRAVESÍA

Either one does not dream, or one does so interestingly. One should learn to spend one's waking life in the same way: not at all, or interestingly.

—NIETZSCHE

We left Lago de Yojoa reluctantly on a beautiful Sunday morning, dodging the market hubbub of Peña Blanca. We had enjoyed every little bit of it: the beauty, the people, the shopping at the markets. On Bob's recommendation, Lloyd bought some hammocks from an older, gentle little man who shuffled around his shop under the brim of an oversized cowboy hat.

We were about to leave Honduras behind. Although I was dreading the trek to the coast, I was glad to see Ivan show up with his son, Carlos, the morning we left. The deep affection Ivan had for his son was unmistakable; they spoke to each other in quiet tones and soft smiles. Lloyd could relate to Ivan on that score. To think that it took coming to Latin America for Lloyd to bond with Jocelyn and Natalie. Back home he'd been conditioned to work long hours, often at the expense of family life. Here, he could spend every minute with them, gently pointing things out, joking about his bad Spanish, and protecting them, as he did by hiring Ivan to take us all safely to Travesía.

We piled the kids into the back of the Peugeot; Lloyd rode shotgun. Ivan loaded the packs neatly into the hatch. "Carlos wants to see the ocean." It made me more relaxed hearing him say that. I could only hope it had an influence on his frame of mind behind the wheel.

He turned out to be a conscientious driver. I will forever be grateful to him for motoring safely along the highway north to the Caribbean. My heart fluttered as we bypassed San Pedro Sula, but it was an uneventful trip with virtually no traffic, as we had opted to travel on a Sunday.

Ivan delivered us to the Costa del Caribe hotel in Travesía, a small Caribbean community tucked in beside the larger port of Puerto Cortés. The hotel was upstairs, above the clapboard, seaside restaurant. Ivan took Carlos down to the water for a swim, and we ordered up lunch for the carload of us. Ivan explained, as we tucked into our meals, that police were cruising the highways now to reduce the numbers of car and bus jackings. Indeed, the sight of so many patrol cars on the road reminded us to be cautious.

Travesía is inhabited by the Garifuna, who are descendants of Amerindian and African people. As we had observed in every Caribbean community so far, the skin of the people became darker, the hair a little coarser. We said our grateful goodbyes to Ivan and Carlos then lounged the day away, eating and gazing out at the sea. Locals looped through the tables, enticing patrons with homemade pastries, chanting "pan de coco . . . pan de coco."

Again, we had bent our rule about eating in restaurants. Every trip was organized to settle the girls with toys, music, and a bag of fruit and bottles of water, but two growing, active children need calories regularly, and it wasn't long before the girls were hungry again.

"I think we need to order again," I said. "The granola bars will not cut it, I don't think, and I have no idea where the market is."

"I wonder what they're eating," Lloyd asked, indicating an older couple.

"Hang on. I'm gonna find out."

Delicious aromas wafted from the kitchen and hovered over their extravagant meal. I pretended to wander around the sandy terrain to admire the sea and cast my eyes down to survey their repasts.

The older man, deducing my ruse, greeted me in Spanish. "Buenas tardes."

Embarrassed, I said a polite hello. "What do you have here?" I pointed to their plates.

I can't remember a thing about their meals, for in the conversation that ensued I found out who this man was. He introduced himself and handed me his card. "Rafael Nietzsche," it read.

I chuckled quietly to myself. "Nietzsche."

"Yes," he smiled. "I am one of his descendants."

Now who is going to believe a story like that? "Yeah, you know one time? In Honduras? I met a descendant of Nietzsche."

The girls were swallowed up by the village kids. They ran around the soft sandy grounds of the restaurant, jumping off logs and climbing trees. They asked us if they could go swimming, but we were so tired and dreamy we held them off. After a time, I relented. "Okay, let's check out the water." No one ever swam until given the say-so, and they accepted this rule without complaint. The restaurant was bound by a low, white canvas barricade. Outside the barrier, mounds and mounds of garbage had been hidden from sight the whole time. Although hundreds of people frolicked at the beach (including Ivan's son) we said a resolute "No" to the girls.

Instead, they tagged along with a gaggle of local children, who became engrossed in the calamity of the public bus loaded with people on their way back to San Pedro Sula that got itself good and stuck in the soft sand.

Lloyd shook his head. "They will be there all day unless they dig out the wheels."

The girls sat on a cinderblock ledge with the local kids and laughed at the men who spent the better part of the day tying ropes to trucks to tow the bus out of the sand. The cables snapped as soon as the driver hit the gas. It didn't seem to have occurred to them to ask the passengers to get out.

OMOA

Based on a good review in our guidebook, we hailed a taxi for the quick trip to Omoa, a coastal town fifteen kilometers away, to find a hostel, reputedly the best in Honduras, featuring camping sites, bicycles, kayaks, hammocks, and a shared kitchen. Our genial Honduran driver dropped us at the door of let's just call it Yohan's Place, where encounters with friendly Hondurans came to an end. A surly woman opened the gate impatiently, and without so much as a hello motioned curtly to the terrain where we could pitch our tent. The carefully tended landscaping attracted hummingbirds to fuchsia bromeliads. The cold-water bathrooms were spotless. We had access to kayaks, bicycles, and ping pong, as the guidebook had promised. If not for the black atmosphere proffered by the nasty owners, it would have been perfect.

We arranged our sleeping bags and air mattresses to accommodate growing limbs. Natalie tossed and turned and complained of a sore ear throughout the night. She could only sleep on one side as a result. My wet lungs had also decided to reactivate, and the congestion extended to the entire respiratory tract. To top it off, Lloyd's air mattress had sprung a leak. He took it down to the beach the next day, and with the girls' help, found a small puncture and patched it up. I stayed out of the water, still harboring the stubborn skin infection on my foot that would not go away.

For our second night, we decided that Natalie and I would rent two indoor beds to get some proper rest. Even with the extra expenditure, Omoa was a budgeter's dream come true, if only because there was nothing for sale. Tuk tuks, those three-wheeled motorized tricycles, shuttled people up and down the road from the main shopping district to the beach.

Back and forth we putt-putted, looking for groceries. The local greengrocer held up his hands apologetically in front of bare shelves, explaining that Omoa was a resort town. He told us that our arrival on a Monday coincided with the migration of shop owners back to San Pedro Sula and suggested I return on Wednesday when the town was gearing up for the weekend.

I dispatched Lloyd to Puerto Cortés where he relieved our bank account of more garage sale money and loaded up his backpack with essentials from a large grocery store. Having no dead body to lug around this time, the ordeal lasted only a couple of hours.

I pounded the pavement of town looking for a pharmacy to buy something to relieve our discomforts. Using the ear scope I'd brought with me (one of our best decisions—it helped locate ants that wandered in and out of auditory canals as people slept), I'd deduced that Natalie's pain was a result of an ear infection, not trauma from the swing at Pulhapanzak, as feared. In addition, both of us were wheezing through the night, so I added allergy medication to the list as well.

The pharmacy was closed, of course, so I impatiently waited until Wednesday, then Thursday before I caught sight of workmen dismantling the interior. The greengrocer, who had become a tourist information service of sorts, told me it had shut down.

"Is there another one?" I wanted to avoid having to go all the way to Puerto Cortés.

"Maybe along the highway," was all he said.

After another fitful night, I resolved to find it. I toiled along the side of the road in the direction I hoped was correct. The heat came off the asphalt in waves, and I kept walking and walking, seeing nothing but industrial sites and the odd gas station. Now I was worrying about my electrolytes, having underestimated the distance from town. I stopped in at a convenience store to buy Gatorade. Between gulps, I asked the girls behind the counter if they knew of a pharmacy.

They pointed to a house across the road.

"At that *house*?"

"Sí," they said.

How in the world would I have found it? I wondered.

I was now weary and angry. How could a decent sized town not have a bloody pharmacy in a central location? The bad attitude of the hostel owners and the complete lack of food in Omoa was making me irritable. *I have two children to feed. Why am I traipsing halfway back to Puerto Cortés on this searing highway looking for a pharmacy?* And so on.

In this frame of mind, after little sleep, I unloaded my frustration on the pharmacist. "I do not understand why there is no pharmacy in town," I said, but I was rude and blunt with this man. He recognized my agitation immediately and treated me with the utmost respect and kindness. I then noticed that he had trouble using his arm and was obviously disabled. Embarrassed, I lowered my voice. Hadn't I taught the girls to be respectful of others? What would they think of my behavior? I was ashamed of myself. I hung my head and apologized to him. "Perdóname."

He waved his good hand, insisting I think no more about it. He gathered up my items and calculated my total, but because of my Gatorade purchase, I was now unable to pay this man what I owed. I had a choice: walk all the way back to town to get more money or give up one of the medications.

He made another suggestion. "I can sell you one adult dose of allergy capsules." He took a pair of scissors to show that he could cut two tablets from the blister package and charge me one-eighth the price. In the end, I bought glycerin drops for the sore ear and a bottle of children's allergy medicine. Natty and I would share it, with me almost having to swallow the whole bottle of the sickly-sweet substance to make up an adult dose.

Lloyd and the girls were waiting for me at the junction so we could take a tuk tuk together back to the hostel. One look at my face was enough for them to know I was not having the greatest time in Omoa.

For the girls, the kayaking and biking all over town was a blast. They went out with their dad every day, lugging the kayaks down to the beach using one of Yohan's pull carts or cycling here and there. Natty had only just learned to ride without training wheels back in Quebrada Ganado, so it was impossible for her to use Yohan's adult-sized bikes. She got a break riding double on Lloyd's seat. I spent my time swaying drunkenly in a hammock recovering from the effects of the medication. After staring dreamily at the trees for hours, I wrestled my way inelegantly out of the hammock, staggered down to the beach, and watched the gang kayaking. The skin on my foot had been blistering off and on since Parismina, some eighteen months ago, breaking a world record, it's safe to say.

The girls took to kayaking like the jellyfish took to the water directly beneath them. I was relieved they had something to do in the ocean other than swim. The filthiness of the beach notwithstanding, they paddled through dozens of jellyfish, which is why I didn't want them in the water.

Omoa's claim to fame was an ancient fort, built several hundred years ago as a lookout for invading Europeans. It didn't hold the girls' interest; they were having a much better time zipping around town with Lloyd or paddling in the water. Back at Yohan's they challenged each other to ping pong games and foosball tournaments when they weren't cringing from the owner's abusive rampages. He lost his mind throughout the day, flinging chairs in a rage to clear a path to the light switch. "Do you know how expensive electricity is?" he screamed. A British couple became the target of his wrath because, rumor had it, his wife didn't like them. They returned from supper and found their belongings in a heap on the grass. The next morning, every single guest checked out. So much for guidebook recommendations.

Since the ferry to Belize only ran once a week, we were stuck in Omoa for three more days. I set out to find alternative accommodations, drifting off to the side streets, most of them covered with a thick layer of sand. Rounding a corner, down a lane two blocks from the beach, I read a sign advertising a hostel. I entered what looked like a factory, and an American expat named

Tommy greeted me. Tommy ran a hostel and operated a handicrafts factory making hash pipes in a large common room on the main floor.

In selling the idea of staying somewhere that made drug paraphernalia I said to Lloyd, "The girls are too young to understand what they're making. Besides, there is nowhere else to stay in this town."

"I couldn't care less," he declared. "I'm never going back to Yohan's."

Instead of rolling every piece of clothing carefully into our packs and unbeknownst to Yohan, we used the bikes one last time to lug our gear, like a convoy of the homeless, over to the new hostel, things stuffed carelessly into plastic bags dangling from handlebars.

Ten dollars a night was all we were charged for a large, empty room. We each staked out a corner, arranged air mattresses and sleeping sacks, and organized our individual possessions—me stacking travel guides and maps beside my pillow, the girls zipping open their pouches to unleash imagination into kingdoms, Lloyd grabbing a bottle of water to hydrate, then secreting the bikes back to Yohan's, in broad daylight.

The atmosphere at Tommy's was light-years different. We all lived communally, eating together, chatting until the wee hours. Luckily for the girls, an American family with four kids was also staying there. Ron, a divorced father of four, had already spent a few weeks traipsing through northern Honduras. I admired his unflappable ex-wife, who had allowed him to take their children, aged four to ten, on a chicken bus tour of their own. He had found a remote Garifuna village and was describing how inviting it was when one of the young artisans, who lived and worked at Tommy's, suggested visiting another.

"Where is it?" Ron asked.

"Past that town you were just talking about," came the reply.

"Oh," Ron said, surprised. "I didn't know there was a *past that*."

"Lloyd nudged me, whispering, "They have definitely earned their traveling stripes."

The next day, the sunny skies of Omoa turned black, so we retreated indoors, reading our collection of novels. The six kids played outside in the rain, happy as clams. The rest of us remained inside, floating on the whisper of Bob Marley playing in the background. When the day came to depart for Dangriga, Tommy taxied us to Puerto Cortés in a deluge.

PUERTO CORTÉS

During our final three days in Omoa, it had rained nonstop. The cool air was not a great motivator for taking a cold shower, and because the girls had been playing in the mud with their friends, we insisted that at least their feet were washed every night. We were looking forward to warmer weather where a cold shower wouldn't feel as torturous on our sweaty bodies. Or, could I dare hope to have hot water at the next port of call?

The day of our exodus from Honduras was miserable and grey, like our moods. Tommy drove us to Puerto Cortés in a run-down van that had not seen updating since the seventies. We sat in the back on the shag carpet-covered bench seat, and Tommy fired up on his eight-track player.

Our ferry to Dangriga, a Garifuna coastal community midway between Honduras and Mexico, left at 10:00. "You know," Tommy shouted over the music, "the boat may not leave at all because of rough seas."

I rested my head against the carpeted wall of the van. I was torn between waiting one more week to ensure better weather or sucking it up and taking the plunge, so to speak. We pulled up to the port as the rain let up, lifting my spirits.

The dock was a hideous mess, with garbage strewn about so liberally that it was a miracle no one sprained an ankle. The boat, sporting a triple outboard motor, could hold about thirty people. In the hull, we sat on benches attached to the starboard and port sides. The overcast day attracted about two dozen people making the journey along with us. The port was calm which helped my nerves. The skipper, I noticed, could not have been more than twenty-five years old. He untied and motored away from the dock. The girls knelt on the bench seats to peer out at the sea. Not long afterwards we entered open water. The boat pitched violently, initiating a fit of giggles from the girls, but within minutes, they were green.

The deckhand motioned emphatically for all passengers to slide carefully along the benches to the stern. The bow was rising and falling so viciously, we were centimeters away from smacking our heads on the ceiling. My heart raced. Even though I had given the whole family three doses of a homeopathic sea sickness remedy, Jocelyn became overwhelmed. The deckhand hauled her like a sack of potatoes to the outer deck where she could vomit in privacy, followed by a staggering Lloyd, who was unable to transfer her for fear of smashing them both into a steel frame or dumping her into the lap of a passenger.

They remained out there for the duration of the trip—Jocelyn's head lolling drunkenly over Lloyd's arms to vomit into a garbage bag with the least amount of effort. I wallowed in maternal guilt for several days afterwards.

Natalie and I clung to each other—me, looking desperately for the horizon, she, exacting a vice grip on my hand. After about thirty minutes she wanted to lie down, which she did and then promptly went to sleep. I couldn't even help her negotiate a comfortable position as my breakfast was at the brink. The deckhand dashed over to help her lie down then stayed by her side so she wouldn't fly off at every bump.

For two hours we endured this, rising then free falling into the abyss until the hard crash-landing of the hull against the water initiated the cycle all over again. I nervously questioned the safety of a sustained elevated heart rate (I was, after all, in my forties). I mentally thanked my local gym back home for allowing me those hours to blunder through my machinations on the Stairmaster. "Maybe my ticker has half a chance," I thought.

Once, I risked a glance down the deck for a check on my other child, but I was forced to rake my eyes back to the window, searching frantically for the undulating horizon. I played mind games with myself, trying to guess how many minutes had gone by since the last time I checked my watch. I questioned every person's sanity that had ever sailed. Ever.

After what seemed like a thousand and one hours, I saw a break in the clouds, and I chanced a look forward. There, before us, lay Belize. Belize with her turquoise waters, blue skies, and glassy sea. The violent pendulum of the boat's journey now evened out. The atmosphere of the cabin lightened. The passengers, at first stonily silent, uncoiled themselves from each other and began chatting and introducing themselves. I left Natalie with the God-sent deckhand and went to check on the two outside. Jocelyn had fallen asleep as well (Will children never cease to amaze?).

Lloyd had his arms around her. "The spray has drenched her to the skin."

I lurched back into the cabin to fish out dry clothes from our packs and when I returned, she lifted her pathetic face and smiled into mine. Natalie had subsequently woken up and was guided to us by successive hands. We stretched out our chilly bodies under the sun's rays, periodically leaning over the side to check our approach to Dangriga.

Lloyd and I barely spoke a word to each other. "I can't talk about this right now," I muttered.

What could be said? We were safe. Hairy moments aside, we were together doing what we had dreamed of doing. The Travel Team had gained another notch on the belt of life.

Chapter 14

Belize

IN DANGRIGA, WE FOUND clapboard houses lining the shore and palms sprouting from well-tended lawns. Folks shouted hello to us as we wobbled to customs on sea legs. In orderly fashion, our group of shell-shocked passengers presented our passports and stated that we had nothing to declare. No one accosted us on the way. No one tried to sell us useless baubles or waved lottery tickets in our faces.

Natalie, alert and gawking after having slept for most of the trip, asked me, "Why are there so many black people here?" I was self-conscious about answering, apprehensive of unintended insensitivity, especially here where English was understood. Alas, my fatigue and history-bereft brain only managed a weak and inadequate response to what is assuredly an interesting and complicated history.

Jocelyn was a wet rag. Waiting our turn at the wicket, she whispered. "Mommy, I have to go to the bathroom."

The professional if not stuffy customs officer shook his head when I asked him if there were washrooms. "No bathrooms for the public here." He perused our passports and scrutinized our faces.

I bent down and spoke softly in Jocelyn's ear. "You'll have to wait until we get to the hotel."

The officer, now realizing my request originated from a child, regarded her rumpled hair sticking to her skull and skinny legs sticking out of an oversized sweatshirt (the first one I could find to warm her up was one of mine) and immediately changed his mind, lifted the counter to let her through, and escorted her to the back of the office.

Seaside cabinas felt luxurious after grungy hostels. The balcony overlooked the azure water spilling over pristine white sand. The reason the beach was kept so clean, it turned out, was because the little man who raked it during the day told the girls to stop ruining his work by playing and digging in the sand. From the balcony, we watched the beach custodian rake the sand, then meticulously smooth it over. When he left for the day, Lloyd told the girls to go down and play, and then later, he smoothed every grain back to its original location, hoping the caretaker wouldn't notice the next morning when he repeated his routine all over again.

The next day, for a lark, we went to Marie Sharp's Hot Sauce factory to study Belizean cultural practices, of course. The popular sauce, topping every restaurant table in the country, comes in the following flavors: *Mild, Hot, Fiery Hot, Comatose, Beware,* and *No Wimps Allowed.* We preferred *Mild.*

An employee took us on a brief tour that strayed right into the middle of the production line. The girls sniggered at each other in their protective hair caps. The hostess then took us back to the office. A desk had been cleared and piled with crackers, napkins, water, and all variations of the sauce for us to sample. From this experiment, we selected gifts for family members back home.

"Papa will be the only one who likes this one," Jocelyn said, pointing to *Fiery Hot.*

Over time, we ate up all the gifts and had to re-buy everything at a grocery store. We had no reason to stay in Dangriga; we were destined for Tikal, our most anticipated destination, so *Star Wars* fans—heads up.

SAN IGNACIO

Leaving the turquoise-water white-sand-beach town of Dangriga for San Ignacio, about twenty kilometers from Guatemala, we observed stark differences in the landscape from the window of the comfy (but still chicken) bus. The road ascended to green foothills and, the guidebook stated, these hills were full of unexcavated Mayan ruins and caves to explore.

Of course, all this was available to the adventure traveler at a steep price. Belize surpassed all other countries in terms of cost. Lloyd commented that we had blown through $400 in five days, about half of that was the cost of the horrendous voyage from Honduras. At the outset, backpacking along the Caribbean coast of Costa Rica, we were living on $600 per month. The current rate of spending was atrocious.

In this vein, San Ignacio presented some problems. It was chock full of persons, like us, making their way to Tikal, further west over the border approximately two hours. The town was overrun with lodgers of all stripes taking up beds at the budget hotels. We sat at a café poring over guidebook recommendations with one of us pacing the streets to inquire into vacancies. Nothing, nada. One entry—in the by now dog-eared *Lonely Planet Central America on a Shoestring*—suggested as a last resort the O'tel Central.

Lloyd read the recommendation out loud to me.

"What, they couldn't even afford all the letters?" I said.

He scanned the street. "It should be nearby . . ." Chalk one up for the Travel Team's map skills, O'tel Central was located directly next door to the café.

"C'mon Natalie." I took her by the hand. "Gotta try for the cute-kid discount."

We climbed a slanted staircase and found a rather sad excuse for a hotel. The linoleum was probably laid in just after the war, and I ducked my head now and again to avoid low-hanging beams, but we'd stayed in worse. Besides, they had vacancies. Cute-kid discount worked, too.

A redeeming feature of the o'tel was the balcony that hung over the main drag of San Ignacio. I studied the hustle and bustle of the townspeople on the street below, judging it an excellent perspective from which to take photos or absorb the rhythm of the community. The bathrooms, stationed down a dark hallway at the back, were clean, if a little outdated. The showers, designed with giants in mind, functioned by way of a shutoff valve anchored on the ceiling. "You are going to get drenched trying to turn on the water for the girls," Lloyd noted.

I tried not to be glum about it. I flopped down on the balcony hammock, sulking. The girls spread out their toys beside me on a little table. I lay there leafing through a magazine, perusing ads for accommodations on Belize's islands, called *cayes*, when Lloyd came out. "I've got two words for you," he said, holding up one finger then the other. "Hot . . . water."

So as crappy as the o'tel was, and despite the rudimentary plumbing, I got my hot shower after all.

Chapter 15

Guatemala

Star Wars fans get ready...

We left organized Belize for the pandemonium of the Guatemalan border. Better prepared than most, we could speak Spanish and Lloyd employed a favorite technique: he changed money on the bus itself when money changers embarked near the border. Then, when we disembarked, both of us were free to supervise the girls in the mayhem. This way he wasn't putting us at risk by exposing the secret locations of our hard-earned garage sale cash. This time, we were over-confident. We successfully changed our Belizean dollars into Guatemalan quetzales on the bus at the same time the Guatemalan border officials were scoping out the rich gringos to scam.

After going all the way through customs, we waited at the side of the road for a taxi. I asked Lloyd, "They charged us the wrong entrance fee, didn't they?"

When we factored it out, the customs officer who could clearly see that we were a family traveling with two young children, had overcharged us by many quetzales. Ironically, this is known as the "gringo discount." We had been duped. Worse still, we learned later that *no one* had to pay to enter Guatemala. This incident would be forbidden in Belize, as the entire process is clearly spelled out by large signs that inform the traveler of the exact amount owing at the window.

The road leading to Flores alternated between gravel, potholes, and speed bumps. The driver gave his best shot at dangerous driving. We endured this trip, mashed in a *colectivo*, a decaying van full of passengers, and pulled up just shy of two hours later in Flores, a town used mostly as a base from which to explore Tikal. The hostel was funky; dorms were furnished with sagging bunk beds and Guatemalan blankets. They were doing a roaring business selling good food and strong drinks. The girls circulated throughout, speaking with people and looking at the ornate carvings on the walls. We ran into old friends from previous hostels who were also following the gringo trail. By now our adventure by chicken bus was becoming well-known, and we felt rather conspicuous, almost embarrassed. Total strangers approached us and said, "I've heard about you guys. You're *that* family."

Conversations went something like this:

Q: Where are you from?

A: Canada

Q: How long have you been traveling?

A: Eighteen months.

Q: (*gulp*) With two kids? The whole time?

A: Yes

After two days in Flores, I suggested to Lloyd that we depart for Tikal from a village called El Remate, the closest community to Tikal, consisting of nothing more than a few guest houses and lodges. I'd been feeling a little under the weather and said, "There's no hurry. Let's stop at El Remate first so I can recover. If I feel better, we can go to Tikal tomorrow."

"All right," he agreed. Then he mentioned, flipping through the guidebook, "There's a guesthouse called El Mirador that overlooks Lake Petén Itzá."

Our taxi drove through a melee of vendors weaving in and out of traffic and deposited us at the tailgate of the El Remate bound bus, or so we thought.

"Wait," Lloyd said. "These guys seem overly happy to see us."

Because backpackers usually travel long distances by chicken bus and short distances by taxi, and we typically travel in packs, a sizable sum for both ayudante and driver materialized before them in the form of the four-person Travel Team.

"Can you ask the ayudante if this bus is going to El Remate?" Lloyd said.

Twice I did so. He nodded his head and mumbled an affirmation, hoisting the packs on top of the bus to tie them down. We were semi-familiar with the route, having passed near El Remate when we traveled from the Belizean border a couple of days before. However, if this colectivo was going back to the border, we would miss El Remate by a couple of kilometers, forcing us to walk the rest of the way.

I walked around to the front of the bus. The destination emblazoned on the bus's window indicated that this colectivo was most certainly *not* going to El Remate. Apparently, we had been delivered to a colectivo that was going to the border. In his determination to fill the van, the driver was willing to mislead us. Lloyd climbed up himself to untie the bags, and we trudged to our correct bus. We stopped off for one night at El Mirador, a simple guest house constructed high up on a cliff across from the eastern tip of Lake Petén Itzá.

TIKAL

This was it. The culmination of our adventure, to see the granddaddy of pyramids at Tikal. We woke the next morning and packed our cast of *Star Wars* action figures and descended to the street where our colectivo was waiting to shuttle us to Tikal National Park, one of the most well-known UNESCO World Heritage sites in Latin America.

Accommodations at Tikal itself were limited and the price exceeded our budget at seventy-five dollars per night. We unfurled the tent, dormant since Yohan's. As Lloyd and Natalie set up camp, Lloyd called out to me, "Both adult air mattresses are leaking, now."

"Do we have any duct tape?" I asked.

It was a strange arrangement, middle- to upper-class vacationers staying at the hotel with backpackers strewn willy-nilly on the lawn, in scruffy tents (some with duct-taped air mattresses), preparing one-pot meals over compact stoves.

Jocelyn and I packed water and snacks for the first foray to see the ruins. Just as we finished lathering sunscreen on noses, a few spider monkeys zipped by, leaping and swinging overhead. One flung itself into the trees above the girls' heads with such reckless abandon that the branch bowed low in an arc to about one foot in front of them. On the backswing, he boomeranged up into the air, catapulting in somersaults to the next limb.

"Show off," Natalie muttered.

After that display, our lackluster method of locomotion advanced us to the procession of people crowding the footpath to the entrance. We would tackle half the park on this afternoon and then spend the next full day exploring the second half. The park is so vast that despite the mobs, one could go without meeting another person for several minutes.

"The girls seem a little indifferent," Lloyd remarked on our way to the Great Plaza. "Have you noticed?"

"Maybe we've done so much already," I said. "What's one more hike?"

They were so indifferent, in fact, that they were unaware of their ridiculous parents.

"Can you translate this sign, please?" Lloyd asked along a shadowy portion of the trail.

"It's something like 'Beware of Pumas,'" I said. "And that's not the first warning I've seen."

Then Lloyd and I both gasped when, out of the corners of our eyes, we both spotted a fuzzy black tail (?) and/or a snarling head (?) in the forest.

Lloyd said, relieved, "Just a bird."

Between Temple I and Temple II on the Great Plaza we assembled our cast of characters to present Chewbacca with his long overdue medal.

"Yes," Lloyd breathed. "This is exactly the place."

Star Wars fans know what I'm talking about. In the first movie, Princess Leia presents Han Solo and Luke Skywalker with medals of bravery for their participation in defeating the Empire. The awards ceremony takes place on Yavin 4, a jungle-covered moon in which Tikal was used during filming as the backdrop for the arrival of the Millennium Falcon. In the final scene, Chewie follows Han and Luke in a procession to the dais. Even though his involvement with the rebel forces was critical to their success, Chewbacca is denied a medal. Many theories exist about why this happened. Let's just say this family of die-hard fans was not going to stand for it any longer. The main players were in attendance: Luke, Han, Leia, Chewie, the droids, still in good shape from Lloyd's forty-year-old collection of action figures that the girls had adopted and brought all the way from Canada for this purpose.

After the formalities, I reposed on the grass, watching the girls hop up and down the steps of the temples. I admit I was feeling a little smug at our accomplishments and sought out Lloyd's praises.

"Can you believe all that we've done?" I asked him as he dropped down beside me.

But his mind was on his first love. "Well, it was worth it, to give Chewie his due."

That night we ate at the cheap staff restaurant while the mosquitoes had their meal of our bare legs underneath the tables. Afterwards, we spent a quiet night at the hotel restaurant playing board games and talking to other travelers. When we went to bed, the duct tape proved inadequate so, overcome by stupidity, I suggested, "Let's leave the air mattresses in their usual positions and turn ourselves ninety degrees, so at least some parts of our bodies are resting on air."

In practice, this meant that each of us was lying on four separate air mattresses, some sections of which were semi-inflated. The girls were intrigued by the novelty of this idea, but after one hour, I had had enough of suffering everyone's smallest adjustments, so I sucked it up and went back to my floppy mattress. In the morning, we were a tumble of limbs and sore necks.

"A good long and hot hike should work out the kinks," I said to the gang overenthusiastically, ignoring glares.

The crowds had swelled to near-full capacity, creating a human traffic jam at junctures. Lloyd was relieved to see that ascending to the top of Temple IV was progressing slowly. Along the gringo trail, we'd met no one over the age of thirty. Most backpackers were young people closer in age to Jocelyn and Natalie than to Lloyd and me. The demographic in Tikal, on the other hand, included overweight Anglos pushing sixty-five. "I hope I can remember my CPR training when it comes time to use it," Lloyd said.

He threaded the girls into the queue leading to Temple IV. Plodding up the wooden stairs to the summit, we stopped from time to time to catch our breath and call out words of encouragement to each other; the climb was *that* steep. The day before, we had become friendly with a traveling family from the US with an adorable three-year-old. The grandfather, a largish man with some form of disability in his leg, was the only member of his clan to confront the ascent. We gave him the verbal pat on the back he deserved as he limped past us on the way down the stairs. He flashed a smile that lit up his face, in an air of self-congratulation.

"See?" Lloyd gasped. "If that old guy can do it, then we can backpack for the rest of our lives."

"Sure." Like I've stated before, if there was one thing we never argued about . . .

One of the tallest structures in the Mayan world, the pyramid was built to mark the reign of the twenty-seventh king of the Tikal dynasty, Yik'in Chan K'awiil. Up there, as in times past, I felt an overwhelming urge to sing, this time I hummed The Carpenters' "Top of the World."

The panorama spread out like a carpet of emerald before us. Only the tops of the tallest pyramids stuck out above the tree line, as if the jungle had swallowed them whole. And it had. Photos indicate that several feet of plant life cover the structures, creating sharp, triangular mountains of green, as we had seen at the Parque Eco-arqueológico Los Naranjos in Honduras. According to the Smithsonian, only 15 percent of Tikal has been excavated. To think how governments of these countries could do so much more for their citizens and the international community if they unearthed more of these ancient ruins and created a living museum.

Atop Temple IV, we breathed in the clear jungle air and mused about the sheer number of people who traveled this far off the beaten path for a momentary glimpse of the top of the world—Central American version, that is. I thought about travel agencies, showcasing glossy pages of white sand beaches and icy cocktails. From the most solitary regions in Costa Rica, such as the island of Parismina, to the isolated monkey sanctuary of Mono Feliz in Panama, we saw the imprint of visitors before us, people like us, who were looking into every nook and cranny to discover the value of other cultures. We had tried our best to learn about a region's history, as we had done in Estelí. We encouraged the girls to become involved in meaningful ways, like participating in the turtle conservation program or offering to teach English.

That day, on Temple IV, it struck me that from now on we would be confronted with mobs of people. We would be visiting some of the most touristed places on earth. After the temples of Tikal, we planned to stay on Caye Caulker in Belize then tour the Mayan Riviera in Mexico. I was nostalgic for the places we visited with few souls about, like Playa Punta Uva in Costa Rica or Volcán in Panama.

Descending from Temple IV, we picked our way through the masses to Mundo Perdido or Lost World. At one time, Mundo Perdido was a "complex for astronomical commemoration," a lofty way of saying "location for star gazing." The structure was much, much shorter than Temple IV, but the climb to the summit was dangerous. Each riser was probably three feet in height, the tread only one foot in width. People raised their arms in victory as they summited, some one hundred feet from the floor of the jungle. I sat on a bench and covered my face with my hands, not daring to watch. I was so afraid someone would topple over, taking several people out on the way down in a macabre form of bowling for gringos.

Lloyd gripped the girls' hands. "We're only going up two steps."

Afterwards, I asked the girls what they thought of Tikal, especially after we had touted it so much. Jocelyn said, "Amazing."

Natalie said, "There was too much. It was overwhelming."

I had a feeling maybe we'd overhyped it. Several weeks later, I overheard her describing Tikal as "great."

We recuperated from two days of hiking and perpendicular camping by rehydrating at a plastic table outside the hotel, waiting for a colectivo to take us back to El Mirador. Now that Tikal was over and done with, the reality that our trip was coming to an end was sinking in. Lloyd was receiving emails from work. More heart wrenching were the messages from friends and family calling us home. By now we were keeping one eye on the forecast back in Canada and the other on the shrinking bank account.

A middle-aged American couple commented to us from the next table. "Wow, is this all you're traveling with?" They pointed to our packs.

"No," I replied. "This is all we own."

EL REMATE

El Remate was heavenly quiet; not even a rooster interrupted our slumber. El Mirador sat at the top of several flights of steep stone steps, far away from the noisy street below. In a feat of admirable Guatemalan feng shui, the owner had designed the open-air rooms and dining area so that they all overlooked Lake Petén Itzá. Each night at dusk one could simply lay on their bed to watch the wavy red ball sink into the crystal water.

Sweaty, tired, and dogs a-barking, we slogged up that staircase. After Tikal, inflicting one last feat of physical exertion on the girls seemed torturous, but we needed peace and quiet after the mobs and the sleepless night in the tent. Not only did the owner have an eye for vistas, he made an honest living attending to the weary traveler, offering comfy beds, hot showers, laundry facilities, and a pretty decent restaurant.

Two days later, we bundled up our gear yet again (by now, we could pack four backpacks and two daypacks in under ten minutes) and got a lift to the crossroads of the busy highway to wait for a colectivo to take us to Melchor, the busy border town.

Jocelyn, Natalie, and I waited at the T-junction on a grassy island to gain a better perspective of oncoming traffic. When we spotted a colectivo, we called out to Lloyd, who was standing facing traffic, on the bend, to flag down the driver, who stopped happily as you can imagine, seeing four gringos standing on the roadside.

Lloyd turned away three dangerously sardined mini-buses. Then, a colectivo disgorged two passengers, but it turned out to be a woman who stepped off momentarily to vomit into a bag. She quickly wiped her mouth, and then got back in the van. After a couple of hours, when we thought about giving up and returning to El Mirador, a colectivo came by that appeared to have some space.

In an almost disastrous turn of events, Lloyd motioned us over to board the van, but when I called for the girls to follow me across the road, Jocelyn stayed behind on the island.

I called over to her. "What are you doing?" She snapped out of her reverie, looked up, saw me waiting, and ran across the road.

Along the highway, in the opposite direction, a large coach was lumbering directly for her.

Lloyd screamed, "Jocelyn!"

I shrieked, "Look! Look!"

She jogged in front of the bus and reached me the moment it coasted past. Lloyd wedged us into the van. I was numb with shock. For the first half of the two-hour trip, I clutched Jocelyn to me, thinking of nothing other than, "She came to me when I called her. It would have been my fault if she had been hit by the bus."

She looked up at me with her brown, puppy dog eyes. "I saw the bus, Mommy. I knew I could make it."

Soon, the horror of that moment wore off because my mind was ripped from its state of shock and jolted into full fight-or-flight mode as it dawned on me that the terrible roads were not slowing our driver down. He drove in madness, unconcerned about ruts or gaping potholes. While we bounced and jarred our way to Melchor, Lloyd threw his hands up in disgust. A small rock, a piece of wood, a darting child, any of these would have been enough to alter the forces of physics we were clinging to on that mini-bus. Wasn't it Newton who declared, "Every object in a state of uniform motion tends to remain in that state of motion unless an external force is applied to it"? Of course, in this case, if the vehicle's path was altered abruptly, the objects remaining in motion would be the human bodies pitching forward (and out the front windshield). What could they be thinking of, to drive that hazardously?

When we refused to ride the local buses because they were too unsafe, did locals think we were spoiled brats? Trying to learn about another culture, especially in the developing world, includes these harsh realities, but there must be limits. The American family we had become friendly with (the patriarch was the slightly disabled grandpa we had congratulated on the scaffolding of Temple IV) had once insisted their driver change the bald front tire of the van before they would agree to get in. He was in danger of losing four full adult fares if he didn't comply. The tire was changed.

Chapter 16

Back to Belize

IN A FOUL STATE of mind, we skidded into Melchor de Mencos, a town adjacent to the border. Crossing back into Belize here was accomplished in an homage to the Keystone Cops. We could have walked to the customs window, but with rubber legs from hiking Tikal, we hailed a cab. The short distance should have made the journey a breeze, but the taxi driver managed to botch the job anyway, letting us all out of the car and driving away with the trunk open and half our bags still inside. He drove around the corner out of sight, and after we caught up to him, he apologized, claiming he was afraid of getting a citation from the border police.

Entering Belize, we sensed an immediate drop in our heart rates. Formalities felt more organized and no-nonsense. For example, negotiating a taxi fare from the border is not an option. Fees to destinations are clearly marked on a large sign at the exit, as our driver pointed out when Lloyd asked him about it.

We stayed over at a hostel known as the Trek Stop for one night. While the girls spent long hours in the onsite insect museum poking around at food chain models and checking out the butterfly garden, I persuaded Lloyd that we should travel to one of the islands, referred to as cayes (pronounced "keys").

Technically, boarding a ferry to putter past islands poking up out of the Caribbean before landing at Caye Caulker should have been a cakewalk. However, competing for a berth with every other pasty-faced vacationer looking for a little sun complicated matters. At the last minute we were refused passage on the first boat because a bus full of all-inclusive holiday makers pulled up. As we became swept away in the mayhem, they were swept right onto the boat, filling it to capacity. Ninety minutes later we jockeyed for position again, trying to fend off late arrivals that suspiciously received preferential treatment. The sun had reached its zenith and was drifting over the horizon by the time a third tour group arrived. They muscled right by our motley group of backpackers who, by now, had been waiting four hours. My mind went into damage control, trying to remember the name of the hotel recommended in Belize City. The guidebook bluntly suggested that one try hard *not* to stay in the city overnight.

The current offense was not going unnoticed by an American couple we had met at the Trek Stop. "Oh no," shouted the male counterpart, "Not again you don't!" He shouldered his way past sweaty, unsuspecting Brits who were unacquainted with our circumstances. He was infuriated; we had been waiting all afternoon for this—the last boat out to the island.

The dockworker calmed us down. "They gonna send another boat." Immediately after that, we were told to line up in front of the Brits and hand over our bags. Then we *all* boarded, which goes to show that information is as cheap as the rum. But it calmed down angry Americans.

Lloyd was disturbed by the grievous overcrowding. As it was, the four of us were the only ones wearing life jackets. He leaned over and shouted above the noise of the motors. "I'll take your pack. Get up to that hostel before anyone else to snatch the last beds, if there are any left!"

Good point. He gave me verbal instructions on how to locate the hostel from what he remembered of the map printed in the guidebook. He needn't have bothered. It sat directly on the emerald shore at the end of the pier.

Without question this was the best location on the island, and at thirty dollars a night for the four of us, a treasure. I hustled in, a little out of breath, and found the congenial manager, who offered us the last four beds in the dorm. By the time the rest of the family showed up, I had claimed a bottom bunk and was taking a tour.

As usual, the presence of our children became an advantage. "I've got an upstairs apartment you can use for a couple of days for the same price if you want," the manager said. The apartment had its own deck, a kitchen, separate bedroom, private bathroom, living room, and television. We had an unobstructed view of the sea with its impossibly blue-green water and sumptuous sunrise.

On Caye Caulker, we expended energy in rigorous endeavors, such as playing chess, reading in a hammock, lying in a hammock, and napping. A small dock next to the hostel's sandy yard jutted out over the water, supporting chaise lounges and hammocks that faced the sea. From this vantage point, you could admire the Caribbean with nothing obstructing your sight line. I'm telling you it was all one could do to keep reading. Every so often, I would lower my book, look out at the ocean, and breathe, "Honestly!"

But Belize does not hold a monopoly on beauty. The ribbon of cerulean-blue Caribbean coastline, extending from the Yucatán, south and then east past the entry to the Panama Canal, was notched with deserted shores and interspersed with overpopulated tourist traps on the one hand and insulated Indigenous villages on the other. This pattern continues along the coast all the way to the tip of South America where the Caribbean Sea washes up onto the beaches of Colombia and Venezuela.

One night back at Rocking J's a bunch of us were swinging in hammocks and sharing stories. A young Scottish woman and her British traveling companion entertained us with tales of teaching English throughout South America, even though, as the British half of the duo declared boozily, pointing to her Scottish friend, "And she can't even speak English!"

In her thick brogue, the Scot told us that Colombia was the country she preferred over all the others. One night, she told us, the two of them had discovered a clearing along a beach where they hung their hammocks in the dark of night. In the morning they awoke, she said, and turning to me with eyes wide, exclaimed, "It was like waking up in paradise!"

Our little patch of real estate on Caye Caulker, protruding out into the middle of the ocean made me feel like we had discovered paradise, too. The entire island was pretty enough, bordered by sandy streets, the main ones pocked with shops and restaurants. Clapboard houses adorned the secondary avenues. The high school students traveled to the mainland every day. From the front window of the apartment, I could see them queuing to board the ferry alongside hundreds of passengers heading back to Belize City and their flight home.

The girls spent their days digging in the sand or examining sea life in the turtle grasses. From my hammock, I could read, admire the view, and supervise the girls in one glance. Even the island dogs expended little energy. On a typical day, two of them wandered into the yard, dug into the sand underneath a hammock, and spent the day sleeping. At times, a concerned traveler would check their breathing. After the sun had set, they popped up and went away.

The north balcony of the hostel faced the community basketball court. On our third night, Lloyd and I had an elevated front row seat for the local league's acrimonious final. The girls, having long been put to bed, were awakened when the crowd went wild during the final minutes. They stumbled out to us on the balcony to watch the losing team walk out in a huff because of a questionable call.

The next day during naps, Lloyd sat up. "Do you smell smoke?"

"Yes! And I hear sirens!" I replied.

We heard shouts in the street and the girls jumped out of bed. The four of us followed the crowd two blocks to a woman's home that had burst into flames due to a leaking propane tank. The manager of the hotel next door balled his hair into fists watching the wind blowing in his direction. Ironically, the firefighters were the same basketball players who had been quarreling with each other the night before. The mob watched in horror as they battled the flames in flip-flops and bare hands. The fire truck whipped down to the beach and sucked up seawater to battle the blaze. The flames had risen high enough to singe the leaves of the tall palms in the yard. Despite a gallant effort, the woman's home was destroyed, even with the opposing basketball players working together to avert an island-wide tragedy. The girls were in shock.

"What will she do now?" Jocelyn asked.

"I'm guessing she will stay with family for a while," Lloyd said.

We walked back to the hostel in silence. Though no human life was lost in the fire, the incident was a tragedy. What a window into human connections, I thought. "People come together when someone is in trouble, don't they?"

Natalie took my hand and her warm, smooth touch ignited in me a sense of overwhelming affection for her, so much so that I felt guilty about my remark, for I did not tell the whole truth. How could I explain to the girls that human beings all over the world are in trouble and no one comes to help them? Are we doing enough by exposing the girls to another way of life so that they would become aware? Lloyd and I often thought the problems of the world seemed insurmountable. The only solution we could think of was to support the microcosm with our dollars. We didn't have very much money, but if our family and other visitors to the island committed to spending money at local businesses on Caye Caulker, perhaps the community would be in a better position to assist this woman.

❖❖❖

Caye Caulker was popular with young party-goers. As parents, or rather, as people who have "been there, done that," we rejected cold Belikins from a couple of American backpackers; we simply could not stomach the vile brew. We integrated when we could, but some parents back home can thank us for taking care of their kids on the road. Our status as the older, more mature residents made us the go-to people for health concerns. Back in San José, at the Costa Rica Backpacker's Hostel, a young woman sought my advice about treating a dog bite. In Nicaragua, an American asked me for something to relieve her agony from sand fly bites. Now, on Caye Caulker, I scolded one of four strapping Aussies who had recently come down from Mexico but was forced to spend a night in the island infirmary. Evidently, having tried to build up his intestinal fortitude, he was felled by some bug he had obtained from the tap water.

"Never drink the water unless it is treated," I admonished.

Later that night, an American was hobbled by an invisible pothole after a boozy party. Lloyd advised him to soak the entire ankle in a bucket of ice water. The damage fouled up his travel plans; he was delayed for days as the purple foot grounded him from going to Tikal with his friends. Knowing Tikal the way we did, we agreed with his decision.

The four Aussies, back at full strength after waiting a couple of days for their mate to recover at the clinic, made a point of speaking to the girls now and then, in their affable Aussie way.

One afternoon, one of them confronted me. "Have you really been traveling for that long?" he wanted to know. "Your older daughter told me you've been on the road for a year and a half. Is that true?"

"True," I answered, "In fact, we're on our way home."

He looked taken aback. Maybe he was pondering the expense, perhaps the effort exerted to accomplish a trip of this magnitude. Here again, we felt our presence was having a positive influence on future parents. Sure, we were doing a scaled-back version of the younger generation's adventures, but we didn't feel that we were missing out on anything. On the contrary, we became caught up in the girls' enthusiasm. We'd gotten over the thrill of taking risks. Now we arranged most activities to spend as much time together as possible. Family bonding would be over soon enough. For some, being stuck with your family members every waking and sleeping minute might seem trying, but these stretches are full of novel and interesting things to do. Downtime on the road can be satisfying, too. Though there is no TV reception and patchy internet connection, there are also no bills to pay, no bathrooms to clean, no mundane nine-to-five. Truth be told, the whole trip was good for our marriage. There wasn't much wrong with it before we left, but traveling like this so intensely for such a long period gave us a sense of contentment that we were compatible under the most trying circumstances. People suggest that the real test of a good relationship is to travel with a partner, to determine if it can withstand the intensity of constant togetherness. In fact, we believe the best test of a good relationship is coping with the mundane. On the road we were energized every day because we were living out our dream, giving our girls the opportunity to learn what it means to be a citizen of the world. Now, faced with a return to our normal life, I wondered how we would manage.

The lack of contact worried our network of friends and loved ones back home. Since entering Belize the first time, after the horrid journey from Honduras, we had been unable to check emails. The last anyone knew, we were in Honduras. Now our parents had heard nothing for weeks. Lloyd was also trying to communicate with his principal, and we needed information on flights. We decided to head north to Mexico where we would return to Canada from Cancún.

I decided that leaving on the early ferry at 7:30 would give us a few hours to see Belize City before catching the bus to Mexico. In hindsight, Belize City could take a person an hour, tops. The girls were somber walking through the main park that smelled strongly of urine and accommodated many homeless men sleeping under cardboard. We frittered away the rest of our time in the bus terminal, staring at the ceiling in sheer boredom, snapping at each other, picking dirt from under our fingernails.

"We had better break out desperate measures," I told Lloyd.

Without a word, he zipped open his day pack and unfolded a pad of *Mad Libs* that had been left behind in our Caribbean apartment. Thus, we spent our morning expostulating verbs, nouns, and adjectives at Lloyd's solicitation, waiting for our bus to Chetumal, over the Mexican border, where we planned to spend the last of our days at the beach until our flight home from Cancún.

Chapter 17

Mexico

The Philip Goldson Highway from Belize City to Chetumal ran parallel to the sea until it strayed inland. Through gaps in the palms we glimpsed the turquoise ocean from the window of the bus. The girls were silent and immobile in their cold, air-conditioned seats, watching a movie. Few were making the trip—the four of us, a group of French retirees, and a couple of Mexicans.

At the border, apart from construction crews building casinos, familiar chaos greeted us: rumbling tankers, convoys of tour buses disgorging passengers, and taxistas honking to gain our attention.

The frenetic pace outside the customs office had no effect on the bored official, who gave us paperwork to fill out only *after* we had waited in line for several minutes, and then insisted we step out of line to complete it. This had never happened to us before in more than twelve border crossings. Fifty or so French nationals from a tour bus waiting behind us insisted on jumping the queue. Lloyd refused to move; we'd been on the road since 7:30 from Caye Caulker and were the only ones in the crowd with children. He was backed up vociferously by the group of French retirees from our bus, and while they ran interference by fiercely arguing the point on his behalf, I scrawled out our personal details on the forms.

The customs officer, who had been staring off into the middle distance, took each passport that was thrust at him, took out the paperwork we had duly completed, and stamped us in without once looking at the paper nor our faces. So much for security.

At the motel, which we chose because of its proximity to the Museo de la Cultura Maya, we encountered the same apathetic reception. The manager flatly refused to let me see a room. All the rooms were "fine." This was another first. We had never been denied this request before. We shlumped to our first room, suspended directly over the busy roadway. Lloyd looked out the window, surveyed the eighteen-wheelers and buses thundering by and said, "No way."

We returned to reception down a narrow flight of iron stairs to ask for a room facing the backyard. The manager, without getting out of her seat, and without saying a word, handed us a key to another room. Back upstairs we trudged, only to find there was no hot water.

Downstairs again, the manager said, "Open the water and leave it running for ten minutes, then it will get hot."

Back upstairs we humped, our legs now rubber from the exercise. I opened the valves and set the timer on my watch. I told the girls, "Don't unpack."

Lloyd noticed a twisting path of copper pipes that led to a collection of water tanks on the roof. "It shouldn't take ten minutes."

"For the first time in my life, I'd kill for a suicide shower." I said.

We waited ten minutes, then gave up and took the girls out for something to eat. When we returned from a strange dinner, we requested a room with a bathroom that genuinely had hot water, as promised. The manager swapped keys for a third room, this time, not looking up from her Bible.

My back muscles were stretched to the limit from all the delays at the border and the slogging up and down flights of stairs with my heavy backpack looking for a suitable room. I spent the next three days taking scalding showers and stretching out my neck.

About that dinner. The slight differences in Spanish we had learned in Costa Rica prevented us from comprehending what in the blazes was listed on the menu. The waiter offered an explanation, which I translated to the Travel Team. "You have a choice between bread smothered with hot cheese and liquidy beans, quesadillas with hot cheese and liquidy beans, and of course, rice and beans."

We ordered all three dishes and in a testament to my extraordinary comprehension skills, we were indeed served bread and tortilla with hot cheese and liquidy beans. Later, we lay in bed passing gas.

The next day we crossed the street to the museum. At the ticket window, recessed past the gift shop, we were told to check everything, including our bottled water. Lloyd handed me a bottle. "Drink it."

Then he directed us all to the adjoining washroom. We didn't get far with that task; each of us returned in need of toilet paper. Now, you're thinking: a good backpacker always carries a roll of toilet paper! And you'd be correct. Alas, ours was tucked away securely along with a bottle of sunscreen and my last packet of suero in our checked bags.

In the exhibit hall, we puzzled over the theme of the artwork displayed in the circular gallery. None was Mayan. Jocelyn paused at each piece, contemplating its merit. The rest of us searched for what we had read about in the guidebooks ("The best museum on Mayan culture"). Then we came upon a courtyard that displayed a rickety, dusty Mayan hut (featuring an electrical outlet) and a few urns.

"Is that it?" I asked aloud.

Filtering out to the exit, we passed reception, and I sought out resource materials for the girls. After much hesitation, two thin coloring books were offered as if doing so would bankrupt their operation.

Lloyd tried to salvage something educational out of this "museum" by taking the girls to the gift shop. "Maybe I can show them some pictures in the overpriced books."

I was so disappointed in the museum and the indifference of the staff that I stayed in the lobby to walk it off. As I paced, I saw two darkened double doors that perhaps led to a theater or seminar room, or maybe the museum's administrative offices. Marked *Sala*, which means "Room," I absentmindedly tugged on the door.

"It's probably locked," I thought. When it swung open, the Mayan world revealed itself to me.

I whipped back to the gift shop and stuck my head in. "I found it!" I cried.

Not one employee, *no one*, had thought to direct us to the entrance. To get to the ticket window, we had walked *past* the museum entrance and had wasted an hour and a half admiring local artwork in the foyer. Even when we were about to leave, the women at the window ignored us.

The museum was excellent. The curators had assembled miniature models of Mayan cities underneath a glass walkway. The girls got down on their hands and knees to peer into the kingdom of Tikal as it once was. Lloyd hijacked a gigantic math board, spanning the entire west wall of the museum. He spent thirty minutes demonstrating the Mayan base twelve mathematical system. A three-floor display elucidated Mayan astrological and spiritual beliefs. Taking in the entire model required climbing stairs to each level. The top floor represented the afterworld and the basement the underworld. And to think we might have missed it all.

Back at the motel, Lloyd choked on a mouthful of beer when I warned him that drinking was expressly forbidden at the motel.

"What?"

"Didn't you see the sign behind the reception desk?"

"No!"

Someone knocked on the door.

Lloyd, wide-eyed, scrambled to hide the offending can in a shopping bag. The knock came from some annoying vendor who had obviously been told which room was occupied by gringos. The merchant rambled on and on trying to sell us hammocks while Lloyd cast furtive glances at the shopping bag.

We were stuck in Chetumal because my back had seized to the point where I couldn't haul my pack, so we stayed. The room was cheap; it had hot water and cable television. So what if we had to drink cold beer under the bed with one person acting as a lookout?

To break up the boredom we went to the mall where we had our first encounter with Dr. Simi, a generic brand of health and beauty items sold at little standalone pharmacies in Mexico. From vitamins to headache remedies, things were laid out at Dr. Simi's stores in bins. And the best part of all? Dr. Simi himself, a gigantic marshmallow of a man (a luckless employee in an inflatable costume) who tried to entice customers by skipping back and forth to a soundtrack whose decibels deafened all who came within his orbit.

We heard Dr. Simi before we saw him. Walking along the corridors of the mall, the blare of music startled us. We turned around to see a white-lab-coated, mustachioed, Muppet-headed, bulbous excuse for a man bouncing over to the girls, arms open wide for a hug.

Natalie shrugged, taking her hands from her ears and extended them wide to accept the embrace. "All right," she conceded.

TULUM

The Mayan Riviera boasted luxurious buses with frigid air conditioning, bathrooms, and movie screens. Could the Travel Team even declare these chicken buses? The answer came a few weeks later.

A slowly building excitement about getting back to Canada percolated as we rolled closer to Cancún. My neck was still tender, so Lloyd offered to lug my packs to the curb and dump them in the trunk of the cab when we arrived in Tulum. When we told the cabbie the address of the hostel he laughed and applied the brakes. It was fifteen meters from the bus station.

The receptionist at the hostel furrowed her brow and expressed reservations about allowing the girls to stay. I told her wearily, "We have been traveling for nineteen months. We're very accustomed to this."

She wrung her hands and nervously clicked on her computer. "I only have dorm rooms available."

"We'll take four beds."

Most of the guests at the hostel were spring breakers. The girls met no one they could interact with and concentrated their attention-seeking on us. Lloyd unearthed a deck of cards while I organized the beds. In the dorm, I met a young professional couple from the Czech Republic named Josef, a smiling bespectacled Charlie Brown lookalike who spoke flawless English, and Denisa, a pouty, athletic woman. Josef and I spoke at length about the changes in the Soviet bloc after the collapse of communism. "Travel agencies are the most successful businesses right now," he said, grinning. "We had been unable to see the rest of the world, now we can't get enough of it."

I don't think his wife liked me very much, monopolizing her husband for so much of their brief two-week vacation. They were far from home for such a short stay, but Tulum lies ninety minutes from Cancún, a city that filters twenty million people through its well-connected airport. Tulum also rests above the ocean—looking down on waves, shimmering like diamonds, and white sand beaches—along the eastern seaboard of the Yucatán Peninsula, a finger of land that separates the Caribbean from the Gulf of Mexico. The stretch from Cancún past Tulum to the Belizean border, known as the Mayan Riviera, was full of vacationers on discount package tours, cheek by jowl, passed out on the beaches, trolling the streets, drunk in bars.

We were unprepared for the crowds. Much of our adventure penetrated outlying districts, where shops, pulperías, pensions, sodas, kayak rentals, campgrounds, and pharmacies were owned by local families. They usually lived in the back and their children ran in and out among the customers, sometimes engulfing the girls and taking them by the hand to play. If we stayed a few days, we got to know the family, and at times we had conversations about our different lives and got to know each other, just a little.

In Mexico, the bulging crowds formed a cultural barrier between us and the locals. Grocery stores were enormous, owned by corporations that hired employees at low wages who must have been tired of seeing us with our fat wallets and loud voices, maybe not even making eye contact with them or asking about their day.

In contrast, we recalled Ricardo and his family back in Quebrada Ganado. Mrs. Ricardo had once become so overwhelmed by grandmotherly pride that she perched her granddaughter beside the cash register in her baby seat so that everyone in town could admire her. And we did. I took to calling her *abuela* (grandmother) after that, which she found delightful. In a touching moment, the family presented us with little gifts the day before we departed the town for good. And I still think about the sweet lady in San

Juan del Sur who called her husband over to meet our "Princessas." Each time we returned and went into the store she flashed a smile and peered around me to look for the girls. I asked Lloyd, "Is this the trade-off?" Because the Mayan Riviera is considered prime real estate for tourism, the level of infrastructure was elevated several notches.

"The development here is grotesque," he protested. "It represents a perfect example of bad planning." Maritime areas were devoured by monstrous hotels, creating dire environmental burdens for wildlife, especially the various species of sea turtle. Towns near these resorts offered the budget traveler accommodations and cheap eats and also housed the personnel who worked at the resorts. Along the coast, land prices had skyrocketed, and locals could no longer afford real estate there.

Back in Canada when I presented workshops on community-based tourism I explained that many family-owned hotels or restaurants were comfortable and provided excellent service. Supporting these businesses meant supporting an entire family instead of keeping locals in underpaid jobs with little room for advancement.

Locally-owned was hard to find on the Mayan Riviera, but doing so meant we could feel good about where our dollars were going. On the other hand, foreign owners addressed the wealthier crowd's desires. For example, at a funky café we ordered yogurt smoothies and watched the hundreds, perhaps thousands of gringos walking in and out of tacky gift shops. I sighed at the charmlessness of it all, even as I seriously enjoyed that yogurt. Some of the restaurant employees weren't even Mexican.

We dipped into our smoothies, making fun of the sunburned bodies and drivers exuding testosterone racing sports cars on the main drag, when a fellow traveler, Mark, whom we had met in Belize, walked by. He stopped abruptly when he saw us. "Hey!"

He turned to his travel companions. "This is the family I was telling you about."

He told us there was a better hostel up the road, within walking distance of the beach and the famous Tulum Ruins. "The crowd staying there are real backpackers. Not college kids here for a week."

We hopped in a cab and went to check it out. He was right. Tulum Hostel, operated by a Mexican family, faced the main highway, away from the strip and the noise of the nightlife. "This was my father's farm," the owner told us. As a bonus, she was happy to see the girls. They rented us an entire dorm to ourselves, right beside the hot water bathrooms. A little pricey at forty dollars, we were at least saving money gorging ourselves on the enormous breakfasts they served up every morning.

Once firmly installed in our new quarters, we beelined it for the beach. In Tulum, as in everywhere else on the Riviera, the beach was located on the east side of a busy highway, which divided the community in half. We crossed multiple lanes tentatively, falling in line with thousands of others on their way to the ruins, which we needed to pass through to get to the beach.

We inched our way to the ticket window sandwiched like fans at a rock concert. Once inside, we jostled among the crowd, encouraging the girls to admire the crumbling structures. They pulled us along, wanting only to see the pièce de résistance: the cliff overlooking the sea. And there it was. This was the stuff of postcards, grey and white cliffs leading straight into the brilliant turquoise of the water.

We hiked down the steep staircase and dug in. Hundreds of towels and water bottles lay waiting for owners to return, dry off, and expose sensitive flesh to burning rays. A newly married couple was having their official photos taken right in the water, the bride still in her wedding dress. While the girls exerted energy bodysurfing with their dad, I sat and listened to a group chatting in Russian beside me.

For the next few days, we walked down to the beach, stayed for a few hours, and came back to have an early supper before bed. I even tried to enter the water; my skin infection had almost cleared up, but because I'd run out of suero, my ill-equipped temperature regulating system broke down, and one night I bucked and writhed in severe abdominal pain, a clear sign I had under-hydrated and unbalanced my electrolytes. I never returned to Tulum's beach. The road to it was just a little too long, the sun just a little too hot.

At our base in Tulum, we scoured the internet for deals on flights and sent emails to friends and family to arrange for pick up. There was one more place we wanted to see: a campground called Xpu Ha that friends back home had recommended. The backpackers at our hostel sped off to see Chichén Itzá or to swim in limestone sinkholes called *cenotes*. We remained relaxed and close to broke and looked forward to the peace of a small town in Canada.

"Lloyd, what do you think about scouting the campground as a day trip?" I suggested. "It's not far and if it's appealing, we can pack for an overnight the next day."

The sole reason for this was because the development of the area made it more difficult to get around. Intertown buses let people off on the side of the highway, and from there beaches were hiking distance away. I empathized with the service workers having to travel these routes every day. "Paved paradise," I complained.

Mega resorts monopolized beaches along the Yucatán. In other countries, notably Costa Rica, the beaches remained in the hands of the public. For ticos, this meant that one of their favorite past times—camping on the beach—remained possible, while corporations fought the government to restrict access. Up and down the coast we saw families pitching tents on the beach, and because developers could not buy up prime waterfront land, small settlements remained along the coast in pockets. Entrepreneurs set up oceanside sodas so campers could have a bite of gallo pinto, and in many cases these eateries provided cheap showers.

Thanks to directions emailed from our neighbors back home, Xpu Ha was easy to find. A short walk from the highway brought us to the campground. The girls stood at the water's edge, digging their toes in the sand.

"We'll need to plan this out carefully," I said to Lloyd. "There is no market nearby. We'll have to carry in all of our food and water."

"We've never camped so close to the ocean. The girls will love it," he said. "But I'm going to see if there is a cabin available. I don't want a sleepless night in the tent."

I joined the girls at the water. "How far can we go in, mom?" Jocelyn asked.

"Hold my hands. We'll go in as far as our shorts."

We waded in and bobbed around a little. Facing the shore, I could see the beach extending for miles, speckled with lounge chairs and knots of holiday-makers. Directly in front of us, the campground hosted a few tents. A plot of cabinas angled perpendicular to the water and the rest of the terrain was sardined with motorhomes driven down from the US and Canada, based on the license plates.

Lloyd returned with good news. "I told her we would be back in a few days to rent one of those cabins."

We retraced our steps back to the highway over a lonely dirt road that served as a delivery route for the adjacent resort. "The owner of this campground stands to make millions if she ever sells," I said.

XPU HA

After more than a year and a half, our packing skills were honed to perfection; we confidently hiked down from the highway with six meals for four people and all necessary drinking water, but we had unwittingly scheduled our stay over a Mexican holiday weekend. When we rounded the final bend, we saw a sea of cars and tents. My stomach pitched thinking that if they were booked up, we had done a lot of work for nothing.

The landlady confirmed my fears. "No space."

We lingered, Lloyd and I reluctant to leave. "What do we do?" I asked him.

He gritted his teeth, took the girls by the hand and made to turn back over the dirt road we had come when we heard shouts. "Señor!" The landlady was calling to us. "My daughter just told me that one cabin has become available. Please wait a few minutes so we can clean it?"

Phew.

After checking in, we lounged on the beach, burrowing into the soft sand under our feet and chatting with our friendly French-Canadian neighbors. The girls went for a swim and I walked the beach, taking it all in one last time. My thoughts were competing for airtime, on the one hand heavy with memories of all that we had done and on the other, bubbling with the excitement of going home.

Going home.

Later, as the girls played with a cluster of children, Lloyd and I strolled down to the beach and sat together in the late afternoon sun, reclining on a mound of sand and gazing out at the ocean.

"Ready to go back to Canada?" he asked me.

"Yes," I said. "I'm burned out. I didn't expect such mental wear and tear."

"The girls' safety has been on our minds for months," he agreed.

"I was sick of our lives when we left, but now I'm looking forward to the boredom."

Lloyd lay back on the sand, his hands under his head. "A comfy bed is all I want right now."

"Have we done enough?" I asked. "Have we shown them what it means to live a different life?"

"We might not know the answer to that for years to come," he said.

Later, in the cabina, I prepared a cold stew on top of the lone piece of furniture, a battered dresser pushed up against a crumbling stucco wall. After dinner, we resorted to desperate measures, letting Jocelyn write out movie titles on pieces of paper to play charades. Before long, Natalie grew sour.

"I'm so hot," she complained.

I felt her forehead. "Lloyd, she's got a fever."

Naturally, we had no remedies with us, so Lloyd loped off to find children's Tylenol. I thought of only two things: *We leave in three days,* and *I hope those French Canadians won't mind giving us a ride to the clinic.*

Lloyd returned with some children's Tylenol he had scrounged, gave her a dropper full, and tucked her in, wrapping her in a dry beach towel.

Instinctively I knew that all kids get fevers from time to time, but feeling most comfortable wallowing in anxiety, I preferred to relive the angst from her previous illness back in Quebrada Ganado. "I'd feel better if one of us stayed awake with her through the night."

Lloyd knew it was overkill, but he was harboring his own anxieties about her well-being and agreed. "We'll each take four-hour shifts."

The sun rose on a glorious day over the impossibly aqua-blue ocean. However, this family of Canadians would not remain to enjoy it; Natalie was still hot the next day, and we were too far from any medical facilities for my comfort level. I begged a ride to the highway from a nice Mexican couple. Natty and I waited at the gas station for Jocelyn and Lloyd to hike out so we could catch the bus back to Tulum together.

That afternoon, Natalie showed improvement only to see Lloyd succumb to the same mysterious ailment. Two days to go and 50 percent of our Travel Team was ill! And then, after nineteen months of "clear sailing," both got Montezuma's Revenge. *Why was there no Dr. Simi in Tulum?*

The hostel's Mexican matriarch whipped up a batch of fresh tomato soup for the invalids, and I delivered it to the dorm in an exaggerated sing-song voice. "Is there anything *else* I can get you two?"

Lloyd gave me a lame smile. "Something to read?"

I gathered up discarded magazines for Lloyd and plopped a baggie of pencil crayons on Natalie's lap.

With those two resting in bed, Jocelyn and I laid out our travel gear and evaluated what did not need to make the flight home.

"What about our air mattresses?" she asked.

"Don't need 'em."

"Flip-flops?"

"Nope."

"Rain poncho?"

"Done."

"Polysporin?"

"Chuck it."

"Hats?"

"Toast."

We cleared a table in the hostel's open-air dining room and pilfered a couple of pencil crayons from Nat. Jocelyn wrote out a sign that read:

FREE!! We're going home after 19 months on the road!

Within the following twenty-four hours Lloyd and Natalie were out of bed, if not a little weak and tired, cherishing their last moments in Mexico. They even felt well enough the next day to browse the shops to buy a gift for Gram, the girls' great grandmother, to commemorate her ninetieth birthday. I scrabbled off last-minute emails and prepared a modest meal of whatever was left over. The following day we were headed to Cancún for our final night.

CANCÚN

This was it, the final day. Our fellow backpackers gathered in the lobby of the hostel to see us off. They gave us rounds of high fives and few of them gave hugs, including the loving owner herself who had tried in vain to get us to stay and teach her son English. At the Tulum bus station, in a true full-circle moment, Lloyd saw in the baggage hold, a live chicken zipped into a vinyl shopping bag. Yes, even first class, air-conditioned, bathroom-in-rear, movie-playing buses can be chicken buses.

As a treat, Lloyd decided we should have a meal at a restaurant in Cancún. That sounded reasonable to me and rather celebratory, but after seeing the restaurants in downtown Cancún and factoring in the still sensitive stomachs on our team, I put my foot down. "You guys can get anything you want at the grocery store for supper."

On the way to the supermarket, we ran right into Dr. Simi. I darted in, picked out a pimply-faced teenager behind the counter and blurted out in Spanish, "Where are the probiotics?" We were *not* going to miss that flight.

That night we pooled the items each of us had personally selected at the grocery store and prepared a meal of mac and cheese, chips, stuffed olives, rice, and Melba toast for supper and ate standing up in the kitchen. I got the girls to settle down by 8:00 in the women's dorm. Lloyd and I checked and triple checked our respective alarms, set for 4:30 a.m. We looked at each other. "Time to go home?" he asked.

I nodded. He kissed me on the forehead and left.

I lay in bed, stared at the ceiling, and tried not to think. *Not to think . . . not to think . . . bam!* I checked my watch . . . 2:30. I tossed and turned. At 4:00 I gave up and silently readied my pack. I bent over beside Natalie's bed to arrange her clothes.

"Hi Mommy." She was awake.

Jocelyn peeped her head down from the upper bunk and smiled. Not a one had slept. I ushered them off to the bathroom and then snuck into the men's dorm to wake Lloyd. He was already up and brushing his teeth.

"Did you even sleep?" I whispered.

"No," he mouthed.

For the last time, we muscled our packs onto our shoulders and gave a quiet "Travel Team!" cry and high-fived each other. We strode out the door and hailed a cab.

At the airport, sunburned tourists still hungover from last night's party stood in line with sour faces. We appeared to be the sole passengers that morning who were genuinely *happy* to be leaving Mexico. When we landed, we raised our arms in victory.

Chapter 18

Home

About a year after we returned from the trip, I wedged in between the girls on our king-sized bed, removed a bookmark from its resting place, and began reading. Jocelyn spooned into me, resting her chin on my shoulder. Natalie rubbed her eyes. It wasn't a long chapter, but they were drifting fast, so I ended it after a few pages. "Time for bed," I said.

They stirred slightly. Natalie tapped me on the arm. "Do you realize it's my birthday soon?" She was stifling a yawn; the words came out in gasps.

"What? You just had one last year."

"Mom," she groaned.

"I suppose you'll be wanting presents?"

"Mom," she laughed.

Jocelyn ran her fingers through my hair. "Tell me about the best present you ever received."

I thought about it for a minute as they cuddled into me. "The best gift I ever got," I told them, "was a French/English dictionary I received one Christmas when I was a teenager."

"Why?"

"Because at that moment I knew for sure I was going to France." It was an unexpected response. The image of me shredding the wrapping paper in rabid expectation popped into my head. Other images crowded my mind. A dozen times I'd relayed the tale of me as a seventeen-year-old sitting in the Gare de Lyon waiting to change trains. I also recalled careening around a mountain road behind the wheel of a friend's blue Renault, five of us crammed in, me having placed in my wallet, only months before, my newly minted driver's license. Or drinking Orangina at cafés in St. Tropez or wandering through Aix-en-Provence to meet up with friends at the Université. Those days in Europe were heady. Those who travel understand this—assuaging your curiosity from the time you rise to the moment you sleep, never succeeding.

Lloyd and I deem travel a vital means of education, a way to expand the mind, to develop empathy for others. In taking our children on this adventure, we hoped to instill a lifelong interest in the miracle of planet Earth. Therefore, when our plans fell through—when Lloyd found himself without work in both countries—we stayed on target, determined to go through with the trip. The powerful, mysterious image that continually flashed through my mind before we left, of an ocean shore in the company of American friends, fueled my resolve because I knew it had some significance.

In March, we returned to the United States, five months earlier than anticipated. Swinging in hammocks on Caye Caulker, sipping fragrant coffee, I'd said to Lloyd, "You know, the girls are nearly fluent in Spanish. We should think about immersing them in French. It *is* one of our national languages." All those young European students speaking three, four, and five languages had inspired me.

He lowered his mug. "Hang out in Québec for the summer?"

"Pourquoi pas?" We clinked our cups together.

Thus, Camping des Forges in Trois-Rivières became our base for a few months. The girls attended the community's day camp where they picked up conversational French so effortlessly that we returned to repeat the exercise for three more summers.

Before that, we accepted an invitation to bunk with Steve, whom we met with his buddy Derek in Puerto Viejo at Rocking J's. The following year they'd returned to Costa Rica and stopped by the villa for a cup of coffee and some catching up. Then they left for Panama to catch a ride on an onion truck. Now, nearly a year later, we were invited to spend a few days with Steve and his wife, Marie, at their home in Maine.

One afternoon they took us sightseeing in Kennebunk. Steve suggested, "We can stop off at the beach so the girls can run around."

"Great idea!" I burst out.

Lloyd raised his eyebrows, leaned over to me and whispered, "Why are you so enthusiastic about going to a beach in Maine?"

"The ocean shore of my waking dream!" I whispered back. "American friends!" All this time I had assumed it was California.

It was a full-circle moment. The six of us walked on the beach in the cool breeze, examining lobster pots that had washed up on shore. I took a picture of Steve explaining to the girls how the lobsters became ensnared in the trap. I put the camera down and grinned contentedly.

The direction of my life took a decided turn that Christmas of 1981 when I pressed a French/English dictionary to my chest and dreamed of croissants and café au lait. In that dictionary on that Christmas morning lay the excitement of a lifetime spent exploring. It spurred me to adapt to other cultures and respect other nationalities by learning their history and their language. In between the pages, it catapulted me to witness poverty and injustice. It provided me the wealth of friends in the four corners of the earth and showered me with exotic memories as I fell asleep. I thought it best to pass this gift on to my own children.

Epilogue

WHEN WE TOLD PEOPLE about our plans to travel with the girls they said, "You're brave." This made no sense to me. Traveling did not require courage for either Lloyd or me. But most people are locked into some financial commitment. If we possess characteristics that render us more able to endure the absence from a regular salary it is because we had a high tolerance for financial uncertainty before we left. We know from personal experience that these commitments can be all-consuming. Leaving a job for an extended period didn't require courage as much as a strategy. We made professional and financial decisions based on how it would impact our ability to travel. We enrolled in courses that conveyed an advantage through the eyes of an international hiring panel (thank you, Professor Mullins). We read books such as *How to Survive without a Salary* by Charles Long.

Many also confessed they felt uncomfortable with the idea of spending 24/7 with their spouse or children. Lloyd and I noticed that those people did not appear to possess the parenting strategies necessary to make it a success. If your children annoy you at home, it will be exacerbated on the road. Same goes with your marriage. Homeschooling trained the girls and me to be tolerant of one another and to behave in a way that enabled us to thrive in each other's constant presence. Whatever your parenting style, an adventure trip will succeed only if you are in tune with your children (for their physical as well as emotional health) and are willing to spend intense hours together.

RISK ASSESSMENT

Families engaging in trips of this nature will face risks. We avoided accidents, but only just. Natalie contracted a serious bacterial infection, probably from the less than hygienic public pool in Quebrada Ganado. She suffered a short, acute illness, was administered the proper medicine, and fully recovered. Jocelyn picked up something that made her cough for weeks and rendered her as pale as a ghost. A bus almost hit her on the El Remate road. But we returned to Canada safe and sound.

Risk needs assessment *every step of the way*. Each segment of our trip was meticulously organized, down to the kilometer. To some it may represent an exercise in extreme stress, and at times, it was. Reintegrating into a Canadian small town included time to recover from the spikes in heart-pounding moments of terror. In a cruel, ironic twist, a startling number of tragedies to several of our friends and family members transpired during the time we were away. This included murders, attempted murder, near-death experiences, fatal accidents, and stays in intensive care. All these in Canada, one of the safest countries in the world. Had fate intervened in all our lives? We were taking much greater risks and were none the worse for wear, yet many of our loved ones suffered terrible tragedies. We'll make it if it's meant to be, I'd think. However, careful preparations can *never* take a back seat.

Unfortunately, despite hours of internet research, we discovered there is a dearth of information available on adventuring with children. Ultimately, we relied on our own previous travel experience and a store of confidence built up from all those years defending our alternative parenting. We simply took a leap of faith and figured things out as we went along. We had virtually no model to guide us. Having confidence is key, and when even that is in short supply, gumption goes a long way.

CHANGES

The night before we left Canada, I laid out our gear on the floor of an empty bedroom. I surveyed our belongings to envision how to cram it all into our packs. Then a wave of anxiety washed over me. Maybe because my Italian grandmother feared my death so deeply when I was growing up, I grappled with anxiety now and then. It bubbled up out of nowhere sometimes, leaving me breathless at night. My grandmother can be forgiven for fearing for my life. She'd lost a child to illness, and when I neared the age of the child's death, my nana began insisting I walk slowly down the stairs and she deboned chicken before I ate it.

On the road I felt guilty for putting my parents through the stress of having their grandchildren gallivanting through Central America, especially for my dad, whose sister it was that died. I also wrestled with the anxiety of ensuring Jocelyn's and Natalie's health and safety. The challenge lay in deciding whether my stress was irrational or not. The turning point came during our interlude at Mono Feliz when Jocelyn came to me and said, "Mickey bit me."

Immediately I wanted to contact the insurance company to evac her to Canada.

"Where?" Lloyd asked her. "I can't see a mark."

"Right here." She pointed to a piece of flesh between her thumb and forefinger. Even with the use of a magnifying glass, we could see nothing.

"He probably just nipped you. You're fine."

I skulked away and curled up into a ball on my bed.

Rabies.

I lay there that night fighting two competing thoughts: *Get her immediate medical treatment* and *Shut up, she's fine*. After sleepless hours, I came to a decision. Knowing I could not weather any adventure consumed by irrational fears, I gave myself an ultimatum. *If you think she may have contracted rabies, then tell Lloyd you want to go to a doctor. Otherwise, shut up.* In the end, my rational side battled to victory.

This is how I managed my stress, by levelling with myself. *If the world is going to end, then take action; otherwise it's simply anxiety—ignore it.* My passion for travel helped me conquer my anxiety. It didn't evaporate after the episode at Mono Feliz, I just chose to disregard it and refocused my attention on the adventure.

Lloyd's resolve to live on this Earth with a minimal footprint was strengthened after experiencing the lengths to which people went to get from point A to point B, as we did on that Panama veggie truck. "I cannot drive my car one day more."

So, we let the tenants stay, and relocated to a community closer to school so that he could ride his bike to work every day, even in winter. A small price to pay, he feels, to honor the people who travel in difficult circumstances and our precious Earth.

How has the trip affected the girls? It's hard to say. I was struck by a comment Jocelyn made at dinner one evening. "I was watching those kids in baggy jeans walking to school today," she mentioned. "I felt sorry for them."

"Why?" Lloyd asked.

"Because they don't have parents like I do."

I laughed. "Go on."

"I mean . . . just the effort you put in to organize the trip."

I was stunned that she would recognize that it took a massive endeavor to coordinate everything. She always seemed to reside in la la land. *Maybe*, I thought, *not always*.

Natalie was five when we set out; we can only hope her young mind was indoctrinated with an appreciation for a different way of life. Though the girls never lived in poverty themselves, will it be enough to have seen it all around them so that they possess compassion for others in dire circumstances?

COMMUNITY-BASED TRAVEL

We'd like to make a plug for community-based travel, which we believe is one of the most responsible forms of tourism. For us it means:

1. Benefiting the local community and its natural environment.
2. Respecting the culture of the host community.
3. Relying on local, family-owned businesses for food, shelter, and transportation.

According to the United Nations Environment Programme, revenue derived from tourists is prone to "leakage," a term that refers to the money that ends up in the local economy. According to UNEP, "Of each US$ 100 spent on a vacation tour by a tourist from a developed country, only around US$ 5 actually stays in a developing-country destination's economy."[7]

We can do better than that! Even people who stay at resorts for a week can commit to leaving the grounds to spend money at businesses nearby. Our garage sale budget prevented us from staying anywhere as luxurious as a resort, and even if we were financially able to do so, Lloyd and I could never bring ourselves to remain sequestered inside the compound while the vibrant energy of the host community beckoned to us. From Parismina turtle patrols to Fossil Land to Da' Flying Frog to family run hostels, we sought to support as many locals as we could. From time to time we supported expats, such as Bob's microbrewery in Honduras, but like Karen and Francisco, Bob hired locals and became involved in the community. Never, apart from visits to the Palí in Siquirres, the chain grocery stores in Tulum and Cancún, and the rental car we drove to get us to the Nicaraguan border did we knowingly support a corporation. We did our best to distribute our garage sale money to as many local establishments as possible.

Backpackers support community-based tourism on key levels. Mom-and-pop businesses within the immediate orbit of a hostel such as grocers, sewing repair shops, launderers, cafeterias, clothing shops, trinket booths, internet cafés, and coffee shops turn a profit because of our presence. Micro-loan programs are an excellent way to support individuals in the developing world. In Puerto Viejo, a community that attracts a large number of tourists, such a program allowed women to purchase washing machines. When I took our laundry to one of these businesses, there was always a lineup.

Other entrepreneurs paced the beach selling slices of mango or selling lottery tickets and could earn a decent wage doing so, as one of my students

---

7. Beckmann et al. *Global Report on Adventure Tourism*, 11.

pointed out to me. By supporting these people, we are affecting their entire family. In turn, they rely on us to sustain the local economy.

As in Parismina, we saw families concocting interesting activities to make a few dollars. The cheese makers of Caño Blanco and Don Rodrigo's coconut oil–making neighbors are a perfect example of this. The same can be said for Tomas and his brother who used their lifelong knowledge of the canals of Tortuguero to make a living by scraping enough money together to buy two canoes. That morning, the two probably made $150 from seven of us. Not bad for a morning of paddling.

Interacting with people at their businesses also teaches us how others live. I thought of Tomas pining for his far-away son, or how we came to know the family of Ricardo and Mrs. Ricardo. Nothing, though, can take the place of chicken buses for getting to know and appreciate a culture. Plying over craggy roads and plunging into rivers does a lot to influence your perception about living conditions. Apart from how it supports the drivers and ayudantes and makes light use of our wallets, riding chicken buses is a wallop of culture shock. Chicken buses acted as a stage with us as the audience, especially how it demonstrated the locals' affection toward children, even as we saw many of them working. Ayudantes picked up the girls and set them down gently. Passengers, teetering down the aisles, stopped to admire them. Over the grinding of the gears, people told us how beautiful they were. Old men in pop bottle glasses patted them tenderly on the head.

Like all children, they were welcomed wherever they went, at all my English classes, at restaurants, stores, hotels, and museums. By comparison, after Steve dropped us at the train station so we could catch the Amtrak to Montreal, we witnessed a young American woman loudly berating her nine-year-old daughter in full view of other passengers. When I turned to view the fuss, I received an angry tongue-lashing. "You raise your own damn kids and I'll raise my own damn kid!"

Yes, chicken buses, crammed full and whistling down a bumpy road, unveil a great deal indeed.

Bibliography

Beckmann, Christina, et al. *Global Report on Adventure Tourism*. Madrid: World Tourism Organization, 2014, 11. https://skift.com/wp-content/uploads/2014/11/unwto-global-report-on-adventure-tourism.pdf.

Marcolongo, Vincenzo. "Message from the Founder." https://www.iamat.org/our-story.

Recio, Patricia. "8 de cada 10 atropellos son causados por imprudencias de peatones." San José: *La Nacion*, 2015. https://www.nacion.com/el-pais/servicios/8-de-cada-10-atropellos-son-causados-por-imprudencias-de-peatones/5LCZXXSAJVGLTPVD5KSIMOERJ4/story/.

Reid, Robert, et al. *Central America on a Shoestring*. Oakland: Lonely Planet, 2004.

Wood, Randy, and Joshua Berman. *Nicaragua*. 2nd ed. Moon Handbooks. Berkeley: Avalon Travel, 2005.